D0962115

GROWING
UP
BASEBALL

An Oral History

GROWING
UP
BASEBALL

Harvey Frommer and Frederic J. Frommer

Taylor Trade Publishing
Dallas, Texas

COPYRIGHT © 2001 BY HARVEY FROMMER AND FREDERIC J. FROMMER

All rights reserved

No part of this book may be reproduced in any form or by any means—including
photocopying and electronic reproduction—without written
permission from the publisher.

Published by Taylor Publishing Company
1550 West Mockingbird Lane
Dallas, Texas 75235

DESIGNED BY JANIS OWENS

Photos on pages 21, 55, 62, 72, 100, 119, 129, 132, 140, 155, and 176 courtesy of
AP/WideWorld. All other photos courtesy of the National Baseball
Hall of Fame Library, Cooperstown, New York.

Library of Congress Cataloging-in-Publication Data
Growing up baseball : an oral history / [compiled] by Harvey Frommer
and Frederic J. Frommer.
    p.   cm.
ISBN 0-87833-186-7 (cloth)
    1. Baseball—United States—History. I. Frommer, Harvey. II. Fromer,
Frederic J.
GV863.A1 G76 2001
796.357'0973—dc21   00-068305

1 3 5 7 9 10 8 6 4 2

PRINTED IN THE UNITED STATES OF AMERICA

To play this game, you've got to have lot of little boy in you.
Roy Campanella

When I was a boy, life was a baseball game.
Al Kaline

For Myrna
Always There for Us
with Much Love

ACKNOWLEDGMENTS

Myrna Katz Frommer, wife and mother, is always in first place. Her reading, commentary, and fine-tuning of this manuscript were invaluable.

Others who make the list for providing leads, encouragement, and support include: Arthur Richman, original mensch, of the New York Yankees, who knows more about baseball than anyone around; Irv Kaze, the best sports radio show host in southern California; Jack Lang; Matt Merola; the Chicago Cubs, especially Benjie de la Fuente; the Baltimore Orioles; the Boston Red Sox, especially Dick Bresciani; the New York Mets; and the New York Yankees.

Editor Michael Emmerich supported the project from the start and was a wonderful constant.

A special thank you is extended to the interviewees who graciously gave of their time and memories.

CONTENTS

GROWING UP BASEBALL

WARM UP

For decades boys have played baseball on city streets and suburban sand-lots, in backyards and cow pastures, in school yards and on Little League ballfields. Whether on makeshift or manicured diamonds, they have dreamed of making it to the major leagues. *Growing Up Baseball* recounts the strivings, struggles, and stories of a sampling of the select few whose dream came true.

Here, in the words of those who lived it, are initial experiences with the sport: the ball, the bat, the glove, the playing field, the glory of early triumphs, the sting of unexpected defeats. Here are accounts of the influ-ence of adults, the growing or sudden awareness of talent, the realization of possibility, the variety of starting points, the years of struggle, the roads taken, the detours along the way, the ultimate successes. Through the memories of nearly seventy major leaguers, we are transported back to the time when everything seemed possible.

The range of storytellers in this book is very wide — from the most illustrious stars to the middle-of-the-roaders to those whose careers were undistinguished and brief. What they had and what they shared was the dream.

So come and meet the youthful Bob Feller, who learned some of his pitching trade on a farm in Iowa; Dom DiMaggio, who was always Joe's little brother; Fred Lynn, a naturally gifted athlete in all sports from the start; Johnny Pesky, whose mother made the decision for him to settle for less money and sign with the Boston Red Sox; Red Murff, whose major league debut came at the advanced age of thirty-five and whose career ended all too quickly because of injury; Dale Berra, Yogi's son, who main-tained, "You can't compare me to my father. Our similarities are different"; Ken Brett, who knew almost from the start that his younger brother would be "the one"; George Genovese, whose major league career consisted of three games and one at bat. . . .

These, and all the others, have stories to tell, dreams to replay. . . .

THE LINEUP

DWIGHT "RED" ADAMS made his major league pitching debut on May 5, 1946, with the Chicago Cubs. Although his total big league career was just eight games, Adams was well known for the distinguished career he put together as a pitching coach for the Los Angeles Dodgers.

JOEY AMALFITANO signed with the Giants as an eighteen-year-old bonus baby in 1954, making his big league debut on May 3. He spent a decade in the majors in the 1950s and 1960s, mainly as a utility player. After his playing career was over, Amalfitano coached for several major league teams and was one of the Cubs' "rotating" managers from 1979 to 1982.

RICH AMARAL has played every position but catcher and pitcher in his major league career, which began with Seattle on May 27, 1991. Amaral played nine seasons in the minor leagues and parts of eight seasons with the Mariners. He signed as a free agent with the Baltimore Orioles before the 1999 season. Many view Amaral as one of the top utility men in the American League.

GEORGE "SPARKY" ANDERSON is a Hall of Fame manager. His 2,194 career wins with Detroit and Cincinnati make him the third winningest manager in baseball history behind legends Connie Mack and John McGraw. Anderson is the only manager to win World Championships in both leagues and was the first to win a hundred or more games in a season in both leagues. His only season as a major league player was with the Philadelphia Phillies, with whom he debuted on April 10, 1959. He played second base and batted .218.

ELDEN AUKER was born September 21, 1910, in Kansas. He made his major league debut on August 10, 1933, and played for a decade in the majors with the Detroit Tigers, Boston Red Sox, and St. Louis Browns. Auker pitched the first night game in St. Louis on May 24, 1940, losing to Bob Feller and Cleveland.

TIM BELCHER made his major league debut with the Los Angeles Dodgers on September 6, 1987, and quickly became one of the National League's top pitchers. In 1988, his first full season, he went 12–6 with a 2.91 ERA. His 3–0 performance in the play-offs helped Los Angeles win the World Series. The next year, Belcher led the major leagues with eight shutouts. He was traded to the Cincinnati Reds in 1991. Belcher has also played for the Chicago White Sox, Detroit Tigers, Seattle Mariners, Kansas City Royals, and Anaheim Angels.

DALE BERRA is the son of Yogi Berra. A highly touted prospect, Berra made his major league debut on August 22, 1977, with Pittsburgh. At first a utility infielder, Dale finally became a regular at shortstop in 1982 and held that starting job for three seasons. Berra played from 1977 to 1987 with the Pirates, Yankees, and Astros. Dale Berra and Yogi Berra held the record for father-son home runs (407) until Bobby Bonds and Barry Bonds broke it.

MIKE BORDICK was not drafted out of high school or college but signed as a free agent with the Oakland A's after an impressive stint in a summer league. His major league debut was April 11, 1990. Bordick signed with the Orioles as a free agent after the 1996 season. One of the steadiest defensive shortstops in baseball, Bordick led all American League shortstops in fielding percentage (.989) and total chances (797) in 1999. In 2000, Bordick was named to the All-Star team for the first time and was traded to the New York Mets later that season. He resigned with the Orioles after the 2000 season.

KEN BRETT was overshadowed by his younger brother, George, but Ken had a long major league career as a pitcher. His major league debut was on September 27, 1967. That year, at age nineteen and one month, he became the youngest pitcher to pitch in a World Series. Brett pitched a total of fourteen seasons with ten different teams.

NELSON BRILES is a vice president for the Pittsburgh Pirates. He made his major league pitching debut on April 19, 1965, with the St. Louis Cardinals. A control artist, Briles pitched for fourteen seasons and posted 129 career victories. He became a starter for St. Louis when Bob Gibson broke his leg in 1967. Traded to the Pirates in 1971, Briles helped Pittsburgh win the pennant and pitched a two-hit shutout against Baltimore in the fifth game of the World Series.

SCOTT BROSIUS made his major league debut with Oakland on August 7, 1991. He never was able to get enough playing time with the Athletics and in 1998 was sent to the Yankees as the player to be named later in a deal that brought starter Kenny Rogers to Oakland. Brosius hit .300 with nineteen homers and a personal-best ninety-eight RBIs and was named to the 1998 American League All-Star team.

BOBBY BROWN was part of the scene for the New York Yankees for eight seasons after making his major league debut on September 22, 1946. He was a hitting star in four World Series. Barely thirty years old when he retired from baseball in mid-1954 to pursue a career as a cardiologist, Brown reentered baseball in 1984, succeeding Lee MacPhail as president of the American League. He remained in this position until 1994.

JOSE CARDENAL was born in Cuba and made his major league debut on April 14, 1963. The outfielder and first baseman had an eighteen-year career that began with the San Francisco Giants and ended with the Kansas City Royals in 1980. He also played for the Angels, Indians, Cardinals, Brewers, Cubs, Phillies, and Mets. Cardenal has also coached for the Reds, Cardinals, Yankees, and Devil Rays.

CLIFF CHAMBERS spent his pitching career with the Cubs, Pirates, and Cardinals. His major league pitching debut was on April 24, 1948, with the last place Chicago Cubs. The 6'3" Oregonian posted a 48–53 career record from 1948 to 1953. He won a career-high fourteen games in 1951. On May 6, 1951, Chambers was a member of the Pittsburgh Pirates when he pitched a no-hitter in the second game of a doubleheader against the Boston Braves. He was traded to the Cardinals in the deal that brought Joe Garagiola to Pittsburgh.

TONY CLARK at 6'7" is the tallest switch-hitter in major league history. A first baseman with the Detroit Tigers, Clark changed his uniform number to 44 in honor of Hank Aaron prior to the 2000 season. Clark has tremendous power and is capable of hitting the ball as far as anyone in organized baseball.

JERRY COLEMAN played nine years in the major leagues with the great Yankee teams from 1949 to 1957. He made his major league debut on April 20, 1949. His career was interrupted twice for military service in World War II and then the Korean War. Coleman was the regular second baseman on three straight world championship teams from 1949 to 1951. He is a longtime announcer for the San Diego Padres.

GENE CONLEY was a pitcher who towered over the competition during his playing days with the old Boston Braves, Philadelphia Phillies, and Boston Red Sox. The 6'9" right-hander made his major league debut on April 17, 1952. He won championship rings as a pitcher for the 1958 Milwaukee Braves and the 1959, 1960, and 1961 Boston Celtics basketball team. Conley also pitched in three major league All-Star games.

BILLY CONSOLO played for a decade in the major leagues with the Red Sox, Senators, Twins, Phillies, Angels, and Royals. His major league debut was on April 20, 1953, with the Boston Red Sox, a team he went to directly from high school after signing for a $60,000 bonus.

MIKE DIFELICE was born in Philadelphia in 1969, attended the University of Tennessee, and made his major league debut with the St. Louis Cardinals on September 1, 1996. He is a catcher for the Devil Rays.

DOM DIMAGGIO is the younger brother of Joe DiMaggio and Vince DiMaggio. Dubbed the "Little Professor," Dom made his major league debut with the Boston Red Sox on April 16, 1940. The bespectacled centerfielder played his entire eleven-year career with the Red Sox and had a lifetime .298 batting average. A seven-time All Star, Dom was an excellent centerfielder and leadoff man.

BOB FELLER is one of the most famous phenoms in major league history. The hardest thrower of his generation, known as "Rapid Robert" because of his great fastball, Feller made his major league debut on July 19, 1936, before he even finished high school. A star for eighteen seasons, the right-handed hurler recorded three no-hitters and twelve one-hitters. He led the American League in strikeouts seven times. He was the winningest and the best pitcher in the history of the Cleveland Indians. Feller, one of the most dominating pitchers in major league history, was elected to the Baseball Hall of Fame in 1962, and in 1969 he was voted baseball's greatest living right-hander. He was selected as a member of the All-Century Team.

JESSE GARCIA is a utility infielder who made his major league debut with the Baltimore Orioles in 1999, playing second base, third base, and shortstop without making an error. He spent seven seasons in the Orioles minor league system.

GEORGE GENOVESE made his major league debut on April 29, 1950, with the Washington Senators. His total career consisted of three games and one at bat. He went on to a successful career as a major league scout signing players like Matt Williams, Jack Clark, Rob Deer, George Foster, Matt Nokes, Elliott Maddox, Gary Matthews, Chili Davis, and Dave Kingman. In 1988 he was given the "Scout of the Year" award.

MARK GRACE is one of the most popular players in the history of the Chicago Cubs, a true icon. He made his major league debut on May 2, 1988. A member of the franchise's All-Century team, the slick-fielding first baseman is a three-time National League All Star and a four-time Gold Glove winner. He led the major leagues in both hits and doubles in the 1990s. Grace has hit at least .300 in nine of his twelve big league campaigns and has finished in the National League Top 10 in batting eight times. He signed with the Arizona Diamondbacks in the winter of 2000.

PUMPSIE GREEN was the first black player on the Boston Red Sox, the last major league team to be integrated. His debut was on July 21, 1959. Green played for Boston from 1959 to 1962, hitting .244 with twelve homers and sixty-nine RBIs. His career consisted of 344 games spread over five seasons, all with Boston except for the last when he played for the New York Mets.

SHAWN GREEN was the sixteenth pick by the Toronto Blue Jays in the June 1991 draft. He made his major league debut on September 28, 1993. A Gold Glove outfielder in 1999, Green was traded to the Los Angeles Dodgers in November of that year.

DARRYL HAMILTON made his major league debut on June 3, 1988. He has emerged as one of the best defensive outfielders in the big leagues. Several times, Hamilton has fielded a perfect 1.000, and in 1996 he set an American League record with the Texas Rangers with 389 errorless total chances. In the early 1990s with the Brewers, he played in 235 straight games without making an error. He joined the New York Mets in 1999.

MYRON "RED" HAYWORTH, a catcher, really had "a cup of coffee" with the St. Louis Browns in 1944 and 1945. His major league debut was April 21, 1944. His career consisted of 146 games.

KEITH HERNANDEZ was the best fielding first baseman of his era, winning eleven consecutive Gold Gloves. He made his major league debut on August 30, 1974, with the St. Louis Cardinals, and he also played for the New York Mets and Cleveland Indians over seventeen major league seasons. The National League batting leader in 1979, Hernandez also won a co-MVP award that year with Willie Stargell. His career batting average was .296 lifetime. He holds the record for most assists ever for a first base-man.

GLENN HOFFMAN played as an infielder with three teams over nine major league seasons. His debut was on April 12, 1980, with the Boston Red Sox. Hoffman also played for Los Angeles in 1987 and California in 1989. A minor league manager in the Dodger system for five seasons, Hoffman managed the Los Angeles Dodgers to a third-place finish after being named manager on June 21, 1998. In 2000, he was a Dodger coach. His younger brother, Trevor, is an All-Star closer for the San Diego Padres.

FRANK HOWARD made his major league debut on September 10, 1958, with the Los Angeles Dodgers but did not play a full season until 1960, when he won the National League Rookie of the Year award. The man they called "Hondo" and "The Capital Punisher," hit 382 career home runs, had 1,119 RBIs, and a .499 slugging percentage over sixteen seasons with the Dodgers, Senators, Rangers, and Tigers. In 1974, Howard went to Japan to play baseball but hurt his back striking out in his first game and never played again. A former manager of the San Diego Padres and the New York Mets, Howard is a coach today for the Tampa Bay Devil Rays.

MONTE IRVIN was already past thirty years of age and had starred for almost a decade in the Negro Leagues before and after military service in World War II when he made his major league debut on July 8, 1949, with the New York Giants. He played for two pennant winners in five full seasons. Irvin batted .458 and stole home in the 1951 World Series against the Yankees. Batting over .300 three times, Irvin's lifetime average was .293. The Hall of Famer worked for many years in the Baseball Commissioner's office after his playing career ended. The Committee on Negro Baseball Leagues elected him to the Hall of Fame in 1973; later Irvin became a member of the Hall of Fame Committee on Baseball Veterans.

GREGG JEFFERIES was one of the most heralded minor leaguers of his generation. His major league debut with the New York Mets was on September 6, 1987. After a late-season call-up in 1988, Jefferies, at age twenty-one, became the youngest non-pitcher to start a League Championship Series game. He played for the Mets, Royals, Cardinals, Phillies, Angels, and Tigers.

ADAM KENNEDY, a second baseman with the Anaheim Angels, is one of the most highly touted prospects in baseball. Kennedy was chosen by the St. Louis Cardinals in the first round of the 1997 draft. In 1999, he was named the franchise's minor league Player of the Year after hitting .327, and he made his major league debut in August of that year. In 2000, the Cardinals traded Kennedy along with Kent Bottenfield to the Angels for outfielder Jim Edmonds.

JOHN KENNEDY homered in his first major league at bat on September 5, 1962, as a member of the Washington Senators. Virtually a model for the classic utility infielder, Kennedy also played for the Dodgers, Yankees, Pilots/Brewers, and Red Sox in a twelve-year career that ended in 1974. He shared the same birthdate of May 29 with President John F. Kennedy.

RALPH KINER made his major league debut on April 16, 1946, with the Pittsburgh Pirates. He went on to become baseball's greatest home run hitter during the years after World War II. Kiner was traded to the Cubs in 1953 and two years later finished his career with the Indians. Only thirty-three when a bad back ended his career, the five-time All Star retired having hit a home run in every 14.1 at bats. For his ten-year career, he averaged thirty-seven home runs and over a hundred RBIs a season. Kiner hit more home runs per at bat than any other player in history except Babe Ruth. His number 4 was retired by the Pirates in 1987. The Hall of Famer has been an announcer for the New York Mets since 1962 and was selected as a member of the All-Century Team.

MAX LANIER made his major league pitching debut on April 20, 1938. He was the winningest southpaw for three consecutive Cardinal pennant seasons: 1942, 1943, and 1944. In 1946, he jumped to the Mexican League and was suspended from organized baseball. Three years later Lanier was reinstated. He completed his fourteen-year career in 1953 as a member of the St. Louis Browns.

DON LARSEN first pitched in the major leagues on April 18, 1953. Though he had a mediocre career record spread over fourteen seasons with eight different teams, Larsen lives on as a baseball legend for his World Series perfect game against the Brooklyn Dodgers on October 8, 1956. Larsen was the last active former St. Louis Brown. A lifetime .242 batter, he had fourteen career home runs and was used sixty-six times as a pinch hitter.

FRED LYNN had ten twenty-home-run seasons, one batting title, and All-Star appearances in each of his first nine seasons. His major league debut for the Boston Red Sox was on September 5, 1974. In 1975, Lynn led Boston to within one win of the World Championship. He also became the only player ever to be named Rookie of the Year and MVP in the same season. The native Californian also played for the Angels, Orioles, and Tigers.

SAM MCDOWELL made his major league debut on September 15, 1961. The tall and lanky left-hander with the high-powered fastball won five strikeout titles and twice struck out over 300 batters in 1965 and 1970. By age twenty-eight, McDowell seemed capable of becoming the greatest strikeout pitcher the game had ever known. But by 1976, he was out of baseball, a victim of alcoholism. McDowell did wind up with 2,453 career strikeouts. His total of seventy-four games with ten or more strikeouts is fourth behind Nolan Ryan, Sandy Koufax, and Steve Carlton. His career average of 8.86 strikeouts per nine innings trails only Ryan and Koufax.

CHUCK MCELROY spent his first full season with the Chicago Cubs in 1991 setting team rookie records for relief pitchers by appearing in seventy-one games and posting a 1.95 ERA. His major league debut was with the Phillies on September 4, 1989. In 1998, he was named Colorado Rockies Pitcher of the Year after appearing in a team-record seventy-eight games and posting a 2.90 ERA. The left-handed relief pitcher was a member of the Baltimore Orioles in 2000.

SAM MELE was a basketball star at New York University in the early 1940s and went on to play major league baseball for a decade with several teams. He made his big league debut with the Boston Red Sox on April 15, 1947, the same day that Jackie Robinson broke baseball's color line with the Brooklyn Dodgers. During his playing career Mele was an off-season sportswriter with a column in the Quincy, Massachusetts, *Ledger* called "The Mele Ticket." In 1965, Mele managed the Minnesota Twins and took them to the World Series. Mele has the distinction of being named to former Baseball Commissioner Bartlett Giamatti's "Italian All-Star Team."

BRIAN MOEHLER made his major league debut with the Detroit Tigers on September 22, 1996. The right-handed pitcher became a member of the Tigers' starting rotation in 1997, winning the most games (eleven) for a Detroit rookie in twenty years. Moehler had two interesting distinctions in 1999. He was the winning pitcher in the final game at Tiger Stadium on September 27, 1999, and he led the American League with sixteen losses that season.

BOB MONTGOMERY played for nine years in the minors before a .324 batting average and fourteen home runs at Louisville earned him a spot with the Red Sox. His major league debut was September 6, 1970. Montgomery averaged fewer than forty games a season in a decade as a backup catcher for Boston.

MANNY MOTA holds the record for the most pinch hits in baseball history — 150. He made his major league debut with the New York Giants on April 16, 1962. In 1966, Mota had the first of seven .300 plus seasons in eight years. A pinch hitter deluxe, Mota recorded ten or more pinch hits in six straight seasons. He retired with a .297 pinch-hitting average.

JOHN "RED" MURFF made his major league debut on April 21, 1956. The tall Texan had a very brief career as a major league pitcher, getting into just twenty-six games in 1956 and 1957 with the Milwaukee Braves and compiling a 2–2 record. He did have an illustrious thirty-two-year career as a major league scout. Murff will be forever remembered as the man who discovered Nolan Ryan.

CHOLLY NARANJO likes to tell the story of how he protected President Dwight Eisenhower from getting hit by a ball in the 1954 season opener in Washington, D.C. The left-handed, Cuban-born pitcher made his major league debut on July 8, 1956, with the Pittsburgh Pirates. His career pitching record was 1–2.

CLAUDE OSTEEN began his major league pitching career at age seventeen with the Cincinnati Reds on July 6, 1957. A three-time All Star, the stylish southpaw pitched for the Reds, Senators, Dodgers, Astros, Cardinals, and White Sox in an eighteen-year career. Osteen won in double figures each year from 1964 through 1973. A longtime major league pitching coach, Osteen began his first full season as Los Angeles Dodger pitching coach in May 1999.

JIM PALMER spent his entire career with the Baltimore Orioles, becoming the greatest pitcher in their history. His major league debut was April 17, 1965. A three-time Cy Young Award winner, Palmer won four Gold Gloves and had eight twenty-win seasons making him, along with Lefty Grove and Walter Johnson, the only American League pitchers to win twenty games in eight or more seasons. He recorded four pennant-clinching wins and two World Series clinchers for the Orioles. The stylish right-hander with a picture-perfect delivery won 268 games and posted a glittering career 2.86 ERA. After his career ended, Palmer became a local and national TV baseball broadcaster. In 1990, Palmer was elected to the Hall of Fame in his first year of eligibility. He was selected as a member of the All-Century Team.

MEL PARNELL was one of the most stylish and successful Red Sox left-handers ever, as well as a consummate gentleman. The native of New Orleans made his major league debut on April 20, 1947. He was very successful in Fenway Park (70–30) even with the Green Monster as backdrop. In 1949, Parnell was the league leader in wins (twenty-five) and ERA (2.77). Parnell pitched from 1947 to 1956 and wound up as the winningest left-handed pitcher in Red Sox history. In 1963, he was inducted into the Louisiana Sports Hall of Fame.

JOHNNY PESKY made his major league debut on April 14, 1942. He played in 1,270 games as an infielder mainly with the Boston Red Sox where he was the tablesetter for Ted Williams, Bobby Doerr, and Vern Stephens. He was traded to the Detroit Tigers in 1952 and finished his playing career with the Senators in 1954. The scrappy left-handed hitter compiled a lifetime batting average of .307. A contact hitter, he struck out just 218 times, never striking out more than thirty-six times in a season. After his playing career ended, Pesky managed the Red Sox as well as their top farm team. For more than fifty years — as player, coach, manager, broadcaster, advertising salesman, and assistant in the Sox community outreach programs — Pesky has been on the Red Sox scene.

TODD PRATT spent seven years in the minors before the Philadelphia Phillies acquired him in 1992. His major league debut was on July 29 of that year. After stints with the Phillies and the Chicago Cubs, Pratt, at the age of twenty-nine, sat out all of 1996, working as an instructor in the Bucky Dent Baseball School in Florida. In 1999, Pratt helped the Mets make the play-offs as he hit a career-high .293 in seventy-one games as a backup to catcher Mike Piazza. But his biggest contribution came in the play-offs, when his tenth-inning home run beat the Arizona Diamondbacks, 4–3, in the fourth and deciding game of the division series.

JEFF REED began his pro career as a seventeen-year-old catcher for a rookie league affiliate for the Minnesota Twins in 1980. Although he was called up in 1984 and made his major league debut on April 4 of that year, it took ten years before he played a full season in the major leagues. In 1990, his second full season, Reed played in seventy-two games for the World Series champion Cincinnati Reds. The left-handed hitting Reed had his best season in 1997 with the Colorado Rockies, hitting .297 with seventeen home runs in ninety games. He joined the Chicago Cubs in 1999.

BILLY ROGELL was born in 1904 and is one of the oldest living former major leaguers. His big league debut was April 14, 1925. He played in the majors for fourteen seasons. The keystone combination of Rogell and Charlie Gehringer was a key factor in the 1934 and 1935 pennants won by the Detroit Tigers. A switch-hitter, Rogell led American League shortstops in fielding from 1935 through 1937. He tossed out the first pitch at the last game at Tiger Stadium. Rogell served with distinction as a Detroit city councilman from 1941 through 1981.

AL ROSEN made his major league debut with the Cleveland Indians on September 10, 1947. The determined and exuberant power hitter led the American League in home runs and assists as a third baseman in 1950, his first full season. Rosen was the American League Most Valuable Player in 1953 when he led the league in home runs, RBIs, runs scored, and slugging percentage. Injuries forced Rosen into retirement at age thirty-two. He reentered baseball twenty years later as president of the Yankees, then the Astros, then president and general manager of the Giants.

NOLAN RYAN pitched for an incredible twenty-seven seasons in the major leagues starting with his debut on September 11, 1966, with the New York Mets. The all-time strikeout leader (5,714) notched a record seven no-hitters; at age forty-two he still threw a ninety-five-mile-per-hour fastball. Ryan pitched for the Mets, California Angels, Houston Astros, and Texas Rangers. He was selected as a member of the All-Century Team.

RON SANTO is one of the all-time favorites of Cubs fans. The scrappy third baseman made his major league debut on June 26, 1960, and remained on the scene with the Cubs for nearly fourteen years. His best overall season was 1964, when he hit .313, with thirty homers and 114 RBIs. Santo was an All Star nine times. An excellent and aggressive fielder, he won five Gold Gloves.

MIKE SCIOSCIA played for fifteen seasons in the big leagues. After making his debut on April 20, 1980, Scioscia went on to catch 1,395 games for the Los Angeles Dodgers, a club record. The man they called "Iron Mike" had his best offensive season in 1985, when he hit .296 to help the Dodgers win a division title. He played on the 1981 and 1988 Dodgers World Series championship teams and was in the All-Star games in 1989 and 1990. Scioscia managed Albuquerque in 1999 in the Pacific Coast League and was appointed manager of the Anaheim Angels in 2000.

CHUCK STEVENS made his major league debut on September 16, 1941, with the St. Louis Browns. A good fielder who lacked pop in his bat, Stevens spent twenty-three years in organized baseball but only three seasons in the major leagues — 1941, 1946, and 1948 with the Browns. After his retirement as a player, Stevens served as director of the Association of Professional Ball Players of America for more than thirty years.

BOB TEWKSBURY had a lifetime pitching record of 110–102 and a 3.92 lifetime ERA. His walks-per-game ratio of 1.45 was the lowest since the Dead Ball Era. The New Hampshire native made his major league pitching debut on April 11, 1986, with the New York Yankees and finished his career in 1997 with the Minnesota Twins. In between, there were stops with the St. Louis Cardinals, Texas Rangers, and San Diego Padres. His career spanned thirteen big league seasons and included a starting assignment in an All-Star Game.

BOBBY THOMSON was born in Glasgow, Scotland. His major league baseball debut was on September 9, 1946. He hit twenty-four or more homers six times in his seven full seasons with the New York Giants. A broken ankle put a damper on his career. But he will always be remembered for "the Shot Heard 'Round the World" — his home run against the Brooklyn Dodgers on October 3, 1951, which gave the New York Giants the National League pennant. In 1969, Thomson was named to the Giants' all-time outfield along with Willie Mays and Mel Ott. He played for the Giants, Braves, Cubs, Red Sox, and Orioles.

MO VAUGHN is one of the most consistent sluggers in the game. He made his debut with the Boston Red Sox on June 27, 1991, but didn't complete a full season in the major leagues until 1993, when he hit .297 with twenty-nine home runs and 101 RBIs. Over the next five years, the first baseman and designated hitter averaged thirty-seven home runs and 112 RBIs for Boston. Vaughn signed with the Anaheim Angels after the 1998 season.

BILLY WILLIAMS is one of the legendary players in Chicago Cubs history. In 1987, he was inducted into the Baseball Hall of Fame. During his eighteen-year major league career, sixteen seasons with the Cubs, he batted .290 with 2,711 hits, 426 home runs, and 1,475 RBIs. His major league debut was August 6, 1959. Rookie of the Year in 1961, Willliams was a six-time All Star. In 1999, he was selected to the Cubs' All-Century team. The man they called "Sweet Swinging Billy" is fifth all time in consecutive games played with 1,117. A longtime major league coach, Williams is in his third stint as a coach of the Cubs.

ED YARNALL is a left-handed pitcher out of Lima, Pennsylvania, and Louisiana State University. In May 1998, he was traded from the Mets to the Marlins in the deal that brought Mike Piazza to Shea Stadium. Then he was traded from the Marlins to the Yankees for top third base prospect, Mike Lowell. He made his major league debut with the Yankees on July 15, 1999. A year later he was traded to the Cincinnati Reds.

EDDIE YOST was called "The Walking Man." Eight seasons he drew a hundred or more walks, leading the American League in that category six times. His eighteen-year career total for walks was 1,614, which ties him for sixth place all time. Yost never played in the minors, going right from the sandlots of Brooklyn and New York University to the Washington Senators. His major league debut was August 16, 1944. His career saw him move from Washington to the Detroit Tigers to the Los Angeles Angels.

TODD ZEILE made his major league debut with the St. Louis Cardinals on August 18, 1989. The direct descendent of two former U.S. presidents, John Adams and John Quincy Adams, Zeile has played for the Chicago Cubs, Philadelphia Phillies, Baltimore Orioles, Los Angeles Dodgers, Florida Marlins, Texas Rangers, and New York Mets.

DON ZIMMER was built like a fireplug and nicknamed "Popeye" for his strength. He made his major league debut on July 12, 1954, with the Brooklyn Dodgers. The affable Zimmer was also an original New York Met and one of the last of the Washington Senators. He managed the San Diego Padres, Boston Red Sox, Texas Rangers, and Chicago Cubs, where he was Manager of the Year in 1989. He has coached for a number of teams including the Montreal Expos and New York Yankees.

DWIGHT "RED" ADAMS

My background was very unusual for someone who went into baseball. There wasn't much I knew growing up about the history of the game or how to play it. I was a typical country kid. I was born on October 7, 1921. The name of the town I grew up in is Parlier, California, in the heart of the San Joaquin Valley, one of the richest agricultural valleys in the world, a lot of grapes, a lot of fruit trees. It was a good place for any kid to grow up in. This was during the depression, and as they said, everybody was poor, but we didn't know it. We had a mom and dad at home and meals at meal time. Some or most of our clothes were hand-me-downs. But we were happy as hell.

My brother, Morris, had a catcher's mitt, and I had a glove. We'd have a catch every day, throw for at least an hour in the backyard, winter and summer. That was where I developed my arm a little bit.

My parents were from Missouri. My dad liked the St. Louis Cardinals, and I liked the Gashouse Gang of Pepper Martin, Dizzy Dean, all those great players. But overall, as I said, I was pretty illiterate as to what was going on in the major league scene.

I went to Parlier grammar school for eight years and then went on to Parlier High School. Charlie Moncrief was a fellow from my hometown who had played professional baseball. I admired him a lot. He gave me a lot of tips about playing ball, gripping a baseball, being a pitcher.

When I was still in high school, Charlie took me to play in Fresno in a summer league called the Twilight League. It was a pretty fast league with most of the guys coming from regular jobs after work. They could do that in the summer time because it stayed light quite late.

We played in different towns where baseball news came over the ticker tape. They would have a big board at the ballparks, and someone would get up there as the news came in and put the scores up. I saw a lot of that.

I pitched three outstanding games in that Twilight League and struck out a lot of batters, and Charlie thought I could play pro ball.

In 1939, when I was eighteen, Charlie told me he was going to take me to a tryout camp at Wrigley Field in Los Angeles. I was surprised. I had been in some softball games and played one year of baseball in that small high school of about 110 kids. That was really all. I had such limited baseball background. I had only been in eight or nine real baseball games in my life. But even though I had no experience, I had a good arm and could throw hard and throw strikes. Maybe it came from throwing the ball with my brother all those years.

I didn't really expect anything to happen at that tryout camp. My brother-in-law bought me a new glove to take to the tryout because I was playing with the first glove I ever owned.

Incredibly — I say that because I truly expected nothing to happen — I was signed out of that tryout camp to a contract in the Chicago Cubs organization. And in 1946, I came up to the major leagues with the Cubs. I pitched in eight games and had an 0–1 record. In fairness to myself, I had a little arm trouble, and during the off-season I did a lot of work, carpentering. That really wasn't the best way to take care of your arm.

That stint with the Chicago Cubs was my total major league playing career — "a cup of coffee," as they say. I was essentially a minor league player spending most of my eighteen-year professional baseball playing career in the old Pacific Coast League.

But everybody has a story. Any name I really made for myself came as pitching coach for the Dodgers in Los Angeles.

JOEY AMALFITANO

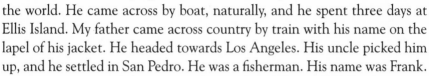

My father came to this country from Italy
when he was sixteen years old. He left his mother
and father and was trying to make his own way in
the world. He came across by boat, naturally, and he spent three days at
Ellis Island. My father came across country by train with his name on the
lapel of his jacket. He headed towards Los Angeles. His uncle picked him
up, and he settled in San Pedro. He was a fisherman. His name was Frank.

I was born in 1934, so I grew up after the depression. I grew up in San
Pedro, which is a fishing village. My hero was Joe DiMaggio, because he
was Italian. Growing up I was a Yankees fan. We didn't have any major
league baseball there, but we had the Pacific Coast League and the California State League. I would go up to Wrigley Field and watch the Los Angeles Angels and the Hollywood Stars play. The Stars were affiliated with
the Pittsburgh Pirates, and the Angels were affiliated with the Cubs.

I got to see the Yankees play an exhibition game at Wrigley Field. I went
up because DiMaggio was playing. He hit a home run. That was a moment
that always stayed with me.

I used to listen to a lot of re-created games on the radio. Whenever I
was fortunate enough and could watch a game on television, like the
"Game of the Week," that was very important to me. Pee Wee Reese and
Dizzy Dean were the announcers, and I learned a lot about baseball listening to them.

When we were real young, we would all chip in and go down and buy a
baseball for the games we played on Saturday. There were five or six of us
who would go into the sporting goods store to buy the ball. You thought
you were buying a diamond ring. We took a lot of time picking out the one
we wanted. Then you'd knock that thing around, and if it went foul, you'd
have to go out and get it. We cherished that ball even though we used to
beat the hell out of it. That's why there were all those times that we used
to tape it up.

The gloves we used were not as sophisticated as today's gloves back then. I still have my first glove. It's a finger glove that my parents got for me. It might have been a Bobby Doerr model, but I can't tell what it was after all these years.

The bats the professional players use today are much heavier than those we used when I was growing up. Naturally, there were no aluminum bats back then. All we had was wood. You used whatever bat that was available that was furnished by the team you played for. You weren't too choosy. You just wanted to go out and play.

When we were young, there was no Little League baseball or Connie Mack or any of that. But we had a little team when we were all fifteen or younger. We would go out and play other teams that were the same age as us. We had a lot of fun.

I played a lot of softball when I was a kid. Then I moved on to play hardball baseball. Different things happened in that game that gave you a thrill. The sport excited me.

I played third base as a kid and all through high school and college. One of the guys who influenced me was Jim Mantellino Sr. He ran a semipro team for the Catholic church in San Pedro. He got me involved in base-ball. Before that another guy who influenced me was John "Red" Zar.

In high school I played baseball, football, and basketball. When I was a sophomore, I ran track because I wanted to improve on my speed. When I left high school, I concentrated totally on baseball.

I could have signed out of high school, but I didn't know if I wanted to play professional baseball. I didn't know what I wanted to do. I went on to college at Loyola University, which is now called Loyola-Marymount of Los Angeles. I played there for two years. The coach was Joe Gonzales, who really helped me. He was a former pitcher in the Red Sox organiza-tion and did spend a little time in the majors with the Red Sox. He would always give me some of his special time and throw batting practice to me trying to teach me how to hit a curve. He kept encouraging me to play professional ball, because I guess he saw some talent or something.

I played two years of college baseball. I just had the fever to play ball. I was having a lot of fun, getting a lot of enjoyment out of it. Scouts were coming after me. Finally, I played in an exhibition game over at Redondo Beach against major league All Stars who were getting ready to go to spring training. I played pretty good, had a lot of fun.

When I walked off the field, a scout for the White Sox came over and started to talk seriously to me about playing baseball professionally. I decided that, jeez, maybe I wanted to do this for a living. So I ended up signing with the New York Giants with guys named Ebo Pucich and Dutch Ruether, who had been a famous left-handed pitcher in the major leagues. I trusted both of those guys. They were fine men.

The scouts came to my house for the signing. Because I was a minor, my parents had to sign my contract. My father was a commercial fisherman who owned his own boat. I had to leave the scouts and go down on the docks to get my father.

He was down in the hatch working on the boat. I went down. I didn't speak Italian, very, very, very little. My father spoke very little English. So I tried to speak to him in Italian and explain that he had to come home. He asked me in Italian, because my mother wasn't feeling well at the time, "Is something wrong with your mother?"

I said, "No, Dad, she is fine, okay."

Then when I got him in the car, I told him in English that I was bringing him home because I wanted to play baseball, that I wanted to sign a contract, that he had to sign it, because I was a minor.

He was in his working clothes. I introduced him to the two scouts, Ebo and Dutch. We sat in the living room. He signed the contract. Then they got up, and my father said to me in Italian, "Take me back to the boat."

So I drove him back. My father asked, "What did you sign for?" — meaning what kind of money did you sign for.

I said, "$35,000."

He said, "America is a great country." I will always remember that.

My first year when I went out to play ball, I had to join the Giants in Phoenix, Arizona, which is the next state over from California. My parents went to Union Station to see me off. I was about set to take a train.

"Where are you going?" my father asked me in Italian.

"Arizona."

And he said, "Oh, my God."

I said, "Dad, my God, when you were sixteen years old, you came across the ocean, then across the country." He never said nothing to me.

My father didn't know much about baseball when I first started to play as a pro. But I'll say one thing, the more I started to play, the more he enjoyed watching the game.

There was a rule back then for what they called "Bonus Babies" like me. It said that if you received over $6,000, you had to stay with the major league team for two seasons counting against the major league roster. That's what I did.

My first year, 1954, was a great year because I got the best seat in the house. The Giants went to the World Series beating Cleveland four straight. I had come to bat just five times all season, but I still collected a $10,000 World Series share. It was not a bad way for an eighteen-year-old kid to start.

I did fish with my father when I was very young, and then, when I'd come back from the minor league season times, he would take me fishing with him. But when I made it to the major leagues, he didn't want me to go fishing anymore.

RICH AMARAL

$\mathcal{I}$ *grew up* in Costa Mesa, California. My dad passed away when I was one in 1963, so I was with my mom and two sisters. It was my uncle, Manuel Escalera, who got me interested in and taught me how to play baseball. I started playing Little League when I was seven. Our team was the Giants. I played everywhere I could — short, pitcher, catcher, everything.

Growing up I liked playing, doing everything. It didn't matter which sport. I played football, basketball, I surfed, and I skateboarded. My favorite sport was skateboarding.

In high school I played second base. I was 150 pounds, I was too small to play anything else. Then I kind of realized that the only thing I really had the chance to play after high school was baseball, so I decided to really bear down.

I was an Angels fan. I liked watching Bobby Grich, who played second base. I liked the way he played defense; he was good with the bat. I loved watching Pete Rose. He wasn't small, but he played a scrappy-type game. He was somebody I wanted to kind of model my game after — the hustle, the diving, all of that stuff.

I thought of playing baseball professionally, but it was so far away, and those guys were so good in the big leagues, you'd never dream that you'd be out there with them. I wasn't scouted in high school. It wasn't until college that I really thought I had a chance to make it. I went to Orange Coast for a year, then I went to UCLA for two. I started getting scouted my junior year by the Cubs and the Reds.

When you're playing during the season, you try to block all of that out, whatever the scouts are thinking, you just try to help your team win. And honestly, I didn't know anything about pro ball. Growing up in California, I wasn't around any minor league teams, I didn't know what the minor league teams were like. I didn't know that they had leagues all around the country. I didn't know about the bus rides. I didn't know any of that. I was just so focused on playing college ball.

Then there I was having a good year in my junior year, I get drafted, and I say, wow, this is a time I will play pro ball. I didn't know what I was going to have to go through. I wound up playing parts of almost ten years in the minor leagues.

There were people who thought and said I should pack it up, but I stayed with it through all those years. And there were plenty of times of doubt. There were times I was going back to double-A for four years in a row, and it didn't look that good for me.

But deep down I felt like I had enough talent to play in the big leagues. I just wasn't getting the opportunity. Sometimes it's tough. There are a lot of good players in the minor leagues, and it's tough to play every day down there. I was also in different situations where I had to share time with other players who were good players. It kept me from putting up some big numbers in the minor leagues and moving up.

In 1991, I was in triple-A and the manager called me in and said, "You're going up."

It was pretty awesome. I was twenty-nine years old. Because I played so long in the minor leagues, it was extra special for me to play my first game in the big leagues. I remember standing out at shortstop and waiting for the guy to throw the pitch, the first pitch of the game, just to say, I played the game.

The game was in the Kingdome, and the Mariners weren't that good, really weren't drawing that many people. But the first day I was there it was Ken Griffey Junior T-shirt night, so they had like 55,000 people there, so I was pretty nervous.

GEORGE "SPARKY" ANDERSON

Baseball is a marvelous fantasy. There will be 40,000 people in the stands, and every one of them wishes he could be down on the playing field.

I was born in Bridgewater, South Dakota, in 1934. I was one of five children, this small kid with big ears. My dad had been a semipro catcher in South Dakota. My uncle had been a pitcher. On Sundays, they would travel around the area playing in baseball games for five or ten dollars. I used to go around with them. I'd be the batboy. It was a lot of fun, and I think that is what really got me started off in baseball. My dad just loved baseball; he had a real feel for the game. He may not have known all the ins and outs of the game, but he loved it, and he instilled that love in me. I couldn't really play well, but I was always playing. Winning to me was always everything.

In 1942, when I was nine years old, we moved to California. It was during the war. My father had gotten a job working in the shipyards. When we moved to California, we lived in central Los Angeles, two blocks from the campus of the University of Southern California. That was the greatest blessing that ever happened to me. There I was living almost next door to a major college, me who, coming from South Dakota, didn't know anything.

The first day of school, I was coming home and I saw this ball come over the fence and land in the bushes. The equipment manager came out to get it. He was looking around and looking around, but he couldn't find it. But I saw where it had landed. As soon as he left, I went and got it.

The University of Southern California ballpark was a combination baseball field and track and field facility. The track circled the whole thing. I walked around the track, and I brought the ball in.

"Who is the boss?" I asked. I did not know anything about a manager or coach. They pointed to the coach, Rod Dedeaux. I gave him the ball. The next thing I knew I became his batboy. I had that job for six years. Rod

Dedeaux was a great coach, and not just a great college coach. He was there at USC for forty-five years, winning eleven NCAA championships with the Trojans. It makes me angry when he's introduced as the greatest college coach in the last hundred years. You're either a great coach or you're not.

I learned everything about baseball from him, all the fundamental things, all the sophisticated things, all the things I used later on in my baseball life. I never forgot them. I always liked to hang around older people and listen to them because they were so smart. What I learned from others I put into my repertoire. And Rod was one of the smartest.

After I left Rod, I became the batboy for the Hollywood Stars in the old Pacific Coast League. Fred Haney was the manager. I'm gonna tell you something. That was a team. That was a team that got a lot of attention and support. The celebrities were always around, all the Hollywood people. They were big baseball fans. I used to see the actor George Raft all the time. He loved his baseball.

Lefty Phillips was a scout for the Dodgers back then. He would work me out during the week and afterwards would drive me home. Dinner would be waiting for me on the table, but I would be sitting in that car talking to Lefty. I just wanted to play, to learn how to play, to talk baseball.

I used a Lonnie Frey glove at first. Then I went to the Bobby Dillinger. The manufacturer of both was Rawlings. The reason I liked my Dillinger was that it was flat. I could toss it about ten feet, and it would land flat like a pancake.

My buddy through all those years of growing up was Billy Consolo. I first met Billy on the Rancho Playground in Los Angeles. We were both about ten years old. We had just moved from South Dakota; the Consolos had come from Cleveland. We were best of friends through high school and American Legion ball. Billy and I were on Crenshaw Post 715, the 1951 American Legion champions that won the title in Detroit in the park that became Tiger Stadium that was then called Briggs Stadium. We had a hell of a team.

We also had a pretty good team at Dorsey High School. I played shortstop. I would say, honest to goodness, by the time I graduated from high school, I really knew how to play baseball. I knew everything about playing baseball. I really studied the game. I just wished I had more talent.

I was taught so well by so many different people, but Rod Dedeaux and

Lefty Phillips stand out as the two people on my list who most helped me learn the game. And it was Lefty Phillips who signed me to play for the Dodger organization.

I started in 1953 with Santa Barbara in the California State League playing shortstop. I loved playing shortstop, but I hated to go in the hole; I didn't have the arm. That Dodger organization had twenty-six teams then, fourteen of them won that year and twelve finished in the first division. You talk about something that Mr. Rickey built.

I got to meet him during spring training. He had seminars that we had to go to twice a week over in the auditorium. Everybody went whether they were discussing pitching, outfield, or infield play. He wanted to have every player know why things happened at every position. He became another one of my incredible teachers. Nobody has any idea today about what went on when the game was the game.

I started out with six seasons in the minor league farm system of the Dodgers. They realized early on that I didn't have a good arm, so they switched me to play second. Of course, not only did I not have a good arm, I didn't have a lot of talent, so I tried to make up for it with spit and vinegar. Talent is one thing. Being able to go from spring to October is another.

There was no room for me with the Dodgers, so they traded me to the Phillies. My total major league experience was with the last-place Philadelphia club in 1959. I was the regular second baseman for Philadelphia. I hit .218 with no homers and thirty-four RBIs. Those were the only 477 major league at bats of my career. It was a disappointment to me but also an eye opener where I had to be honest with myself.

Thank God, I was honest enough to have common sense and realize I wasn't good enough to play in the big leagues.

ELDEN AUKER

I come from Norcatur, Kansas, a little town of about 350 people out in western Kansas, about twelve miles from the Nebraska line and eighty-five to a hundred miles to the Colorado line. It was just a country town, a cow town about three blocks long. It was in wheat country. We had one restaurant in town, but we had no recreation facility, except the high school gym.

I was born September 21, 1910, and I was an only child. My father had a steady government job as a mail carrier. He was a rural route carrier for about forty-six years or something like that. I think the most he ever made was $60 a month, and he had to pay all of his expenses out of that.

We had four horses. When he first started out, my dad rode horseback to deliver the mail. Later on he used a motorcycle. When I was six weeks old, as I was told later, my mother got on the back of that motorcycle with me, and we went around with him on his route. His route was about twenty-five miles long, and he probably had twenty-five patrons on the whole route. I guess he took us around the route because he wanted to show those twenty-five patrons his new son.

We didn't have too many kids in town, but there seemed to be more during the summer time. We'd play catch and then choose up sides and have baseball games.

My father didn't play baseball. My father was not athletic. He could have been if he wanted to be, but he just never took it up. He just wasn't that kind of a guy. My Uncle Frank, who was married to my mother's sister, was a wrestler in those days. He and his brother, Ed Brunk, were noted for their wrestling and boxing skills. Frank liked athletics. He played a little baseball, pitched and played the outfield, just country baseball. He was the one who showed me how to throw a curveball. He also helped me a bit with my fastball, which I could throw hard as a kid.

When I was in high school, they had a town team. It was a bunch of men in town who got together and formed a baseball team. It was no secret that I could throw the ball pretty hard. So they asked me if I would pitch for them. They played on Sundays against the other towns around that particular area.

When I was pitching for the town team, I remember several Sundays out there in the summer time when there was terrible heat, like 100, 115 degrees. But no humidity. The wind would be blowing so hard. We had terrible winds. In fact, that's what created the Great Dust Bowl that they had in those days. I knew a lot of the people moved out of Kansas and moved west, a lot of the farmers, you know, they just blew out. It just ruined their crops and took all their topsoil off, and many of the farmers around there lost their farms. A lot of them moved to California like in *The Grapes of Wrath.*

During those days, we had no radios. This was before radio came out to the area I lived in. We never had a daily paper nor a local paper. The closest cities to where we lived was Denver, which was about 250 miles west, and Kansas City, 300 miles east.

I'd read once in a while a story about Babe Ruth hitting home runs, and that's about all, because there wasn't much sports news out in that part of the country. I was never caught up as a fan in baseball. I never knew anything about baseball, except just playing it. I never knew anything about the major leagues. I really wasn't too interested in it anyway; I was too busy playing.

I don't know or don't remember where I got the first glove. The first ball I ever started with was an old tape-ball or something like that. We never had too many baseballs. Even the town team that I played with had very few baseballs.

The baseball fields we played on were just cow pastures, really. They were out in the pastureland on open ground. You could see from there for miles around. We had some kind of gunny sacks or something that were the bases. When we did have a baseball field in town, which they eventually built, it was all just dirt — dirt infield and outfield, no grass.

We never had any high school baseball. There just weren't enough kids in the high school. My graduating class in 1928 was twelve members. We had a football team, and I think we had twelve players. You didn't dare get hurt, because if you did, you had to keep playing.

I kind of got my growth spurt in high school. I was a tall, skinny kid. In fact, my sophomore year in college, I was 6'2". I weighed 165 pounds. And the next year, my junior year, I weighed about 175 pounds. My senior year in football season, I weighed 202 pounds. Football really was my game then. I was pretty successful and captain my last year.

My plan was to become a doctor and go to college to study medicine. But there was no way I could go without getting a job, having some way to get money. I talked to Charlie Corsell who was the baseball and basketball coach at Kansas State University. He got me a job that paid me $1 a day.

I swept out a drug store and mopped it every day, for the four years I was in college. I had to have the drug store all mopped up, all cleaned up, by eight o'clock in the morning. I got up at five o'clock every morning. I lived about two miles from the drug store. I would run to the drug store, since I didn't have any transportation except running. And I did that for four years.

Now that sounds foolish that $1 a day would help me in school. But in those days, you could buy breakfast for 15¢, and lunch was probably 25¢. You could get a good dinner in town for 35¢. A 50¢ dinner was a big dinner.

I was so busy. I was taking premed. I was playing three sports and working. I didn't have much time to read the newspapers, or anything else. In my sophomore year, we were opening up against Purdue University. About ten days before, I hurt my shoulder. But they fixed me up putting a kind of steel brace over it. I went in and I played.

I played football for the rest of the season. The next year, I had the shoulder injured again. Then in the spring of the year when I went out for baseball, I couldn't throw directly overhand. So I began to throw kind of sidearm. I did that for three years in college, lost only two games.

After the football season was over in my senior year, Bronco Nagurski from the Chicago Bears and a fellow by the name of Bert drove out to Manhattan, Kansas. They wanted me to sign a contract with the Bears for $500 a game, and a twelve-game guarantee. That was $6,000 to sign with the Chicago Bears. I did not give them my decision then, because I knew there was a lot of interest from major league baseball teams.

Truth be told and not to appear immodest, I won nine varsity letters — three each in baseball, basketball, and football — during my career at KSU. I was also the first athlete to be an All American in three sports. So there was a lot of interest in me as an athlete from different quarters.

Bill Essick of the New York Yankees was a famous scout. He wanted to sign me. The St. Louis Cardinals made contact with me. They were interested, too. I was scouted by and had an opportunity to sign with the Brooklyn Dodgers. I still have about four or five letters from Casey Stengel, who I was dealing with. The Dodgers offered me $500 a month to play in the minor leagues for them. Tiger scout Steve O' Rourke watched me a lot as I was coming up. The Tigers offered me $450 a month. I went with the Tigers over the Dodgers because Steve O'Rourke said Detroit was building a young baseball team.

When I signed with the Tigers, I could not tell you who the teams were in the American League. I knew absolutely nothing about professional baseball. The only reason I signed a professional baseball contract was that it was an opportunity for me to earn some money. I thought, if someone was willing to pay me to pitch — I was all for it. Four hundred and fifty dollars a month was a lot of money to me.

My parents were supportive, but they didn't know what it was all about. They knew I was going to get paid $450 a month. In those days, that was outlandish money.

I reported to Detroit right after I graduated from college. It was the next day, in fact. I left on the train from Kansas City. The next morning, I was in the office of the Tigers in downtown Detroit. I met Mr. Navin who ran the ball club. He said to me, "I understand you're thinking about playing football this fall."

I said, "Yes, I've been offered a contract with the Chicago Bears to play for them for $6,000."

He didn't say anything, so I kept on talking. "I thought after the baseball season's over, why, I'd try to play football."

Then he said, "Well, look. We think you have the makings of a major league pitcher. But if you're thinking about playing football, I'm not interested." He said that with some firmness and then continued: "You're going to be a liability to us if we send you to the minor leagues to get you experience. I don't have a lot of money. If you're going to play football, I'm not going to spend one penny on you. I'm going to leave here for a few minutes, and when I come back in this room, you tell me whether you're going to play baseball or football. If you say you're going to play football, I'll give you a ticket back to Kansas. Because I'm not interested in trying to support you in baseball, and then having you go out and play football. I just can't take that chance."

He went out of the room for a couple of minutes. Then he returned. "What is your decision?"

I said, "I'll play baseball."

He said, "Well, you're not going to play football this fall."

I said, "OK."

They sent me to Decatur, Illinois, which was in the 3-I League. Bob Coleman was the manager. He was quite a well-known minor league manager. He held the record for the most wins for a minor league manager up until just a few years ago.

Bob saw me throw, and, as I explained, I threw sidearmed. He said, "Elden, if you're going to pitch in the major leagues, you'll have to get the ball over the plate, you have to have control. Throwing the ball from sixty feet, six inches, and trying to hit a seventeen-inch plate, sidearm — that will be very tough to do consistently. So many sidearmers have trouble with their control.

"There used to be a fellow by the name of Carl Mays with the Yankees," he continued. "He threw directly underhanded. Did you ever have a chance to try throwing directly underhanded?"

"No, I never did," I told him.

Coleman said, "Well, you're fast enough, and you've got a good curveball. I'd like to see you throw directly underhanded. You can line up with the plate better. It's just like overhanded, except it's reversed. Then all you'd have to work on is your height."

Well, I pitched batting practice for four or five days. Bob watched me. Then he said to me, "Elden, I'm going to start you against Quincy, Illinois, which is leading the league. You're going to pitch nine innings underhanded. I don't care how many hits they get off you, or how many walks, but you're going to pitch nine innings. You're going to pitch it underhanded."

So I did. And I shut 'em out. We beat 'em, I think, 1–0 or 2–0. I struck out something like fifteen men. That was the last time I ever threw a ball any way except underhanded. That's the way it started. That's how I got the nickname "Submariner" because of what they called "this highly unorthodox underhanded delivery." It all came about because of that shoulder injury in college.

I came up in 1933 and made my major league debut on August 10. Tiger Stadium was Navin Field, and there were no light towers. Games started at three o'clock in the afternoon. One of my great early moments was coming into Yankee Stadium for the first time and facing Babe Ruth for the first time. They called me in from the bullpen. I struck him out on four pitches. He didn't like that too much.

TIM BELCHER

I was probably three or four years old the first time I played baseball. I kind of grew up around slow-pitch softball, which my dad played. My dad was really good. He played outfield.

My mom and dad were always doing something athletic — softball or bowling or whatever. More than anything, they just taught us the value of participation, playing games with other kids and things like that.

I grew up around those slow-pitch softball games in the parks of Ohio my father played. We were there every weekend all summer long. It was me along with other players' kids all getting together in a baseball or softball game among ourselves.

My dad wasn't like a tennis dad starting me out as a three-year-old in classes and camps and all kinds of stuff like that. Just being around my dad, watching him play, got me into the game.

My favorite team back then was the Cincinnati Reds, even though we lived actually closer to Cleveland. We went to Cleveland, too, but most of the time we went to Riverfront to watch the Reds. The Indians weren't the team then that they are today. The Reds were in their heyday — the Big Red Machine of the early to mid seventies. My hero was Johnny Bench, because I was a catcher as a kid.

I played catcher from the time I was seven and played Little League all the way through my sophomore year of high school. I liked the action of the position. My throwing arm was always good, so the position was kind of a natural fit.

I grew up thinking I'd be a big leaguer. My mom still has a note that I wrote her when I was like nine years old asking her to get me up at a certain time one morning during the summer. At the bottom I wrote, "P.S. — save this, it will be worth something some day." She still has it.

It's not something that really you talk about a lot when you're a kid growing up in a small community, like, "I'm going to be a big leaguer."

Other kids laugh at you — "Yeah, right." And actually, as I got older, into my teens, I probably talked about it and thought about it less, but it was still in the back of my mind, still something that I wanted to try to do.

I went from catching to playing shortstop in high school, probably for the same reason that most kids play shortstop in high school. They're the best athlete on the team and have a good throwing arm. It's also a pretty important position on the field. Then I played a little bit of third base at Mount Vernon Nazarene College. I didn't really pitch full-time until my second year in college.

Following my junior season in 1983, I was named the right-handed pitcher on the *Sporting News* college All-America team. That's when I started thinking I had a real shot. I went to a couple of professional try-outs. I made the Pan Am team and then began seeing a bunch of scouts showing up. I figured, "Well, they must like what they see."

I was drafted in the June 1983 amateur draft as the very first pick in the first round by the Minnesota Twins. But I didn't sign. Negotiations just didn't go well. That was at the end of the Calvin Griffith ownership period. They were really stingy with money and really cutting back. They left three of their top picks unsigned that year.

I was selected by the New York Yankees in the secondary phase of the 1984 free-agent draft, but I became the center of controversy before I ever pitched in pro ball. The Yankees didn't have the chance to protect me. I was taken by Oakland from the player compensation pool after Baltimore signed Type A free agent Tom Underwood. That incident pointed up the problems of the compensation system, which was later abandoned. I was traded by Oakland to the Dodgers for Rick Honeycutt.

My first major league game was September 6, 1987. I came in in relief at Dodger Stadium against the Mets. It was a Sunday afternoon, extra innings. I had been in the bullpen the two previous days and didn't get in to pitch, but that day I wasn't in the bullpen. I was in the dugout because I was going to start on Wednesday on the upcoming road trip. But the game went into extra innings, and we started using up the bullpen. About the thirteenth, fourteenth inning I was told, "Hey, you may need to get your spikes on. Go down to the bullpen."

By the time I got my spikes and got down there, the phone was ringing in the bullpen. The voice on the phone said, "All right, you're in the game in the fifteenth." So I really didn't have time to get nervous. It was a good first outing. I pitched the fifteenth and sixteenth innings. We won on a wild pitch. I pitched two shutout innings and got the win.

I began in 1988 in the Dodger bullpen and worked my way into a starting pitcher role. I wound up with the 21–6 record and a 2.91 ERA. We won the pennant, and I was National League Rookie Pitcher of the Year.

DALE BERRA

My growing-up time was mostly spent playing sports, basically with my brothers. Baseball to
me was playing Wiffle ball, throwing pop-ups to
myself, thinking of throwing the ball against the house, being all
the different players on all the different teams, getting to play against
older kids when I was younger and — and this was a big difference between me and other kids — going out to a major league ball park and being able to catch fly balls during batting practice hit by big league hitters
and being able to be around big league players.

But also I would like to say I played all sports. Dad was a big advocate
of playing all sports. As soon as the baseball season ended, I played hockey.
As soon as hockey ended, I played football. Whatever sport was in season — I was playing it.

Growing up in Montclair, New Jersey, I was aware of my father's great-
ness as a baseball player but not cognizant of it. I don't know. That might
be a Yogiism. I didn't think too much of it. I think one of the reasons we —
meaning my brothers and I — handled it so well is that we stayed in one
town when we were kids. We weren't moving around and having to make
new friends. We weren't a novelty except for maybe a little while.

When I tried out for a local team, I might have been Yogi Berra's son.
But I knew all the kids already, so it wasn't like they were ready to see what
I could do. They were not waiting to see me. They saw me every day in
school and on the playgrounds.

I was a Mets fan growing up. This was when Dad was the coach and
manager of the Mets. I remember going to spring training and seeing
Casey Stengel down there. He was very friendly and talkative.

I was a batboy when I was about nine years old. It was very exciting. I
became friends with Tom Seaver, Bud Harrelson, Ron Swoboda. I remember even the early Mets — Tommy Davis, Ken Boyer, Nolan Ryan. Dad
said Nolan threw real hard.

When I was a kid, a day did not go by when I didn't think I was going to be a professional athlete. I didn't even know which sport. But I knew I was going to make a living playing sports. I didn't think of doing anything else.

I really didn't think about what a privilege it was growing up as Yogi Berra's son. I just looked forward to going to the ballpark. I didn't like watching the games. I went to the ballpark with my dad not for the games but for the batting practice, playing the outfield and going after grounders. To tell the truth, the games were boring to me. During the games I used to go under the stands and throw the ball against the walls. I would go down to the clubhouse and help the clubhouse man. I liked playing much more than watching, much more.

I remember the Mantles coming over to the house in Montclair, the Fords coming over for a cookout in the summer. One thing I did notice was that me and my brothers, Timmy and Larry, were much better than the other players' kids. I noticed this when I was nine, ten years old. I remember going in the backyard and playing Wiffle ball with the Mantle kid. I thought he was going to be better than he was.

My dad was signed with Spalding, which was a great glove maker at the time. We used to get good equipment, good stuff. Every once in a while we would get a glove from a major league player. I had started playing infield in Little League, and Chuck Hiller, who was on the Mets then, gave me a glove. I loved that glove, I cherished it. I did not use it as a memorabilia piece. I used it to play with. Dad told me Chuck Hiller was a good fielder, and I used that glove all throughout Little League.

In school when they were choosing teams, I was the first one picked. That was in every sport. I guess it was a combination of natural ability and the fact that we played so much. Dad never did anything with us, never put pressure on us. I remember asking Dad to have a catch with me when he came home from a game and he said, "That's what you have got broth-ers for." He didn't play with us. My mom, Carmen, was always there for us. She would take me to games, pick me up, take me to soccer, take me to Pop Warner.

I started at shortstop as a freshman at Montclair High School — which nobody had ever done before. By my junior year I knew I was getting good and that the scouts were coming around. I was first-team All State. I had power and a good arm. Average speed.

After my junior season in baseball leading into the summer break, scouts told my dad that he would be wise not to let me play football and hockey in my senior year because they projected me as a high draft pick. My dad said, "The hell on that. Go ahead and play. If you are going to get hurt, you're going to get hurt." That was what he had done. He played all the sports. He always said, "Play 'em all."

I was the eighteenth pick in the draft, first-round pick. I got a phone call from Joe Brown, who was the general manager of the Pirates. He congratulated me. I was hoping I would get drafted by the Mets, because Dad was still with the team, but it didn't happen.

Howie Haak and Gene Baker were the scouts from the Pirates. They came over to the house. There were discussions. I got $50,000 to sign. This was 1975. At that time that was a lot of money.

I was excited at the idea of going away to play baseball. I had never been away from home for any period of time until then. Two weeks after high school graduation I was playing in Niagara Falls in the New York Penn League — a seven-hour drive from Montclair. I had my own car, my own apartment — $95 a month. We were only making $500 a month.

It was a rude awakening that first year in the minors. I was hitting .550 in high school. When you face college pitching and other first-round picks, you realize how difficult the game really is. I hit .260 there. I had never hit less than .400. But I led the league in RBIs. I was eighteen years old, and I won an award from the sportswriters there as the outstanding player in the league. The time was successful from my point of view. I enjoyed the experience.

Those were the first ballparks I played in — Albany, Elmira, Oneonta. They were nice little ballparks. Newark, New York, the little town where the farm team of the Milwaukee Brewers played, was odd. When it was a perfectly clear night, the game had to be stopped in the second or third inning because the sun would go down right in centerfield. We would wait a half an hour because it was impossible for hitters to see under those conditions.

When Dad was the manager with the Mets, he could always follow me through the minor league reports. But he got fired that year of 1975, and he was able to have time to come up and watch me play for about six games. They made a big deal up there having Yogi Berra in the ballpark. It was a big perk having a Hall of Famer in the ballpark. They turned it into a promotion. I remember I hit a home run the first time he saw me.

I went to A ball in Charleston, South Carolina, the next year and really learned how to play. The manager there was Mike Ryan, who had been with the Red Sox and Phillies. He taught me how to play. I played every day and expected to play every day.

I was then with Columbus, which had a lot of players who made it in the majors. The manager of the team was Johnny Lipon. He was great. I was good then, played every day. I was twenty years old, but I was leading the International League in home runs and RBIs.

Rennie Stennet broke his leg in the middle of August 1977, and I got a phone call that night: "Report to Pittsburgh." That is pretty much when the adversity began.

My major league debut was August 22, 1977. The game was against the San Diego Padres. They had Gene Tenace, Dave Winfield, Cito Gaston, Rollie Fingers, Willie McCovey. We had a great team — Stargell and Dave Parker and Al Oliver. All those guys. That was the beginning of the "We Are Family" team.

I batted against Bob Shirley. I flew out to leftfield my first time up. Now it got tough. I was pinch hit for my third major league at bat, which never obviously would have happened before. The next game I didn't even start. So all of a sudden you go from the guy who comes to the ballpark every day knowing you're going to bat third, knowing you're going to play, knowing you're leading the league in RBIs and home runs. Then you are in the big leagues, and you don't even know when you are going to play. As I said, now the adversity starts. Now it's difficult.

I played nine years total in the majors — Pittsburgh, Houston, and the Yankees. But my formative years were in Pittsburgh. I played three years every day in Pittsburgh. That is where I got a chance to play. That was the highlight of my career.

As I once said, "You can't compare me to my father. Our similarities are different."

MIKE BORDICK

When I was four, my mom bought me a left-handed glove. That didn't work out. She was just trying to help out. But I was right-handed. After we got by that little hurdle, things started to improve as far as baseball was concerned.

My dad was a big influence on me as a kid. He taught me how to play the game. We played in the backyard; it was like a sandlot type of thing in good old upstate New York. A bunch of kids would come by to play. We would break windows and all that great kid stuff.

I remember getting a baseball for my seventh birthday and thinking it was the greatest thing in the world. Then we played a game that day. Somebody hit that ball into the cow pasture across the field. My birthday ball was lost. It was devastating.

We would play three-on-three baseball. Our neighbors had four or five kids. There were also a couple more who lived across the street. We'd run the bases. The only fence was that cow fence out in rightfield. It was kind of a short porch out there. There was a garden out in leftfield; sometimes you'd have to chase the ball into the garden. You had to go get it, pulling carrots and all that going after a ball.

Even though we had only three guys on a team, we were able to cover the entire field because as a younger player, you really started understanding about hitters' tendencies. You knew that this guy was going to pull it, or that guy would hit it the other way.

My dad was a catcher. He always kind of promoted that spot, so I liked playing catcher. Every little kid wants to touch the ball as much as he can. What position can you touch the ball more than as catcher or pitcher? So when I started playing organized ball when I was five and then Little League, I used to catch and pitch. But I also played short.

I remember getting beat by a kid that I never thought could hit. I was pitching. I said to myself, we got this game won. Then this kid got a base hit off me. I learned something about baseball that day. I also cried.

My father was in the Air Force, and we moved about frequently in my growing-up years. I was born in Michigan, spent parts of my early childhood in Maine and also in upstate New York. My dad ended up retiring, and we settled down in Winterport, Maine, where I went to high school at Hampden Academy.

I used to like the Dodgers. One of my real favorites was Steve Garvey, just because of the way he stood up at the plate. But when we moved up to New England, I became a Boston Red Sox fan. Carl Yastrzemski, when I was hitting left-handed playing Wiffle ball, was always my favorite.

If there was a day in Maine that you put a jacket on and it wasn't snowing, we'd be outside playing baseball. For high school practices, if the wind was blowing and the snow was moving around a little bit, we'd be on a hardwood gym floor getting ground balls. But anytime you could get outside, we'd be outside.

I pitched, played shortstop, and played outfield a little bit. It was cold most of the year, so you'd play when you had the opportunities. A lot of the playing was indoors. We'd turn double plays and bunts and things like that. You'd just learn the fundamentals of the game. We'd start up in February in the gym, and then everybody would just hope for the snow to get off the field. Once the snow left, it didn't matter how cold it was, we'd be outside throwing the ball around. It snowed a few times when I played, and we'd play right through it.

Our high school team played only twelve games a year. There were not many pro scouts that came around. You don't get that much exposure in Maine. Plus, I wasn't even close to being ready.

After high school, I went to the University of Maine on a partial scholarship. At the start of winter practice, the campus was generally covered with snow. But I was able to do a lot indoors, and the facility there was much better than the high school setup. The field house had a floor of synthetic turf, two batting cages, even a net around a kind of makeshift infield.

Snow, though, affected everything. The outfielders on our team got out onto the parking lot when it was plowed and caught fly balls. But the infielders like me couldn't do much with snow covering the ground.

The first home game I played in for Maine took place during a snowstorm. I made four errors, but I pressed on. I batted .201 as a freshman but raised it all the way up to .364 when I was a junior and we made it to the College World Series.

The June 1986 draft saw 982 players selected including seven from my college team. I was not picked. I guess I couldn't blame anyone. I was a scrawny shortstop who had hit but five homers in three years of college play.

The summer of my junior year I played in the Cape Cod League for college stars. J. P. Ricciardi, a scout with Oakland, was down there checking somebody else out. I just happened to be putting in a pretty good weekend of baseball.

Ricciardi was persuasive. He told me that I had done everything I could as a college player, that I hadn't gotten drafted, that the Oakland organization wanted to sign me and give me a $15,000 bonus.

He asked if I was interested in signing. I was and I did.

The date was July 10, 1986. I was signed by the Oakland Athletics as a free agent to a minor league contract. I was very excited and scared, but very naïve too about the whole process. Being in college, and especially in Maine, you basically do it one step at a time. Not many from Maine have made the big leagues.

So I didn't know what to expect, really. When I went out there, playing rookie ball was pretty amazing. All these kids trying to get the same spot. The next year you go to spring training seeing everybody trying to reach the same goal. You really start understanding what you have to do. It truly became a matter of focusing in more, instead of being such a free-spirited, fun-loving baseball player.

I wasn't prepared for the travel and the baseball demands that are put on you every day. In college, you're playing on weekends, doubleheaders and stuff like that. In professional ball, that's your job. You're playing every day. If you feel bad, you can't say, "Oh, I don't feel too good today. I'm not going to play." They expect you to be out there and play every day. You learn that. I loved playing, and I enjoyed the minor leagues. I think the reason I did was I didn't know what was ahead. There was a little bit of a culture shock I guess in rookie ball because everything was new. Then boom, I get promoted to single-A. You still had the travel, but it just seemed better because you're climbing the ladder.

Then I get promoted to double-A. The travel in the Southern League was terrible. I mean, you're on sixteen-hour bus rides. But it seemed better, because you're in double-A.

I was in spring training with Oakland in 1990. That was the time they expanded the major league rosters by two players. Spring training was going all right for me. Then Tony LaRussa, the Oakland manager, called me into his office.

"We're going to keep you on the roster," he said. I was very surprised, very excited. Tony LaRussa made it clear to me what my role was on that team. I was a utility guy who could play second, short, or third. If I got a hit, it would be a bonus. I was the one that he would use late in the game for defensive purposes.

The year before, the A's had won the World Series, so I got to be a part of their celebration that first game in Oakland when they handed out the rings. What an experience. It was great. It was like a dream. Fireworks are going off. Lights go down in the Coliseum. Fifty thousand fans cheering on the world champion Oakland A's. Mark McGwire, Jose Canseco, Rickey Henderson, Dave Stewart. You name it, they were all there. I was twenty-four. I was real lucky to come up with that team, because I learned so much from those guys. Of course, I had probably the best manager in the game, too, Tony LaRussa.

It took me a while to get my first major league hit — about six months or so, fourteen at bats. I actually didn't get my first hit until September, because they sent me down after April, and I got called back up in September. My first hit came in New York at Yankee Stadium. It was a line drive up the middle. I remember Carney Lansford came out of the game in the fifth or sixth inning. He had back spasms or something like that. I came up. I got the hit. It was great.

KEN BRETT

The main place I grew up in was El Segundo in southern California. It was a town with a population of 15,000 then. It's still 15,000. But before I got there, I lived in a couple of other places.

I was born September 18, 1948, in Brooklyn, New York. When I was six to seven years old, my accountant father moved us to West Virginia for a couple of years to a place fittingly enough called Moundsville. Three of the four boys in the family had been born by that time. There was really no place to play a lot of baseball in Brooklyn. That was why my dad moved the family. I have vague memories of getting my first baseball glove in Moundsville. It was a trapeze glove, like a first baseman's mitt because I was left-handed.

The California baseball memories are more vivid. The baseball field I played at was on the corner of a busy intersection. I remember playing baseball in my standard outfit — a green T-shirt and jeans. I don't remember a lot about the equipment that we used except that the catcher's equipment was always too big. The bats, of course, were all wood.

The Angels in my growing-up time in California were a minor league team. I didn't pay much attention to them. I was a huge LA Dodger fan. Since I was a left-handed pitcher, I looked up to another left-handed pitcher, maybe the greatest of all — Sandy Koufax. I thought that he was a dominating type of pitcher. I would go to the ballpark and get my binoculars out to watch him warm up. It was incredible to see how good a pitcher he was.

I never had real good seats; in fact, we always bought the cheap seats. But I went to a lot of games because my friend's brother loved baseball and he took us to games all the time. From those great experiences at Dodger Stadium and from growing up in El Segundo where I got such good instruction, I developed a real love for the game.

My father was not much of an athlete and neither was my mother. They both worked the whole time we were growing up. We were very middle class. We never lacked anything. I needed a glove, I got a glove.

Although my father never played with any of us, he could be very stern and very demanding at times about the way we played. He encouraged our playing ball. There we were — the four Brett brothers playing baseball. We played every night, I think. It must have been hell for my parents to adjust to our different schedules. We were all two years apart, just far enough apart where we didn't play much together.

Most good athletes at the high school level end up being pitchers. I was real good in high school and won a lot of games taking advantage of my strong left arm. I played the outfield or first base when I wasn't pitching. I had good grades in high school and could have gotten a full scholarship to virtually any of the top baseball colleges. But I wanted to play professionally.

The two big influences on me were Ed Helvy, my Babe Ruth League coach who has passed away, and John Stevenson, my high school coach who is still the coach, believe it or not, at El Segundo High School. When I was fifteen years old in Babe Ruth baseball, our team won the national championship. We were good, really good, and it wasn't just me.

I was drafted by the Boston Red Sox right out of high school, and I was scouted by Joe Stephenson, who still does some work for Boston. His son Jerry Stephenson is also a scout now and was a teammate of mine on the Red Sox.

But the first time Joe Stephenson came to my house the summer of 1966 and made an offer, things were not that cordial. My father said, "Get the hell out of here — just get out." Joe came back two more times, and the second time he came back I signed the contract in my living room. The funny thing about signing that contract was that I had a pair of jeans and a T-shirt on and was in my bare feet — the easy-going California look.

I was drafted in the days before they had agents, so my father kind of handled everything. He had a lot of experience in business and knew what he was doing.

There was a kid named Steve Chilcott, who lived in Santa Barbara and was the number one draft pick in the nation that year of 1966. The Mets had drafted him. My father got on the phone with Steve's father. I was the number four draft pick. The fathers, as the story goes, compared notes about money. My signing bonus ended up being $100,000. I guess my dad's comparing notes paid off.

When all the contract and signing details were over, my father, who had a way with words, said, "Joe, now that you have signed Ken for the Red Sox, this is the one you really want," and he pointed to my brother George, who was twelve years old.

I never saw that kind of ability in my brother George. Seventeen-year-olds do not play with twelve-year-olds. My father was able to see what George could do. I was not. I was usually practicing or playing when George was playing. My father knew what my younger brother had in him.

As for me, I was just thrilled to be on the road to a big league career. I started to pitch in the majors in 1967. I was just a kid. My first major league win was against the Yankees. I also got three hits including a home run. That October, it was Red Sox–Cardinals in the World Series. I became the youngest pitcher to appear in a World Series game. That was how I started.

There was also a little postscript. A television camera panned the crowd at Fenway during the 1967 World Series. An excited 14-year-old mouthed the words: "Hello, I'm Ken Brett's little brother, George."

NELSON BRILES

I grew up primarily in Chico, California, a hundred miles north of Sacramento. It is just beautiful country where you have the advantage of great weather so you are able to play sports the year round.

From the time I was eight years old at the start of the 1950s, I had a dream of playing major league baseball, and I never really lost that dream. I played all the other sports — it just seemed a natural thing to do. However, my real strength and interest was in baseball. That's where I excelled the most.

I was blessed with a good strong arm, something that you can't create. I was always a pretty husky guy who could throw the ball hard compared to other kids my age. My father used to catch me in the side yard. He could catch me when I was eight, when I was nine. When I was ten years old, I pitched to him, and he didn't get the glove up in time. The ball hit him in the shoulder. "I think you are going to have your brothers catch you from now on," he said.

There was no pressure to play, to do better. I was just allowed to play, and that helped me more than anything else early on. I developed a love of the game. I was able to enjoy that first. Then as I got older the importance of winning and excelling came along.

I never had one major league baseball player as an idol. I admired all of them because they were what I wanted to be — a major league baseball player.

Even though I grew up in northern California, I was first a Brooklyn and then an LA Dodger fan. That was probably because everyone else was a Giant fan. I didn't actually follow major league baseball until the Giants and Dodgers came west.

One of the influences on me was watching the "Game of the Week" on Saturdays with Dizzy Dean and Pee Wee Reese. From time to time I'd listen to the Pacific Coast League and follow the Sacramento Solons. I never saw a game in person but listened on the radio with my father. He was a sports fan but not a participant. My mother, on the other hand, was a world champion athlete. When she was in her late teens, she trained for endurance swimming in Arrowhead Springs, California, and broke the world record for swimming in a pool without touching anything — thirty-two hours, twenty minutes, something like that.

My mother always worked. She worked, along with my father, in the lumber mill. They were basically hourly wage people. They set an example for hard work, honesty. The family was in debt. Nevertheless, we always had a roof over our heads even though we lived in rented houses, never anything very upscale.

I can remember the first baseball glove I ever had. It cost $13, and I bought it at a local sporting goods store with my own money. I had worked for weeks to earn the thirteen bucks. It was just a tan leather glove, a Wilson, with a metal button on the strap and no autograph. I had heard all the rumors about what you had to do with a new glove. You have to oil it — so I oiled it. Then I heard you needed to put it in water. So I did that. I also wrapped strings around it to form the pocket. I don't know if I ended up with a good glove. But I did end up with a heavy glove.

The bats I had were those I reclaimed from a high school or college game. If they were cracked, you'd put little tacks in them and wrap them with some kind of tape to make them usable.

Early on, it was my Chico High School coaches who made a difference in what I was and would become. One was Bush Dalrymple. The other was Skip McDonald. Both also helped coach football and were behind the scenes for basketball. I was with those coaches basically for all three sports for my whole high school career. They really concentrated on making sure my mental approach to the game was correct. They worked me like a dog to see I was in shape. They instilled in me the habit of working hard.

I stood out in high school. In my junior year, I was 17–1, 15–1. I threw a couple of no-hitters. I struck out sixteen, seventeen a game. The scouts started coming around. My senior year the scouts were talking about the three killer B's — Bob Bailey, a guy the Pirates signed for big money, $125,000; Frank Bretania, a left-handed pitcher Baltimore signed for about $75,000; and Nelson Briles. But for me, the offer was only $8,000.

I said, "Wait a minute, you told me there was three of us, all in the same category. How come I have only been offered $8,000?"

The answer was, "Well, you're up here playing in a small area, and you really haven't faced great competition."

There was all the baloney. This is 1961. No agent. No lawyer.

I ended up getting a full scholarship to Santa Clara University, which was in the old CIDA League, at that time the best baseball league in the country. So I positioned myself to go against top competition. I did extremely well in my freshman year. Then during my sophomore year my father passed away. It was a terrible blow. He had lived through me.

I left college after my sophomore year to take care of my mother, whose health wasn't good at the time. I signed with the St. Louis Cardinals and paid off all the bills when I signed my major league contract. For the first time, our family was out of debt.

I spent one year in the minors and came up at the end of the 1964 season and sat on the bench watching the Cardinals beat the Yankees in the World Series.

I did not have that ninety-eight-mile-per-hour fastball. Mine came in there in the low nineties. But I had discipline and desire. My major league debut was April 19, 1965. I wound up spending fourteen years in the majors, a long and enjoyable career.

SCOTT BROSIUS

I always dreamed about making the major
leagues. From the time I was three, four years
old, I used to talk to my mom and dad about it all
the time. I pretty much played baseball my whole life growing up.

I was born August 15, 1966, in Hillsboro, Oregon, a rural, small town
south of Portland, Oregon. We had baseball fields right next to our neighborhood, and I had a neighbor who was a Little League coach. He let me
come over and play with his team before I was old enough to play for real.
I was playing with older kids in the neighborhood. In the summertime, I
played baseball all day long, every day.

I never had one player as an idol. They were all my idols, because they
represented what I wanted to be — a major league baseball player. But my
favorite player growing up was Dale Murphy.

All the baseball playing I had as a kid was a lot of improvising. Whatever kids were available, we made do. If we had two kids, it was one-on-
one. If we had ten kids, it was five-on-five. We played out in the street. We
just made up games. If we didn't have a baseball or a tennis ball, I mean I
remember we played games where we hit a basketball, and I mean did all
sorts of things. They weren't all organized, Little League–type games. We
just used to play any kind of games we could think of.

Our backyard was used so much for ball playing that it had base paths
worn into it. But we used mostly a tennis ball — we weren't allowed to
play with a baseball back there. We had a firm rule. If you hit the ball off
the house, that was three outs automatically, because we didn't want broken windows.

I always loved to play and thought of the challenge of making the major leagues. I never saw the downside that says that most people don't
make it. I never considered failure. I just felt like I was going to play some
day, and it all just worked out.

I was drafted in the twentieth round in 1987 by Oakland. Surprisingly, at that time, I had never seen a major league game in person. The single-A team I was on was invited to play an exhibition game at County Stadium against the single-A affiliate of the Brewers. First they played the Twins.

I was sitting in the stands watching the game with my teammates when Tim Laudner of Minnesota hit a foul ball right to me. I caught it without any trouble. Then all these kids in the stands started screaming for the ball. They wanted me to give it to them. I told them, "Hey, it's my first major league game, too." That was how much a novice I was at the time.

I was called up to Oakland for the first time on August 4, 1991. It was my father's birthday. You can imagine what kind of a kick that was for him and for me. I made my major league debut three days later. My dad's favorite player had been Mickey Mantle. Later on I would actually wear Mickey's number 7 with the A's because of that feeling my dad had for the Mantle tradition.

One thing I think I had probably done a hundred times in my backyard as a kid was to fantasize about being a member of the New York Yankees. In my wildest dreams, I was always there. And then it happened. I was the player to be named later in the Yankee trade of Kenny Rogers to Oakland. That was November of 1997.

Little League, high school, all the teams I played for through the years had never won championships or anything like that. It really wasn't until I got to the Yankees that I was part of a championship team.

BOBBY BROWN

I had my first major league tryout when I was thirteen years old. Three years later I was brought to Detroit and had a tryout along with Rex Barney and Art Houtteman. The things you remember . . .

I was born on October 25, 1924, in Seattle, Washington and spent my first twelve or thirteen years there. My dad enjoyed baseball and was a good ballplayer himself. He taught me how to play. Dad started me as a left-handed hitter, and I continued to hit left-handed. I started playing baseball before I can remember. I know that when I look back to when I started the first grade, I could hit the ball better than any of the other kids in the class.

In Seattle, you couldn't play too much in the winter time because of the rain and the chilliness. But whenever the weather was decent, I played a lot in the park, on lots, and in the school yards.

We moved east to East Orange, New Jersey, when I was in the seventh grade and lived there halfway through my sophomore year in high school. Interestingly enough, while I was in junior high in East Orange, Monte Irvin was in high school. I saw him play basketball. He was a terrific athlete. Later on I would spend one World Series seeing line drives he hit go over my head.

My dad took me to quite a few major league baseball games when we lived in East Orange. I saw both the Giants and the Yankees. I saw one game in the 1936 and 1937 World Series. I had hoped to be a major league player ever since I could remember. Being there seeing those teams play just whetted my appetite.

I liked the Yankees but I liked the Giants, too, so I didn't have any burning desire or dream to one day be with any one team. But I followed both New York teams very closely. In those days you got most of your news about baseball from the *Sporting News*. There were a tremendous amount of minor league teams and players. I always avidly read that newspaper and checked out the box scores of all the minor leaguers.

When I was a high school sophomore in New Jersey, the baseball coach told my dad he wasn't going to use me that year. It just so happened at the time my dad had this good job opportunity in California. He was weighing the decision whether to stay in New Jersey, where he was doing quite well on his own, or to take the job offer in San Francisco. He decided we'd move to San Francisco. What certainly played into the mix was what happened with me. In San Francisco, I began playing more and more baseball. I settled in as a shortstop. I was a decent hitter. I identified with Arky Vaughn, who played for the Pirates. Other than that, I really did not have any real heroes.

I was pretty successful wherever I played baseball. The scouts kept up with my moving around the country. The primary scout was a man named Joe Devine. He was a decent guy, and he could really spot talent.

Joe Devine put together a team that was essentially composed of the kids he had scouted. We were all in high school, and we played on Sundays. Seven of us went to the major leagues, so that really showed that Joe Devine knew what he was doing. They were Jerry Coleman, Charlie Silvera, Bill Wight, Fenton Mole, Carl DeRose, and Artie Shallock. All Bay Area kids. Most of us would end up with the Yankees, and some got traded on.

Baseball was a big deal in San Francisco back then. I played on the best high school team I ever saw, and that was more than fifty years ago. They had two great high school teams in San Francisco at the time, my school Galileo High and Mission High School. We ended up playing for the championship the two years I was there. We played the championship games on a Thursday afternoon at Seals Stadium, and 10,000 people came out to see the action. We won both years.

In addition to the team Joe Devine put together, I played a lot of other semipro baseball in San Francisco. The quality of play was extremely good, because they had so many minor league players in the area who came home for the winter and played all winter long. So I was able to get a baseball education coming up against all kinds of guys who had professional experience.

I went from high school to Stanford University where I was premed. During World War II, I was in the navy, and since I had been premed, I pretty much was kept in school when I was in uniform. I also played a lot of baseball against service teams — which were all comprised of professional players, so the competition was extremely good. That sharpened my skills.

Larry MacPhail was one of the owners of the Yankees then. At that time he was a colonel in the service and just happened to be in San Francisco. He paid a visit to my dad and asked him what it would take for me to sign a contract with the New York Yankees. At that time my dad was an executive with the Schenley Distilleries in San Francisco, so he knew something about business. He told MacPhail what he thought was an amount.

Colonel MacPhail said, "Fine." They shook hands, and that was it. It was pretty simple. There wasn't anything written.

But I couldn't sign at that time, because I was in the navy. When I got out in January of 1946, I was eligible to sign a baseball contract. The Yankee offer was the best — a substantial bonus and a deal allowing me to continue my education and also to play ball. That really swung the decision for me to sign with them.

I loved to play baseball, and fortunately I could play it reasonably well. I didn't think it was so odd that I could do that and also be a medical student. The balancing of it was tough, but I worked at it. It was just a question of not having much time off.

The Yankees assigned me in 1946 to Newark, their top farm team in the International League. We had a good team with Yogi Berra, Vic Raschi, Allie Clark. But it was Montreal, a Brooklyn Dodger farm team, that won the pennant. They had a super team. They had Jackie Robinson. He was not easy to play against, and he could aggravate another team. But he was a heck of a player. I think we ended up one-two in the batting race that year. He hit .349. I hit .341. I was right there with history happening. Incidentally, when I was in the navy, they sent me to UCLA where I spent three semesters. I saw Jackie play football for UCLA against Stanford.

That 1946 season the Boston Red Sox had clinched the pennant, and the Yankees were in second place. So I, along with Yogi and Vic Raschi, was brought up. Yogi and I and another player named Frank Coleman all drove over from Newark to the stadium for a Sunday doubleheader against Philadelphia. Vic Raschi also was there. The four of us all joined the Yankees on the same day. Joe McCarthy had started the year as manager and resigned in mid-season. Bill Dickey was in charge for a while, but he didn't like it. Johnny Neun was the manager the last few weeks on an interim basis.

My major league debut was on September 22, 1946. Yogi and I played every one of the remaining ten games. Vic Raschi pitched in the regular turn. That was how it all started.

My career was 548 games for the Yankees and also seventeen World Series games. They claimed I was the hitting star in four World Series, which was a nice thing to say. I retired from baseball in mid-1954 to practice medicine.

I always felt that I could have some kind of career in the major leagues. I guess every kid feels that way at some time. I never dreamed that later on I would have an executive position in baseball — coming back in 1984 and becoming president of the American League.

JOSE CARDENAL

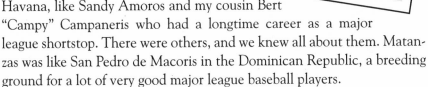

A lot of very good players came from Matanzas, a province of Cuba ninety miles from
Havana, like Sandy Amoros and my cousin Bert
"Campy" Campaneris who had a longtime career as a major
league shortstop. There were others, and we knew all about them. Matanzas was like San Pedro de Macoris in the Dominican Republic, a breeding
ground for a lot of very good major league baseball players.

I was born in Matanzas on October 7, 1943, and grew up there. I was
the baby in the family of three boys, two girls. My father worked as a carpenter and only made about $5 a week. My mama was a housewife.

The whole family was involved with baseball in some way or other. My
daddy had played. My older brother played in the Army League. My
brother Pedro Cardenal signed with the St. Louis Cardinals in 1954 and
played for a while in the minors. My older sister was the only female official scorer in all of Cuba.

Most of the kids I grew up with sold newspapers and shined shoes to
help their families get some money. I never did that. Since I was the
youngest, my father took care of me. I just went to school nine to four,
came home, put on my short pants, went to the ballpark, and played until
the sun came down. I played baseball all year round.

Being a good baseball player in Cuba in your growing-up time meant
having prestige and popularity. People envied you. When I was a teenager
and coming into baseball, there were all the Cubans in the majors like
Tony Oliva, Camilo Pascual, Pedro Ramos, Luis Tiant, Tony Perez. One
time we had about twenty-seven Cuban players, star Cuban players, in the
major leagues. Baseball in Cuba was and is the number one sport —
boxing is second. We are too short to play basketball and not big enough
to play football.

The playing fields in Cuba were just great. When I was growing up, I
played with no shoes, because my family could not afford to buy me a pair
of shoes. We were poor. I was ten, eleven years old —running on grass and

rocks. I didn't feel anything. When you are poor and hungry, you play any-where. The only glove I had was an old beat-up one that my brother brought me from the United States. It was a Rawlings. It was a great glove for a kid to have back then.

When I was starting to play ball, Batista was in power. Castro took over Cuba on January 1, 1959. But the revolution did not have any effect on baseball. Politics is politics and baseball is baseball. They don't mix.

I was a second baseman in Little League, Pony League, and high school. I knew that my family would never be able to send me to college. My hope was at least to finish high school and get to the United States and try to make it through baseball and help my family that way.

The only teams we followed in Cuba when I was a kid were the Dodgers and the Yankees. In the late fifties and early sixties it seemed those teams were in the series every year. Not too many in my neighborhood could afford television. But I would go to a private club owned by a company and watch games there on their TV.

On Saturdays and Sundays as I got up in my teens I used to catch the train and go to Havana to play. It was known by everyone that all the ma-jor league scouts would come to Havana to watch young kids play base-ball. Sunday nights after the games were over I would catch the train again and go back to my hometown.

When I was fifteen years old, my coach and also my friend, Larry Ruiz, told me that this famous scout guy — Alex Pompey of the San Francisco Giants — was interested in me. I believe he had signed Willie Mays and a lot of other famous players. I stayed in Havana for three days working out. At the end, I was signed up for the Giants along with three other guys.

When I signed with the Giants in March 1961, I finally did not need that Rawlings glove anymore. It had served its purpose. And even though Castro already was in power, there was no problem in my leaving Cuba.

But I was lucky, because after I signed the government came out with a ruling that no more baseball players could go to the United States because they wanted the best players around for the Pan Am Games and, later, the Olympics. Only those already signed to contracts could go. I was one of the last to get out legally.

Though I was sad to leave my family and friends, I wanted to go to the United States. I figured baseball was the way I could help my family. I came to the United States looking for a better way of life.

I spent three and a half years in the minor leagues. They were success-ful years. Finally, in 1963 the Giants brought me to the big leagues just for "a cup of coffee." I stayed twenty-eight days, and they sent me back to the minors because they wanted me to play every day. The Giant outfield of Willie Mays, Willie McCovey, and the Alous was a tough place to get playing time in. In 1964, I ran out of options so the Giants traded me to the California Angels.

From that point on I played in the big leagues. I never went back to the minors. It was a very good career. I played for nine teams in eighteen major league seasons, 2,017 games and a .275 batting average.

CLIFF CHAMBERS

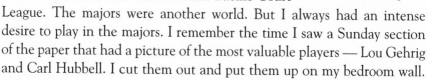

As a kid I was not a fan of any major league team because I was too far removed from them. The closest team was Seattle in the Pacific Coast League. The majors were another world. But I always had an intense desire to play in the majors. I remember the time I saw a Sunday section of the paper that had a picture of the most valuable players — Lou Gehrig and Carl Hubbell. I cut them out and put them up on my bedroom wall.

I was born January 10, 1922, in Portland, Oregon, but grew up in Billingham, Washington, on Puget Sound, about fifty miles from Vancouver, British Columbia, and twenty-five miles from the Canadian border. I was a depression kid who lived in a fairly poor neighborhood. So there was a lot of economics involved in my wish to become a major leaguer.

I had no brothers or sisters. I did not come from a background of athletes. But I went to an elementary school where the principal was one tough guy. Most everyone was afraid of him. He had us playing sports all the time. We played all the sports, and we beat everybody in town.

I got really involved in the sixth grade league. Forty-foot bases and a small softball were used. That's when I started pitching in earnest. From there, I went to the hardball, always throwing the ball with my left hand. "Lefty," that's what they all called me as a kid.

Equipment, bats, balls, gloves, they were no big deal to me. You hear all these stories about how players would oil their gloves and whatever. I was more concerned with how I was equipped, developing my physical strength. I used to have a couple of soft rubber balls and would squeeze them fifty to seventy-five times a night to get a strong forearm. Then I would put them under my pillow. I noticed how the guys who milked cows had strong hands, strong forearms. You needed that to grip a ball. I was trying to get milker's muscles.

I began playing junior American Legion ball while I was in high school. I had skipped so I was a year ahead of myself, but I was a pretty big kid so it was no problem. Before I was sixteen, I played semipro ball for money under an assumed name up in Vancouver, Canada. Baseball was just getting started as a semipro thing up there. I would just jump the border and that was that.

Vancouver is a beautiful part of the world when it isn't raining. You get two good months up there: July and August. The rest of the time, it's either foggy or raining. But we didn't get rainouts. We'd just play in the rain. That semipro league had teams in places like Tacoma, Victoria. We used to bounce around and play traveling teams like the House of David, a group of bearded ballplayers, most of whom were Jewish.

When I was eighteen, I pitched against Satchel Paige, who was playing with the Kansas City Monarchs. Satchel, they said, was born old. He seemed old even then. But pitching against him meant nothing to me at that time. They told me his name and how great he was, but I knew nothing about him. I didn't know who anybody was.

My parents were okay about my playing semipro ball. My dad painted for wages until I was about out of high school. Then he became a contractor. I used to work for him in the summertime. But even then, everything I did was geared to baseball. I worked with my dad to build up strength in my shoulders and arms swinging a paint brush all of the time. I lived baseball twenty-four hours a day.

I pitched with Bob Feller on a little barnstorming trip, and I could throw as hard as he could. I struck out as many as he did in one game. I was a little wild because my ball moved so much, but I had what was undoubtedly a hundred-mile-an-hour fastball in those days before the radar guns. Scouts and others came to me with offers right out of high school. But I didn't go professional at that time because I was after a bonus. Back then you got a bonus for signing and that was what I was after, that or a sale price. All the talk in my area was about Freddie Hutchinson, who signed on with the Seattle Rainiers, and the big bonus money he got when they sold him.

I went to Washington State University and played semipro ball on the side. Then I was approached by the Chicago Cubs chain. They offered a $2,500 bonus, and I signed with them. The contract also had a sales clause that specified that I would get an additional ten percent on any sale of my contract to another organization. I was assigned to the Pacific Coast League Los Angeles team, which was owned by Wrigley.

Then the Japanese hit Pearl Harbor. I went into the service. When I came out, I went to spring training with Los Angeles in 1947 and made the ball club. I had a great year there. We won the pennant.

Then I went up with the Cubs the next year. I made my debut on April 24, 1948. The Cubs were not a great team, but they were a major league team. I was the only one from Billingham to make the big leagues except for a guy named Clarence Marshall, who was a part-timer with the Yankees.

One thing I learned — baseball is a total dedication thing. I saw a lot of kids who had the ability and should have been in the big leagues but never had the drive to fight through a slump or a bad time.

TONY CLARK

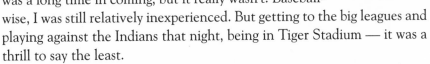

My first major league game was in 1995 against the Cleveland Indians. It seemed like it was a long time in coming, but it really wasn't. Baseball-wise, I was still relatively inexperienced. But getting to the big leagues and playing against the Indians that night, being in Tiger Stadium — it was a thrill to say the least.

You can't help but be nervous. You're talking about Tiger Stadium, you're talking about a lot of players who have been there before, who have walked down the same hallway, played on the same field. I came in for a pinch-hit appearance the night I got called up and struck out. The next day, I went 2-for-5, which was my first start. I was on my way.

I was born in Newton, Kansas, on June 15, 1972. My mom and dad were playing in a coed softball league when I was a kid, and I'd go to games and run around, hit the ball and throw the ball — all that fun stuff. I was probably three or four. So it just seemed like a natural progression that they got me started as soon as I was able to play T-ball. They signed me up for the Lemon Grove Little League in San Diego when I was five.

When I was a kid, we'd play with everything. You name it, we hit it. We hit Wiffle balls, tennis balls, taped balls. If a bat wasn't handy, we used a broomstick. We played in the backyard and in the driveway where across the street was a home run. We weren't supposed to do that, but with Mom and Dad away at work, we got away with it. A couple of times we broke some windows — which I will still deny. But we never got into any big trouble.

We'd play Little League baseball games on Saturday mornings down at the ballpark. I was a shortstop and a pitcher. My first Little League coach was my father, Arthur Clark. He was a three-sport star in football, basketball, and baseball at Bethel College in Kansas. He taught me everything about sports. He was very competitive. I like to think I've acquired some of his traits.

I was a right-handed batter as a kid. When I was eleven, I told my dad one day I wanted to try left-handed because I hit pretty good that way playing Wiffle ball. He let me try, and wouldn't you know it? I got a hit. That was when I started to learn to switch-hit.

They would make Little League cards of you when you were ten, eleven, twelve years old. You had to pick your favorite team, your favorite player, your favorite position — all that fun stuff — for the back of your card. My favorite player was Hank Aaron, because he was the home run king. As I got older I had a much greater appreciation for the things he accomplished besides the home runs — the perseverance and discipline he had.

My favorite team was the Yankees. That was the team on the back of one of my Little League cards. I don't know why I chose the Yankees. I don't even remember following them. I didn't follow baseball that closely. I was too busy and always had to do a lot of homework.

Basketball was always my first love. I was taller than most kids and more talented than the others in basketball. When I was in high school, I played forward and was focusing my attention on a basketball career. People are still impressed when they hear that when I was a senior at Christian High School in El Cajon, California, I led the state in scoring and averaged 43.7 points per game.

Before the Tigers drafted me, I told them that I was going to play college basketball and if I was drafted by an NBA team, I planned to play pro basketball. But they took a chance on me anyway and drafted me in the 1990 draft, in the first round, second pick overall. I had it written in my contract that I could go to school and play basketball and then come out and play baseball in the summers.

I went to the University of Arizona for a little while, and then San Diego State. I couldn't play baseball, because I had signed with the Tigers out of high school, so I'd go to school from September 1 to the end of May and play basketball. Then from June 1 to the end of August, I played baseball in the minor leagues with the Detroit organization.

But basketball was still my focus. Baseball was something I did after basketball season. Basketball was something I did year-round. I had to make a decision. The Tigers were trying to convince me to go along with a baseball career. They said the earlier I started playing baseball year-round, the sooner I would get to the big leagues.

Then fate intervened. I injured my back the second week of basketball practice in college. I had surgery on my back, and afterwards I wasn't the same player on the hardwood as I had been before. I couldn't jump as well. I wasn't as quick. I was a step behind everything. I could still shoot — which was my mainstay — but it was a lot more difficult for me to get things done, offensively and defensively. After my junior year, therefore, I figured it was time to give baseball a fair shake.

The injury didn't bother me in baseball. Where the running and pounding and jumping on the hardwood was difficult, the rotation stuff didn't bother me. I think I would have had a shot at the NBA if I hadn't gotten injured. I'm not naïve enough to say that I would have definitely been there, but I would have had a shot. Still I have to say that I am glad to be doing what I am doing.

JERRY COLEMAN

$\mathcal{I}$ *was born* on September 14, 1924, in San
Jose, California, but grew up in San Francisco.
Catholic Youth Organization baseball was my first organized
baseball experience. Holy Cross was the church. We played at a place
called Ewing Field, an old dump with bases that were pure cement. I was
an infielder. I also did some pitching like most kids do.

My father had played professional baseball in the Pacific Coast League
very briefly. He was a catcher. In his time you could make more money
working than playing, so he got out of baseball after he got married.

My mother pushed Lou Gehrig on me as an idol when I was in grade
school. Then just before I was in junior high, Joe DiMaggio was running
his course with the San Francisco Seals before he went to the Yankees. Of
course, the Yankees became our team because DiMaggio was the big star
in New York.

There was a man by the name of Anton Orr who was an old-timer out
at Golden Gate Park in San Francisco. He liked me, and I guess he
thought I had some talent. He presented me with a really good glove. I
had never had my own glove — so if someone had dropped a pocket full
of gold in my pocket, it could not have been more exciting for me.

In California we played all year long. There were winter leagues and fall
leagues. There was baseball every Sunday. But I never thought of being a
professional baseball player any more than I thought of being a naval avi-
ator. I made the teams I tried out for but I was not the star. I was not big.
In ninth grade I was 5'2". In high school I was 5'6". I did not get to my
present height until my late teens.

I was not what you would call a student. I went to school because it was
the law. But I got to take my baseball and basketball shoes with me, and
that made it interesting.

When I was in high school, it was Joe Devine who told me he thought
I had a chance to be a big league ballplayer. Devine was the Yankee scout
for northern California. There were not many scouts in those days. Bill

Essick was the Yankee scout in southern California. That was about it. Anyway, Devine ran a kid team called the Kenelly Yankees. The team was sponsored by Neil Kenelly, who owned a bar, although he himself didn't drink. Every Sunday a bunch of us kids would pile into two or three cars. That was the Kenelly Yankees being transported all over the San Francisco Bay Area to play baseball. One of the nice things about the experience was that we all got to wear ex-Yankee road uniforms. I got Frank Crosetti's.

When World War II began, I was attending USC on a baseball-basketball scholarship. I was only seventeen. I wanted to get into the V 5 program for naval aviators, but I couldn't get in until I was eighteen. I had this whole summer to kill, so I ended up signing a Yankee contract and taking off for Wellsville, New York, to play baseball for the summer in the class-D Pony League. This was 1942. I signed for a $2,800 bonus. That was a fortune coming right out of the depression. The contract to play was $75 a month.

I had never been farther south than San Jose. Bob Cherry, who was my bosom buddy, and Charlie Silvera, out of St. Ignatius High, who later became a Yankee, went with me. It took forever to get there — forty hours, more. We got into Wellsville, New York, about midnight or so, put our luggage on the station platform, and all the lights went out. Pitch black. We didn't know where we were. We finally found the main street. The town wasn't very big — only 5,000 strong. We groped our way to the hotel. We then got a room at 120 Maple Avenue. It was a really big room with three beds for $7.50 a week. We used to eat at the diner where a steak dinner with all the trimmings and dessert cost a dollar. I spent part of July, August, and September playing in Wellsville and wound up saving a hundred dollars because of those dinners.

We played on an infield that was all dirt. This tall, silver-haired man who was working for the Yankees arrived one day. He had on a pair of khaki pants, and he would go out there and take off his shirt and rake up all these pebbles, put them in little piles, take the wheelbarrow out, and take away the pebbles. One day he said to me, "Hey, you want to know how to 'hit and run'?"

"Sure."

So we showed up the next day. He was on the mound, "Now I throw the ball," he said, "and you hit it." He throws high, and he throws low. The idea of a 'hit and run' is that you have to make contact. I slashed away. This went on for about four or five days. I learned how to 'hit and run,' and then he disappeared.

I went to Roy Brandenberger, our general manager. "Mr. Brandenberger, what happened to that man who was pitching to us?"

"Oh, you mean Chief Bender."

I had no idea who Chief Bender was. Then I found out — he was Connie Mack's greatest money pitcher back in the early days of the century.

Our team was called the Wellsville Yankees. They gave us the hat, the pants, the belt, and the shirt. That was it. Everything else you supplied. I wore number 12. We never changed uniforms, never had them washed. They were filthy.

It's still painful for me to remember the first week. I played a bad shortstop, so bad they moved me to third base. I was using an old high school glove and maybe that was part of the problem. I struck out my first six times, and my seventh time I got hit right in the ribs. We were right in the middle of a beanball battle.

We were not there two weeks when the river overflowed behind the ballpark. The ballpark was like a gigantic bathtub filled with about eight feet of water. We had to go and play in Belfast on a field that had no fences, no nothing. Just a field. Then we went back to Wellsville.

The owners of the club had two daughters, and we cozied up to them so we could raid the refrigerator every night. That was how we ate. Otherwise, we played out the season without incident, except we were disappointed that we missed the play-offs. I took the train back home to California. I turned eighteen on the fourteenth of September, and on the fifteenth I was at the Ferry Building getting into the naval aviation program. I was in for three and a half years in World War II and flew fifty-seven bombing missions over the Solomon Islands.

When World War II was over, I went back to the Yankee organization and ended up in Lake Wales, Florida, under manager Bill Meyer who was a wonderful person. From there I was sent to Binghamton for a full year and then Kansas City a full year, under Bill Meyer again.

Spring training of 1948, I was in Florida trying to make the Yankee ball club. Bucky Harris was the manager. I was at Miller Huggins Field when Joe DiMaggio walked into the clubhouse. It had been a long way for him and for me from San Francisco. He had on a Hawaiian shirt, a pair of slacks — and in those days they wore the shirts out, they hung down around the hips. I just looked at him. I didn't know what to say. He looked bigger than life. I don't even know if we played in the same games that spring.

I was the last man cut by the Yankees in spring training in 1948. The thing I remember most coming up from Florida was that they dumped us at Penn Station, which was like a zoo. I didn't know where I was or what I was doing. But I spotted one of the other players and followed him and got to the hotel.

I played for the Newark Bears in the International League in 1948. At the end of the season, I came up to the Yankees. I didn't even think I would be brought up. I'd had a poor season at Newark, only hitting .250. I'd never played second base before — it was new to me.

My first major league game was April 20, 1949. We were playing the Washington Senators. The first batter hit a ground ball to me, and it went right through my legs. The next guy up was Sherry Robertson. He hit a one-hop shot at me. I caught it, turned it into a double play, and the day was saved. That's how I began with the Yankees.

The way we were indoctrinated . . . the Yankees were not our team, they were our religion. That was what we lived for. It wasn't money then, it was winning or losing. If you came in second place — you lost. It was the glory of winning and the ring.

GENE CONLEY

$\mathcal{I}$ *was just a* jock all the time. I enjoyed all
sports but especially basketball and baseball. I
played both well enough to excel. I never had it in my mind to be a professional athlete even with all the accomplishments. But that is getting
ahead of my story.

I was born on November 10, 1930, in Muskogee, Oklahoma, a pretty
good-sized town that had a minor league baseball team. What comes back
is YMCA. All the free time I could get I would spend there. They had a
little Sunday school, and if you attended you could get a free pass for
Wednesday nights. You bet, I never missed Sunday school.

My father never played ball or took part in any kind of athletics, but he
loved baseball. From the time I was nine years old, he would take me to
the ball park to see our minor league team, the Muskogee Reds, a farm
club of Cincinnati. We would sit in the bleachers. One time he told me:
"There's a kid playing tonight for the class-D Springfield Cardinals, Western Association ball. His name is Musial. He's only about nineteen years
old, but I am watching him because he is a real good hitter. He is hitting
about .400 for Springfield."

So I concentrated on Musial. He struck out at least twice that night.
I turned to my father. "I don't think that Musial is going to be that
good." Later on I wound up pitching against him for about seven
years.

When I was about thirteen, we moved out to the West Coast to Rich-
land, Washington. I was so busy playing all kinds of ball on my own that I
did not give the major leagues too much thought. I went to Columbia
High School. I was a sophomore when I started playing high school ball. I
wasn't that big then, but I started to grow real fast as a junior. I was 6'3".
Then I was 6'6½" as a senior. We had some real good basketball teams in
my junior and senior years. We won the league championships of what
they called the Yakima Valley. We even went to the state tournament in
Seattle.

I also have a lot of good memories of high school baseball. Those were the real glory days for me. I was chosen from teams that made up the Yakima Valley League to pitch in the championship game. I started the game as an outfielder. I could pitch very well, and I was also a pretty good hitter. The starting pitcher needed help, and the coach called me in. I pitched three or four innings and struck out six or seven guys. I also hit the only home run ever hit by a high schooler out of Seattle Stadium. Our team won the Yakima Valley championships.

I was voted the outstanding player in the game and chosen to represent the state of Washington in an exhibition game at the Polo Grounds in New York City sponsored by the Hearst newspapers. It was New York City high school baseball all stars against all stars from all over the United States.

My dad put me on a train. One of the sportswriters from the *Seattle Intelligencer* went along with me to cover the game and do a story about me. That was a hell of a train ride. It took three or four days to get to New York City — all the way to the Roosevelt Hotel. I was about seventeen years old and quite thrilled to be there.

All of us from the United States team worked out at Yankee Stadium during the day and then watched the Yankees play the night before our game. The coaches for the United States team were Oscar Vitt and Max Carey, the old base stealer. I seem to remember that Rabbit Maranville was a coach for the New York club.

I was fortunate to be voted in as the captain of our team. I was the starting pitcher in the game against Frank Torre, Joe Torre's brother. Frank was a left-handed pitcher. I pitched several innings, struck out four or five, and was credited with the win. I only batted once in the game and was runner-up for the Most Valuable Player award. There were about four or five, from that game that went on to the major leagues.

When it came time for me to graduate from high school, I had a lot of offers for baseball and basketball scholarships from all over the place. Hank Iba from Oklahoma and Adolph Rupp from Kentucky used to write me letters. But I wanted to go to a college that was big enough and close enough to home. I chose Washington State University.

It was a very good experience. The two years I was there we won the league championship in both basketball and baseball. I led the Pac-8 in scoring in my sophomore year and led the Cougs to the All Coast championship. I believe Bill Sharman led the Southern League in California. We went to the Coast play-offs against Johnny Wooden's UCLA Bruins. They played both games in that old Westwood court with about a thousand people, mostly rooting for them. It was a downer — we were close, but they beat us in both games by a total of three points.

In baseball we won the Coast championship. I got a win against Stanford. That gave us a chance to go to the NCAA College World Series in Omaha, Nebraska. I pitched against Frank Lary, who later became a Yankee-killer. I pitched a full game and beat him 9–0. All the scouts were after me. Then we went up against Texas in the championship game.

At the last minute our manager told me, "Gene, I'm going to fool them. I am going to start a left-hander against them and have you ready in the bullpen." I was very disappointed. They got a couple of runs off the left-hander, and he stuck me in. We still lost, I think it was 2–0.

After the NCAA tournament, I played semipro ball out on the West Coast for a little money, $35 a game, just enough to keep the car going. Now I was 6'8", stronger, more confident, pitching against some good ball players. Now the scouts were really after me. There was Bill Marshall, who was the scout for Lou Perrini's Braves. There were several scouts for the Yankees, including Carl Mays, who used to follow me around Washington. He came to my house and everything. There was a pitcher named Tommy Bridges, who had played for the Detroit Tigers.

I signed with the Braves for $6,000. They called it a bonus, but I was only allowed to make $2,700 because they were sending me to an A league in Hartford, Connecticut. I took some of the money and bought a cream and blue colored Pontiac Chieftain four-door car for cash. I thought I was the richest person in the world having my own car. I went to spring training with the Braves. One of my friends from high school drove the Pontiac to Hartford when I settled down.

I have a lot of wonderful memories of that time. It was my first year of pro ball. A ball was fast ball. I had just gotten married. Tommy Holmes was my first manager. He had played with the Braves.

I was going for m, twentieth win at Hartford, and we were playing the Wilkes-Barre Bears who had players like Sam Jones, Frank Malzone, guys who had real talent and were soon going to be major league players. They called that night "Gene Conley Night." The park was jammed. There were maybe about 5,000 people in the stands. I was pitching in the fifth inning when I heard the announcer say, "We are now passing around the bucket in the stands so we can draw some money for Gene Conley on his night."

I thought, I better win this game. Sure enough, we won 2–0. That win gave me a 20–9 record for the season at Hartford. I was the Minor League Player of the Year for 1951.

Maybe more important than that was the $600 they collected for me on my night. That money helped a lot.

Making $500 a month in the minors, the money was gone pretty quick. I remember one year my wife, Katie, and I came back and stayed in a trailer in North Richland. I got a job as an iron worker making $1 an hour. One year, we had to stay with my wife's folks in Spokane. It was tough going.

The Braves brought me up in 1952 and tried to force-feed me into their rotation. I was essentially a big strong guy but not a pitcher — a thrower. I was 0–3, and they sent me back down to the minors. That winter I played the last half of the season with the Boston Celtics. I made the connection through Bill Sharman from my college basketball days.

Playing professional baseball and basketball was hard both physically and mentally, because you never really get a rest. I did it because I needed the money. All professional athletes back then worked during the off-season to make ends meet.

In 1953, I pitched for the Milwaukee Brewers in triple-A and was the Minor League Player of the Year again. I was the only player ever to win the award twice.

I was back with Milwaukee again in 1954. But this time with the Braves. The Boston Braves had moved there. I won fourteen games and was third in the Rookie of the Year voting and went on to have a nice major league career.

Injuries cut into things, but I really have no regrets. I was the biggest guy in the minors and the majors for a long time.

BILLY CONSOLO

My family moved from Cleveland to California in 1943, and my father bought a home in a brand-new settlement in Los Angeles. My brother Horace was four years older than me. He started going to the playground to play baseball, and I wouldn't let him out of my sight.

We loved baseball. We showed up and we played — somewhere. When the big kids showed up, we had to shag. That was the way it went. I batboyed for my brother's junior league teams and senior league teams. Any time they got a lead, they'd stick me in rightfield or whatever.

On the Rancho Playground we used mostly city equipment. You couldn't break those bats with a hammer. That was how strong they were. We used to saw off the ends to make them more usable. We always had balls and cracked bats that we nailed together. It was not an organized and upscale scene the way it is today. We played in Levi's. We even slid in Levi's.

Jimmy LeFebvre's father was the playground director. For 50¢ they put you on a team. The first team I was on was the Tigers. Sparky Anderson was my best friend. Only then his name was George. He was on the Tigers, too.

The MGM studio lot was about four blocks away, and all the little kids that were in the movies would come over to the playground during their breaks. We got to know all the little kids on the "Our Gang" series. "The Little Rascals" and other child stars of the day often played sandlot ball there with us. I don't remember if Spanky played with us, but Buckwheat was our rightfielder. Another movie kid, Leonard Landy, was our first baseman. That was all in our Midget League time. Then we played Junior Baseball there on the playground, and then it was our high school time right next door. The whole playground environment was an absolute baseball Mecca.

American Legion baseball was very big at that time. We won a national championship in 1951 from that playground. The name of our team was Crenshaw Post 715. You had that right across the chest of your uniform.

We left California and went to Arizona, to Hastings, Nebraska — all by train. We ended up in Detroit, Michigan, at Briggs Stadium. We played White Plains, New York; Jacksonville, Florida; Cincinnati. We beat them all. Seven of the kids on our team eventually went on to sign professional contracts.

I didn't know anything about major league baseball growing up. All I knew was the Pacific Coast League, and that was because two kids on the playground were with the Hollywood Stars. Sparky Anderson, my best friend, who would play infield with me on the same high school team, was their batboy, and Elmer Amones was their ballboy.

There were the teams like the Hollywood Stars, who were owned by the Pirates, and the Angels, who were owned by the Cubs, in the Pacific Coast League. It was an open classification. There were also independent teams like San Francisco, Sacramento, and the Oakland Oaks, who had their own minor league system.

It really started to take off for us when we got to play semipro baseball. We played for a traveling team run by a man named Bill Gray, a frustrated baseball player. He was the guy! He provided us with the best of everything. We had brand-new uniforms, the best gloves, bats, uniforms. I never walked out without sanitary socks, a cup, and a jock strap. We were just kids, but we played against major league players in Los Angeles in the off-season. You really got a chance to measure yourself that way.

Our high school, Dorsey, was right next to the Rancho Playground, and our school invited the thirty-six best teams in the city of Los Angeles for the Dorsey High School Tournament. It was the city tournament. All the scouts showed up and walked around these four diamonds. They drooled. They were able in one fell swoop to cover just about every good high school baseball team in the city in a three- or four-day span.

I was High School Player of the Year in Los Angeles in 1951. I was also Athlete of the Year twice in my high school career. I ran track and played basketball. I was pretty good in track. They made me first man on the relay because I never worked out with the track team, as our baseball schedule conflicted. The scouts all told me not to play football, not to swim, not to lift weights. Those were the things they did in those days. They would never, God knows, look at a player who wore glasses, so guys hid them when scouts came around.

Lefty Phillips was the Dodger scout in that area. He also ran the Dodger

Juniors, whom I played for about five years. He signed most of the kids right out of that playground.

In January of 1953, I graduated from high school. A rule had just been put in that said if a kid was signed by a team for $4,000 or more he would have to count as a member of the big league roster. I just happened to be the first kid who was affected by that bonus rule. Instead of all sixteen teams bidding for me, only eight bid because the others felt they could not carry an eighteen-year-old kid with no experience. Joe Stephenson was the Red Sox scout who signed me. I got a $60,000 bonus and an explanation from him that Boston was going through a youth movement and could wait for me to develop.

I went from high school to spring training in Sarasota, Florida. I ran onto the field and knew no one. The first man I played catch with was Dominic DiMaggio. Ted Williams was there. He was thirty-eight years old. It gives me goose pimples even now talking about him. He led the American League in hitting that year. The Sox had other players like George Kell, who had an over .300 lifetime batting average. There was Johnny Lipon, Billy Goodman, Mickey Vernon.

Joining that Red Sox team was culture shock for me in many different ways. East Coast versus West Coast was the least of it. I was all-everything growing up in Los Angeles. But being on the Boston Red Sox was something else. This was the big leagues.

Nobody questioned me, made fun, got on me. I had an attitude about me. My major league debut was April 20, 1953. I was in rightfield, Jimmy Piersall was in center, Ted Williams in left.

I got into forty-seven games that season. That was all. That was the way it was in my career with Boston. They were a first division team, and they couldn't and wouldn't play kids. But I knew I could play no matter what the record shows.

MIKE DIFELICE

I was the youngest of the four sons. We lived in Philadelphia when I was born. But even after we moved to Georgia, we were big Phillies fans. Mike Schmidt was kind of my idol when I was a young kid.

I played a lot of Wiffle ball with my brothers. Wiffle ball turned into Little League, and Little League turned into high school baseball.

At the house in Georgia, we had a long driveway. We set up a home plate in the middle of the driveway. If you hit the ball across the street, which was a pretty far distance, it was a home run. That was the perfect setup for Wiffle ball. I attribute a lot of my baseball skill to those Wiffle ball years.

We used to tape the ball up, so we could throw it harder, and then we'd tape the bats up. Most Wiffle balls that we used, one side would have all the holes, or some of the balls would have a lot of dots all over them. If you taped up the balls a certain way, covering up a certain amount of holes, and put enough weight on them — once you let them fly, the wind going through would make them do different things.

A taped-up Wiffle ball would do a lot of things. You were winging it as hard as you could. Basically it was just like baseball. And, man, we would develop skills in hitting breaking balls. It really built a lot of reflexes, instinct, and hand-eye coordination.

Another thing we used as kids that was kind of unique and helped a lot to develop baseball skills was a hunting stand that we'd use as a catcher. We got that from my dad, who was a hunter. We had a ghost man on each base. If it was a ground ball, it was a single, that type of thing.

My family moved on to Tennessee, and there we had a backyard. A tree came into play for our ball playing. If a ball was hit at the tree, you'd play it off the tree. If you caught the ball in the air, then it was an out.

Past the first tree was a single, past another tree was like a double. I'm not sure we had triples. We actually had a fence near the tree. Getting the ball over that was a home run.

One guy would pitch, and one guy would be behind him kind of in the outfield. It was always the youngest and the oldest against the two middle ones. I always played with my older brother, Johnnie, against Angelo and Anthony. Nice little Italian family. My brothers were a real big influence in my career. Even to this day, I ask them for advice.

We had a big basement. We'd just invent games there. My oldest brother was really awesome. When you're oldest in the family, sometimes you can just forget your brothers and do your own thing. But he was always there. We'd play knee football in the basement. We'd put knee socks on our knees and we'd play football. We actually played little baseball games in there; we'd ball up a sock, and we'd have bases across the room. My brothers would have to play on their knees. I was so young I could play standing up. You could hit with the back of your hand. The way you'd get an out was you'd throw the sockball at the runner. Those were real good years, and they really helped with my competitiveness in sports, my desire to play baseball generally.

In Little League, I played shortstop, pitched, caught a little bit. I was the only one who could catch the ball and block the ball. In Wiffle ball, I was catching with my brothers taking full swings — no mask or nothing. Nobody wants to get behind the plate, because they are pretty afraid of the ball or afraid to get hit.

I remember my first Little League home run. I was ten years old. My brother was on my team. I think he was twelve. We were in the city play-offs. It was our first play-off game. In the bottom of the sixth, the game was tied. I hit just a skying pop-up. The ball just barely cleared the fence. We won the game. I remember being real excited about that. My mom was there, the biggest baseball fan ever, so you could hear her screaming from a mile away, cheering the whole game. My dad was a coach. So it was a special moment. I think we had a pizza party afterwards.

By the time I was twelve, I was probably the best pitcher in our Little League. I threw pretty hard, threw a couple of no-hitters. I really didn't have much failure. I'd give up one hit, two hits, that kind of stuff.

When I was in baseball summer camp, I pitched for our All-Star game. The whole camp was there watching, and for the first time ever I was nervous. I was pitching and walked like ten guys in a row. That was the first time that I knew what baseball pressure was. I was wearing my brother's spikes. I remember taking them off in the second inning and saying that's why I pitched bad — it was the spikes. I think I cried. It was terrible.

People were actually there to watch and root for me; still I didn't handle the pressure very well. So from that day on, whenever a big moment came, I focused on having confidence in myself.

I kept on playing baseball through Bearden High School in Knoxville, then the University of Tennessee. I was selected by the St. Louis Cardinals organization in the eleventh round of the free-agent draft on June 3, 1991. I moved up the minor league rungs. My major league debut was September 1, 1996 — a moment my whole life had been geared to.

DOM DiMAGGIO

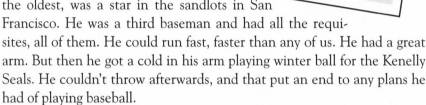

There were four DiMaggio brothers. Tom, the oldest, was a star in the sandlots in San Francisco. He was a third baseman and had all the requisites, all of them. He could run fast, faster than any of us. He had a great arm. But then he got a cold in his arm playing winter ball for the Kenelly Seals. He couldn't throw afterwards, and that put an end to any plans he had of playing baseball.

I was the youngest and the smallest of the remaining three DiMaggio brothers, all of whom played in the majors. I was born on February 12, 1917, in San Francisco. Joe was three years older than me, and Vince was five years older. I was always the little brother who wore these big round eyeglasses. Call it what you will, but I never felt handicapped.

I don't know if the DiMaggio brothers were competitive with each other. But we certainly enjoyed playing baseball with each other. We would play catch on a rather steep hill. San Francisco has a lot of them. We would try to throw the ball in scoops and short hops and that sort of thing. If the ball got away from the one of us who was on the downhill side, he would have to run two blocks to retrieve it. That was one of the ways I developed my fielding skills. If you were on the uphill side and missed the ball, you had to change places and become the guy on the downhill side of the hill. The hill was just outside our front door so it was pretty easy to get out and play catch there.

The playground was a different story. That was a far more organized experience. We played softball and hardball and chose up sides. I spent as much time as I could on the playgrounds of San Francisco, especially the playground that was recently named after Joe — the northeast playground which was just a block away from my home. We played there morning, noon, and night. After the playground closed for the night, we would jump over the fence to go swimming. But baseball was the game of choice. It seemed we played it, or a version of it, any chance we had.

I used to read about all the outstanding stars in the major leagues. From the time I was a kid, I'd follow the stories, the statistics, the box scores, the whole works. At first it was just the San Francisco papers. Later on we got into the *Sporting News.*

I don't know as I had an idol in my growing-up time, but I did have favorite players like Paul Waner. I enjoyed watching players like him perform in old Recreation Park. We would go there whenever we had a chance. I recall very distinctly they had a tall rightfield fence. On it was a very large ring. If a player batted a ball and hit the ring, he won a prize of $5 or whatever.

Despite all the baseball interest of the DiMaggio brothers, all the ball playing and the time devoted to the sport, Dad was not overly enthused. He thought his sons were wasting time playing so much baseball. But then Vince signed a contract and went on to play professionally, and Dad said to me, "They pay you for doing this?"

I said, "Yes."

Then Dad realized that playing baseball was a form of working and not just playing and having a lot of fun. When Joe broke in and had his great success, Dad asked me, "When are you going to start to play as a professional?"

I didn't go out for baseball in Galileo High School until my final year when I made the senior team. Each year at that time the San Francisco Seals and the Cincinnati Reds held a tryout period at Seals Stadium, Sixteenth and Bryant.

I was working at the Simmons Bed Factory at the time, but I thought, well, this is an opportunity for me to find out if I have any ability to play professional baseball. So I entered that tryout. They paid each kid $2, probably because many of them came from outlying areas. But I lived nearby, so I got no money. One hundred forty young men came down, and I was one of those the Seals thought well enough to sign.

Until that tryout, I had been an infielder. I entered that tryout camp as a shortstop but changed to centerfield during the tryout. The Seals had lost their centerfielder the year before and needed one. As for me, they thought a shortstop with glasses was not going to work. I made one throw when I went deep into the hole after a ground ball. The ball ended halfway up in the stands. They thought I had a good arm, so they put me in centerfield. Maybe the fact that Joe had also broken in as a shortstop but had gone to the major leagues as a centerfielder had something to do with what happened with me. Who knows?

My older brother, Vince, had been signed by the Seals and was sent down to their farm team in Tucson, Arizona. He had lost a tremendous amount of weight after playing down there for a year. And since I was of such a slight frame, the people who ran the San Francisco ball club decided that I should not be farmed out to Tucson. They probably worried I would just shrink away in the heat.

My primary objective when I entered professional baseball was to play one year. That would have satisfied me. But one of the newspapermen of the time who did not think very much of me took the time to go into detail about that in a column he wrote. He also wrote that Joe was the greatest baseball player that ever lived, justifiably so. I believe that column gave me the determination to go beyond just the one year in professional baseball.

I batted .306 that 1937 season with the San Francisco Seals. Then the Boston Red Sox came into my life; they bought my contract from the Seals. Glasses for major leaguers was a no-no for coming into professional baseball. There were guys who had played and then resorted to them. But I don't actually recall anyone actually coming in off the sandlots into triple-A baseball wearing glasses and then jumping, as I did, to the major leagues. But that is what happened to me.

The "Little Professor" nickname came out of the blue. Some said it was because of my slight build (5'9" and 168 pounds) and round spectacles. I think it probably came because I looked more like a student or a teacher.

While I don't remember my first glove, I do have a strong memory of the one I used at the end of my stay with the San Francisco Seals. In fact, I brought it up to the majors with me. I would break in new gloves — and wind up with a locker half full of gloves. But I always resorted to the old-time glove. By 1940, when I joined the Red Sox at the start of spring training, my old glove had been sewn a number of times and had a patch on the thumb.

My first view of Fenway Park was of a ballpark filled with a lot of ice and snow. It was a bit unusual for someone who had spent his growing-up years in California. I thought we would never get to play a baseball game there, never open the season.

My first game in the major leagues was in Washington, D.C. Sid

Hudson, who won seventeen games that year, pitched against us. I thought I hit a ball pretty hard. Gee Walker was the leftfielder, and he went back and caught my shot.

My first game at Fenway was against the Philadelphia Athletics. It had rained and the field was slippery. I had sprained an ankle in spring training and had missed a good part of it. I played rightfield instead of center-field because Doc Cramer was the centerfielder at the time. I went after a ball, skidded, and hurt my ankle. Manager Cronin thought that he had better be careful with me, especially with the wet grounds. He put a guy named Lou Finney in my place in rightfield. The pitchers couldn't get Finney out from then on, so I rode the bench until the Fourth of July or sometime like that.

The only way I got back into play was because of a collision between Ted Williams and Doc Cramer. In a road game, they ran into each other in left-centerfield on a ball hit by Ray Mack. Ted and Doc were both knocked unconscious for a bit. Williams left the game, and I took his place. When we came home to Fenway, Cronin inserted me in centerfield and put Cramer in leftfield because Ted was injured.

The things you remember. When I was working in the Simmons Bed Factory, I wanted to satisfy myself after having played around the sandlots. I thought if I didn't find out how good I was I would miss an opportunity. So I decided to tell my boss that I was leaving. I gave him two weeks notice, because it was piecework. He was very nice. "We'll have someone take your place," he said. "And if you don't do it, if you don't make the grade in baseball, come back and we'll have your job waiting for you."

BOB FELLER

My earliest baseball memory is throwing a rubber ball through the door into the living room of our house. My dad would be sitting on the couch in the living room, and he would stop the ball with a pillow. Since I was much too young to catch the ball, he would roll it back to me. When I threw the ball to him, I'd go into the big windup that he had taught me. Sometimes I'd miss the door and hit the wall and knock some of the plaster off or jar the lamp that was attached to the wall. All of that did not make my grandmother happy or my mother for that matter. But it didn't bother my father too much.

I was born on November 3, 1918. I grew up on a farm just west of Des Moines, Iowa, in a small town named Van Meter. My sister Marguerite came along when I was ten. My father, William, and my mother, Lena Feller, gave me time to do things and develop. So I consider that I had a great childhood.

My father's dad died when my dad was nine years old. His mother never remarried. He had four sisters and a sick brother who died at the age of nine. All of that shaped my father and his work ethic, how he treated people. It also influenced me.

I grew up during the depression, the dust storm era. But I did not grow up poor. We never missed a meal. My parents had a self-sustaining farm that consisted of over seven hundred acres, and they worked day and night taking care of it. They never took a vacation in forty years.

From the age of five, I started throwing a ball. I threw in the pig lot or tossed a ball off the outhouse. I threw in the winter cold. Snow was piled up everywhere except where we shoveled to get a flat surface. We always had about a dozen balls around, and if they got wet in the snow, we would put them into the wood stove and dry them out. I also played some kind of ball in the barn all winter. My dad hung lights in the barn and would open one of the doors to let in some light. We had a basket there, and I would shoot baskets.

I played catch in the barnyard, which we called the "hog lot," and between the outhouse and the house. The stitches on the balls would break fairly often from being batted around, so we would tear off the entire cover and stitch things together with harness thread and curved needles, drawing the thread through a big ball of bee's wax. I would do that kind of sewing chore evening after evening after evening with my father in front of the old potbellied stove. We'd sew those balls up good and use them again and again.

It wasn't all baseball. We lived the life of a farm family. We stored the hay and the native lumber up there in the barn as well as some of the grain. Underneath were the horses and some of the livestock and the straw to bed them down. We milked the cows there in the stanchions. We had a pair of running horses that we put on a buggy with a sleigh. They were Belgians and Clydesdales. I curried them and cleaned the barns out every Saturday.

But whenever we could, we played baseball. As time went on, my dad pitched batting practice to me and hit grounders. I also had a little dog called "Tagalong" whose job it was to field the balls. Saturday nights we'd go over and take the butter and eggs in. Then we would go to town and do some shopping and listen to the band and get home early so we could play a ball game on Sunday.

I have been told that my story of growing up on the farm and getting into baseball is very dramatic. But I really don't think of it that way. My mother was very intelligent and responsible; she was a registered nurse. Both my parents were on the school board. My parents let me know where the stakes were set. I never had to ask what to do next. I knew when to clean out the barn, when to play ball, curry the horses. All of that helped me to learn a sense of proportion, build a work ethic, develop stamina, complete my games.

When I was about eight years old, my dad was throwing batting practice to me. I picked up one of the balls to throw back to him and just snapped my wrist when I did it. My dad told me to do the same thing again. That was how I started to throw the curveball.

My father made a home plate in the yard, and I'd throw to him over it. Dad caught me all the time. He even built me a pitching rubber. When I was twelve years old, he built a complete baseball field out of a pasture on our farm. We had a diamond, an outfield with a fence, a scoreboard. We fenced the pasture, put up the chicken wire and the benches, a backstop, a little grandstand behind first base, and refreshment stands.

We called the place Oakview because it was up a hill overlooking the Raccoon River and had a beautiful view of a grove of oak trees. We formed our own team and played other teams from around the community on weekends. My father paid for the loan of the uniforms from the school. People would come and pay 25¢ to watch us play. Most of the players were in their late teens and twenties except for me.

We had the first Field of Dreams over there on our farm in Iowa. Our Oakview team started playing fifty-seven years before they had the "Field of Dreams" up there in Dyersville. We were there four years before I started playing for the Farmer's Union team in Des Moines that won the Iowa State Championship.

My heroes growing up were Rogers Hornsby, Walter Johnson, and Babe Ruth. My first glove was a Rogers Hornsby, the old three-fingered kind. Hornsby was my idol because we could get the Cubs' game on our radio on the farm in Iowa. I even took up second base as my first position because that was where Hornsby played.

All my heroes meant a great deal to me. I followed them very closely and read everything I could in the "Pink Sheet" of the *Des Moines Register*. My dad bought me all the baseball books that were around and also the *Sporting News*. I did a lot of baseball reading.

I guess all the farm chores made me strong. At Van Meter High School, I pitched five no-hitters. I had a live fastball. I could throw hard. Since I started throwing a curveball at age eight, it was no surprise to anyone that I had a great curve in high school. I taught myself how to throw it and got better with it through the years.

My windup was geared to get as much speed out of my arm and as much fear out of the batter as possible. I pivoted away, turned my back on the batter, and then let it go.

When I was sixteen in 1934, I saw major league baseball competition for the first time when we went to St. Louis for the World Series. There were four games in Detroit that year, but I saw the three played in St. Louis. I saw Dizzy Dean and his brother Paul Dean pitch and Schoolboy Rowe and Tommy Bridges. Frankie Frisch was the manager of the Cardinals then.

But I had seen many major league exhibition games before then in Des Moines. There was a Cub farm team there — the Des Moines Demons. The Kansas City Monarchs out of the old Negro Leagues would play a lot in Des Moines, too. I saw Satchel Paige; I also pitched against him when I was sixteen years old. We went on to become great friends. Satchel could throw hard, had great control, had the great motion. He would have been one of the top ten pitchers in history if he had played in the big leagues in his prime. Later when I was on Cleveland, he played for us in 1948, but by then he was already forty-two.

The scout who signed me was C. C. Slapnicka of Cleveland, the same scout who signed Mel Harder, Herb Score, Lou Boudreau, and a lot of others. It was July of 1935. I was sixteen years old. Slapnicka had come to Des Moines to sign Claude Passeau from the Demons for the Cleveland Indians, but he came by to see me pitch in a tournament in an early morning game. He never did get to see Passeau, who wound up being signed by Pittsburgh.

I was a bonus baby. I signed for a dollar bill and an autographed ball. It wasn't even new. But I was very confident that I'd make good, and opportunity was more important than security.

That ball was signed by the 1935 Cleveland Indians. The contract was written on the back of a piece of hotel stationery. It called for me to go to Fargo-Moorhead of the Northern League. The Indians were going to pay me about $175 a month.

But Baseball Commissioner Landis said what the Indians did was a violation of baseball rules, because I signed before completing high school. Commissioner Landis fined the Indians $7,500 and ruled that I was free to sign with any team. The bidding might have reached $100,000, a very large sum in those days, but I respected my contract with the Indians.

This was 1936. I started playing semipro ball in Cleveland for a team called the Rosenblooms, sponsored by a clothing store located at 321 Euclid Avenue. I played in six games for them. Then I was asked to pitch in an exhibition game for the Indians when the Cardinals came to town on July 6, 1936.

I pitched the fourth, fifth, and sixth innings against the Gashouse Gang managed by Frankie Frisch. Durocher was the first hitter I faced. I remember that. I struck out eight out of nine and instead of going to

Fargo, North Dakota, to start my career, I was put on a train to join the Cleveland Indians in Philadelphia. I met Connie Mack there, and he became a great friend of mine; I loved him.

I was taken care of very nicely by the Indians. Steve O'Neil, the manager, he was like a father to me. Wally Shang, the coach, who had been a catcher with several teams, was a wonderful man and helped me a great deal. He was kind of my buffer and advisor.

My first big league start was in Cleveland in League Park. It was August 23, 1936, against the St. Louis Browns. I struck out the first eight men to face me and then seven more for a total of fifteen. That was one less than the American League record. I won the game 4–1. I was in games in relief in July and August, but that was my first start. I was seventeen years old. I was the youngest pitcher to ever win a major league game. I struck out seventeen Philadelphia Athletics in a game shortly afterwards, establishing a new American League record. Then I went back to Van Meter to finish high school. It's all storybook, but it's true.

My father had a cancer that started in 1936. We had big bills at the Mayo Clinic for the radium and X-ray treatments. The Indians took care of the bills, giving me $10,000 that winter for his care. Mayo was about 220 miles from Van Meter. I would drive him up.

I did graduate from high school. I took two weeks off in 1937 and had a tutor in spring training in New Orleans where we trained. I went to school every day in my room at the Hotel Roosevelt. After, I went back home, graduated, got my diploma, and rejoined the Indians.

At the start I was with the Indians between my junior and senior year. I came back to Van Meter and had a homecoming. I went back to school that winter but could not participate in basketball because I was a professional.

I used to do simulations all the time with my dad. Man on third. What do you throw? When do you have to bear down? That's why when I first got to the Cleveland Indians at such a young age, I wasn't the greatest pitcher, but I had a good idea of what was going on and what to throw when, because I had done those simulations.

Just as Edison said: "Find out what you like to do and you'll never have to work again." I was about nine years old when I started to think of being nothing but a major league ball player. I wasn't a cocky kid, I was very quiet. I just worked at it with my father helping me all the time.

I have been asked what was my greatest moment in baseball. Well, I enjoyed playing catch with my dad. Those were the better days than the days of pitching three no-hitters, twelve one-hitters, or striking out eighteen men. Those were the days.

JESSE GARCIA

$\mathcal{I}$ *was an* Astros fan growing up in Texas. My favorite players were Nolan Ryan and Dickie Thon. Just watching Dickie Thon play the infield — he never missed a ground ball — I was like, "Wow, this guy is good! He never makes a mistake." I wanted to be like Dickie Thon and never make a mistake, catch every single ball that was hit to me. I also admired Nolan Ryan because of his arm and how hard he threw. I wanted to try and throw hard like Nolan Ryan did. He was the strikeout king.

I was born on September 24, 1973, and grew up outside Corpus Christi, Texas. My first T-ball team was the Orioles. I wore uniform number 15. Ironically, in 1999, I made it to the big leagues with the Orioles. My first number with the big league team was 15 as well, so that was really ironic.

My favorite position was shortstop. Then when I went to Robstown High School, I was moved to second base. I did very well there. Along the way I got into boxing in Golden Gloves and won several titles as boxer. But baseball was my thing, that's what I was serious about. Still, it really was not until my senior year of high school that I realized I had a chance of becoming a major leaguer.

There was time spent at Lee Junior College and then being selected by the Baltimore Orioles organization in the twenty-sixth round of the free-agent draft on June 3, 1993. And then there was all that long time in the minors . . . the California League, the Eastern League where I led all second basemen in fielding percentage in 1997. *Baseball America* gave me recognition for the second straight year as the best defensive second baseman in the league. But even with that, I was looked upon as "good glove, not so good bat."

Finally, after seven minor league seasons, after going through every level of the Baltimore organization, I was called up by the Orioles. I had been a second baseman all through the minor leagues. Then when I got to the major leagues, I was moved to shortstop, because they liked my arm strength.

My first game was at Camden Yards on April 4, 1999. It was against the Blue Jays. My family was here. I'd always dreamt of hearing my name called at Camden Yards, with Cal Ripken and other guys that I watched growing up. It was such a thrill for me and my family. I was like a kid in a candy store, taking it all in.

Everybody talks about the fact that you're always going to remember your first at bat. I wanted it to be special. I was fortunate enough to get a base hit, right back up the middle. The first home run I hit in the majors I hit in 1999 in Texas, back home. My friends and my family got to see me do it.

I was watching all these guys, watching Cal Ripken, and then I became Cal Ripken's locker roommate. It was pretty exciting.

GEORGE GENOVESE

When I was growing up, Bill Terry was the player-manager of the New York Giants and Mel Ott was the star. The St. Louis Cardinals always seemed to have some real standouts in those days, the early thirties. I would get to go to Ebbets Field or the Polo Grounds or Yankee Stadium with the Police Athletic League or the newspaper boys. We always sat in the bleachers.

I would read the *Staten Island Advance*, the *Daily News*, the *Daily Mirror.* The *Journal* would come out in the afternoon, and there were the late scores there. There was always a lot of good sports coverage in that paper.

My father was a hardworking Italian. His job was in the shipyards where he was an excellent riveter. My mother took care of the family. I went to Public School 19 and then Port Richmond High School. My parents encouraged me to play ball all the way through school. My last year in high school I was the baseball team captain, a popular and pretty good player.

I still remember the glove I used. It was the Lonnie Frey model put out by Rawlings. It became the real standard for infielders, and I was always an infielder.

Back in those days not too many scouts came around. Most of the time players had to go to tryout camps to get noticed. It was 1940. I was eighteen years old, about 5'6", and had just graduated from high school. My CYO director recommended that both the catcher on our high school team and I go to a St. Louis Cardinals tryout camp in Waterbury, Connecticut. My parents knew I was interested in playing baseball, but they would never have let me go. My brother, however, gave me a dollar, and I had 25¢ of my own. I wrote a note to my parents and left it on the kitchen table.

The catcher had a car. In those days there were no freeways, so it took us four to five hours to drive from Staten Island to Connecticut. In those days White Castle restaurants sold hamburgers for a nickel. You can imagine how many hamburgers I had.

We finally arrived in the area of the tryout camp and went up the road to try to find a place to sleep. The first place we stopped at was a farm. The farmer said we were welcome to stay in the barn in the hayloft as long as we did not smoke.

We slept well that night. In the morning we got down to town, went into a little grocery store, and got a pack of crackers and a bottle of Pepsi-Cola. That was our breakfast.

There were two guys who ran the whole St. Louis tryout camp operation: "Pop" Kelchner, one of Branch Rickey's right-hand men, and Roy Dissinger, a scout who was the younger of the two. I marveled at how Roy held up in the heat because he must have hit fifty to seventy infield grounders a day. All he did was sweat and drink Coca-Colas.

The whole enterprise was one big survival contest. I survived for four days along with my friend, the catcher. Then they cut him. I told "Pop" that I had only 10¢ left. "If you are planning to cut me," I said, "you might as well do it now, because I would then at least have a ride home."

"Stick around a little longer," he said. They put me up in a hotel. I took my friend with me to the hotel. I got the bed. He slept on the floor. Since I could sign for meals, we both had a big steak and I signed for it. I am sure they thought I was a real big eater. My friend ultimately went on his way back home, but I was taken good care of for the next few days.

Finally, the camp, which had run all week, ended. It had been a process of elimination. Three of us had survived out of about 700. Roy Dissinger told me to go home. "We will get in touch with you," he said, and then he asked, "Do you need any money?"

"No," I told him. "Just give me 50¢ and I'll get on the highway." Boston Post Road ran behind the ballpark. There I was in my baseball uniform and my little bag carrying my other clothes. I had never hitchhiked before, but now I put my thumb out. A truck driver pulled up and asked me where I was going. "New York City," I said.

He said, "Hop in. I'm going there, too." At that time the 1939 New York World's Fair was on. He was bringing some stuff there. He took me right into New York City. On the way we stopped, and he bought me a nice dinner. Then he dropped me off at a subway station in the city. "Home you go," he said.

Mind you, I had 50¢ — a nickel for the subway, a nickel for the ferry boat, and a nickel for the bus, which left me off about half a block from my house. I got home with 35¢ to spare.

Three days later my brother got the telegram: "George Genovese report to Fred Lucas Wentworth Arms Hotel in Hamilton, Ontario." It was class-D, lowest classification, but it was the beginning.

My brother got me a train ticket. I had been told they would reimburse me for it. The train got in about five in the morning. I got to the hotel at about six A.M. and rang the team manager: "Mr. Lucas, I am here." The team had just gotten in from a road trip. I woke him up.

He was all right about it. "I will see you in the coffee shop at noon. Have them give you a room."

I don't think I slept a wink. I was on pins and needles.

Finally, it was noon. I went to the coffee shop, and one of the waitresses pointed him out. I don't know what kind of an impression I made, because I wasn't very big. We spoke for a while, and the wrap-up was that he told me to meet him at three o'clock and we would go to the ballpark. We took a local bus out to the ballpark. I was fitted out with a nice white home uniform for the Hamilton Red Wings.

The manager asked me if I wanted to sit around for a few days and watch. I kind of sensed that he wasn't too thrilled with my size. So I said, "No, Mr. Lucas. You can put me in the ball game, and if you don't think I can play you can send me home tomorrow."

There was a player on our team, Hank Redmond, who had arms on him like Popeye the Sailor. He was about 5'8" and 210 pounds. Just square like a granite block. He was the captain of the team, and he could hit, and he always had a big wad of tobacco in his mouth.

Here I come out to the field with this brand-new white uniform on and the first thing he did was splatter it with tobacco juice. It was disgusting.

I asked, "What's that for?"

And he says, "Good for the linen, kid."

You gotta remember — I was Joe Rook. Now we're lining up before my first game. They played "God Save the Queen," and also "The Star-Spangled Banner." We sang both national anthems. While we're doing that, Hank decides to spit on my shoes.

So I ask again, "What's that for?"

And he says, "Good for the leather."

That was my introduction to professional baseball. My first time at bat — it was against the London Pirates — I hit a double to rightfield.

I played the rest of 1940, and the next year I was back there with a big $5 raise to $85 a month. In 1942, I went to Asheville in the Piedmont League where I played against Tony Lazzeri. He was the player-manager. Ben Chapman was the player-manager of Richmond. The draft age that year was lowered from twenty-one to eighteen, and all of us playing ball there had to register in the town of Asheville, North Carolina. It was a small town, and it was cleaned out of twenty-one-year-olds. Half our ball club was drafted.

I was able to finish out the season, went into the army that fall, and was in the service three and a half years. While I was in Okinawa, I came across the grave of Frank Zera, one of the buddies I had on that team.

I got out of the service in 1946 and started all over again. I went from Lynchburg to Omaha to Denver, which was turning independent. I had a fine year for Denver in 1948, made the All-Star team and was sold to Hollywood in the Pacific Coast League in 1949. We won a championship.

In 1950, I reported to spring training with the Washington Senators. Bucky Harris was the manager. I was ticketed to be a utility infielder, but I got impatient. I was in only three ball games and told Bucky I was not happy and would just as soon go back to Hollywood.

They sent me down to Chattanooga in double-A. I made my way back to the Pacific Coast League where conditions were better than in the majors — playing a week in each town. Every Monday was off.

I had one of the briefest careers in the major leagues ever — that was partially of my own doing. But I had a long career in organized baseball.

MARK GRACE

$\mathcal{W}hen\ \mathcal{I}\ was$ growing up in Nashville, Tennessee, my favorite players were George Brett and Keith Hernandez, because I was a first baseman and left-handed like them.

I was born on June 28, 1964, in Winston-Salem. I am the only professional athlete in the family. My father and my brother played sports in high school, but I'm the only one that went further.

I grew up as a Cardinals fan listening to KMOX radio, to Jack Buck and Mike Shannon. I did not expect to be a major leaguer. I did not aspire to it. My father was a realist. He always told me, "Go get your education. Get ready for the real world." But it turned out that I was good enough to play the game.

Our family was middle class. Dad worked hard for Union Pacific Railroad. We were never in need, but by the same token we did not have the best of everything.

We moved to California when I was about junior high school age. I graduated from Tustin High School in 1982. The Minnesota Twins selected me in the fifteenth round of the 1984 free-agent draft. But I did not sign. I was a twenty-fourth-round pick in 1985 by the Chicago Cubs out of San Diego State, where I had a baseball scholarship, but again I did not sign.

Instead, I went up to the Alaska League. I played so well up there that summer of 1985 that the Cubs came back and made a significantly better offer. This time I signed.

In 1986, I won the Midwest League batting title with a .342 average at Peoria in single-A ball. The Cubs moved me to the Eastern League the next season. With Pittsfield, I had a bang-up time hitting .333, driving in the most runs in the league, winning the Most Valuable Player award.

I played in only twenty-one games at Iowa in triple-A in 1988 when the Cubs brought me up. My first big league at bat was May 2, 1988, in San

Diego against Jimmy Jones. I hit a little old ground ball to third base and was out. My next at bat I got my first major league hit — a line drive to rightfield. That sure felt good. Funny thing, during that first major league series that I played in from May 2 to May 4, 1988, at San Diego, I wore uniform number 28. I did not begin to wear my regular number 17 until our team returned to Wrigley on May 6. I won the *Sporting News* National League Rookie of the Year award that 1988 season and went on from there.

I have to give a lot of credit to my dad and my mom. I am lucky that my parents stayed together through all the years. There was just an older brother and myself, and my parents ran a tight ship for us. They weren't strict beyond belief, but they taught us right from wrong. They've encouraged me throughout my baseball career.

Wrigley Field is the office. But it's also home. I can't think of any better place to play or fans to play in front of. Win or lose, they love you.

PUMPSIE GREEN

My given name is Elijah Jerry, but I have always been called "Pumpsie," the nickname my mother gave me when I was a couple of years old.

I was born in 1933 and grew up in Richmond, California, where baseball was, what you might say, a natural part of life. All the kids in the area, the young and old, men and women — everybody played baseball.

I never thought of playing pro ball. To me, baseball was just a game to play and have fun with. That was all. I used to see this big picture of Stan Musial on the side of the highway in the neighborhood. That was just about the only association I had with major league baseball.

But the Pacific Coast League was really big. I listened to Bud Foster doing every Oakland Oaks game and followed a whole bunch of people on that team. It was almost a daily ritual. When I got old enough to wish, I wished I could play for the Oakland Oaks.

We were just an average family living in an apartment. I had four younger brothers, and a couple of them really excelled in athletics. Cornell was especially good in football and later became a Dallas Cowboys' defensive back. Another brother played for the Packers for a year. I had my own crowd and was a little older, so I didn't compete that much against my brothers. I also always played against guys a little older than me so that when I was ten, I played against guys who were thirteen, fourteen and also against grown men.

We played a team from another neighborhood that was crosstown who beat us 44–0. But we had a return engagement, and we had an idea: "Hey, let's do everything opposite of what we normally do."

Everybody just switched around. I was a right-handed hitter, so I turned around and batted left-handed. That moment in time is what began the switch-hitting for me. I had a heck of a day with the bat. We still lost, but we improved. The score this time was 35–10.

For a while, I didn't have a glove of my own. I talked my mother into buying me a glove at a time when the family really couldn't afford one. I was one of her favorites, if I must say so myself, because I was the oldest.

To get the glove I worked every day around the house, on the farm, and did whatever I was asked to do. Finally, she saved the money — seven or eight dollars — enough to buy me a brand-new glove. Boy, did I love that glove! When I could, I took a couple of baseballs and wrapped them into the pocket of the glove. I tied the whole thing up into a neat package and greased it and so forth. I used it and used it until I wore it out.

The glove was what we called Caledonia those days, a three-fingered glove. The guy who played shortstop for the Oakland Oaks, Artie Wilson, used a three-fingered glove. I played shortstop mostly out of school and wanted to be like Artie Wilson. But when I was a senior in El Cerito High School, our team didn't have a catcher, so I switched to that position.

We had a good high school team coached by a man named Gene Corr, who went on to become the baseball coach at Contra Costa Junior College after my sophomore year.

When I was getting set to graduate from high school, I planned to go to Fresno State, which offered me an athletic scholarship. But Gene Corr promised me that I could play shortstop if I joined his team at Contra Costa, so I switched plans and went there.

In my senior year at Contra Costa, Gene Corr got a tryout for me with the Oakland Oaks. It was like a dream coming true. I got into his car, and we drove from Richmond to Oakland, which was about seven or eight miles away. I tried out with the team for a week.

As a kid I had a policeman friend who loved baseball and took me to a game every once in a while. I would watch Artie Wilson, Billy Martin, Jackie Jensen, and all the rest. Now I was there on the tryout schedule. Augie Galan was the manager. But the guy who ran the hell out of me was a coach named George "Highpockets" Kelly, who had been a major leaguer for many years. He grabbed that fungo bat and kept hitting balls to me. I ran around. I was whipped. I was tired.

My workouts would take place before the regular team did its exercises. Then when the game started, Gene Corr and I would sit in the stands and watch the games. I'd talk to the Oakland third baseman, Spider Jorgensen. My favorite player was Piper Davis, who made it to the majors.

The people in charge of the Oaks finally came to a decision about me. It was just sign and go play ball. Oakland was an independent team, so there was no draft as far as I was concerned. I got no bonus, just a regular salary of three or four hundred dollars a month.

Unfortunately I never got a chance to play with Oakland. I played in Oakland's minor leagues with Wenatchee, Washington, the apple capital of the world, and in 1955, I was moved up to Stockton, California.

It was June. We were in first place. I was having a great year. Then one day my manager Roy Partee told me, "Hey, Pumps, the Red Sox bought your contract. You are going to their organization, to Montgomery, Alabama."

I did not want to go. I wasn't ready for it. One of the reasons Boston wanted me to go to Montgomery was that Earl Wilson, the only black in their organization, was there. They wanted me to be his roommate.

I managed to get permission to finish out the season with Stockton and was named the Most Valuable Player in the California State League. I hit about .300 and drove in about eighty-something runs.

In 1956, I went to spring training with the Red Sox in Florida. I was street-smart and knew I could take care of myself. But any young black in those days going to the South had some kind of feelings. California was an integrated experience. There were some problems, but there weren't signs all over the place about where blacks and whites could go like there were in Florida.

I roomed all by myself. I knew that all the major league teams had been integrated except for the Red Sox. People made me aware. They wouldn't let me forget it.

About a dozen years before, I was just happy to hear that Jackie Robinson had broken baseball's color line. The second year after he broke in, he barnstormed with an All-Star team, and they came and played at the Oakland Oaks' ballpark. I scraped up every nickel and dime together that I could — and I was there. I had to see this game with the Jackie Robinson All Stars. They were all black — Suitcase Simpson, Minnie Minoso, and the others. They played an Oakland team that was put together specially for that occasion.

But now I did not think of myself as another Jackie Robinson, as a pioneer with the Red Sox. I just wanted to make the team. As long as I had that chance, I was going to try and do the best I could. It got to be sort of tiring when the media kept asking me questions about being the first black on the Red Sox and what it meant to me, and what was my opinion as to why Boston had never had a black player before.

I met all the guys, including Ted Williams, at spring training, and they acted fine to me. I had the best spring training of anyone on the whole team, including Ted Williams. Yet, after such a great spring, I was sent down to Minneapolis. That caused a lot of writing in the newspaper, and that was when I got tired of it all. People were asking me too many questions about things I had no control over. I told them, "You are asking the wrong person."

They kept me in Minneapolis until 1959. That year I was having a great year, hitting about .330 or .340. On July 21, I got a call. I headed off to meet Boston in Chicago. It was exciting. But I had a little laugh walking out this long dungeonway in Comiskey Park. Passing the White Sox dugout, I saw an old junior college and high school teammate — Jim Landis. He yelled, "Hey, El Cerito. You have a good season."

I got to play immediately; I started my first game that first night. I will never forget my first at bat. I faced a guy who really shook me up. His name was Early Wynn. I had seen him on television pitching in the World Series. He had a big name. It was the end of his career. I know he did not throw me one strike, and yet I had two strikes called on me. I finally grounded out to second base because I stepped forward and just flicked the bat. I didn't want to strike out or hit something to a guy named Nellie Fox at second base.

That first at bat was the worst I ever had in the major leagues, made comfortable outs the rest of the game. There was only that night for me in Chicago and then we went to Cleveland. My first night in Boston was July 24. I had never been to any of these cities before. Fenway Park just felt small because it is small. Even Minneapolis, where I played for two years, seemed bigger.

There was now more media pressure than ever. I was trying to make it as a player and as the first black man on the Red Sox. I had no roommate. It never crossed my mind to have a roommate, since I was the only black on the team. It wasn't a rule. It wasn't a law. But it was unwritten that blacks did not room with whites.

The Red Sox got me a room in a hotel. I didn't even know if I had to pay for it or not. I got to meet Mr. Yawkey the second day that I was in Boston. He was a very gentle, short, round man. He told me why he called me up, said he wanted to get to know me, and wished me well. "If you run into any problems or need any advice on something, you don't have to go to the coaches or manager. Come directly to me," he said. I thanked him, and we shook hands.

The first night I got to Fenway there was such a crowd, the park was full. A lot of blacks wanted to come to the game. They didn't have a seat, but they were accommodated. The Red Sox roped off a corner part of centerfield. The whole thing made me feel special, but it made my blood pressure go up, too. "I can't fail. I can't make a mistake." That was how I felt.

When I first got to Boston, I got in touch with guys from the University of San Francisco — Bill Russell and KC Jones, who were stars on the Boston Celtics. Russ would take me around and talk to me. He told me where I should and shouldn't go.

The reception in Boston was good. It was just like anyplace else. If you are doing a good job, you get the "Yea." If you are not up to snuff, you can get the "Nay."

Around the first of September, the Red Sox flew my wife up to Boston. That made things a lot easier for me. We had been married since 1957.

I had good friends on that team — Pete Runnels, Frank Malzone. Jackie Jensen and also Ted Williams were friends and fellow Californians. I was able to function, I really was. Some of the pressure and nervousness I put on myself. I know the people expected a lot, especially the black community, which wanted me to do good.

There were overtones of racial things. These overtones could be heard not only at Fenway but at any other ballpark. Sometimes terrible things would be yelled out, racial epithets. Some people said I must have felt like killing somebody. But I never did. I got where I could divorce it from my mind, cut it off. I told people I had enough troubles trying to hit the curveball. I wasn't going to worry about some loudmouths.

Growing up, although I knew about the Brooklyn Dodgers and Jackie Robinson, I did not know how much he had to endure. Funny thing, he was retired for a couple of years when I began my time in the major leagues with the Red Sox.

I didn't have the kind of career that I would have loved to have had. Still, if I had it to do over again, I would do the same thing. I never thought about the major leagues at all. I would have been happy just to have had the chance to play for the Oakland Oaks.

SHAWN GREEN

My place of birth was Des Plaines, Illinois, the date: November 10, 1972. When I was a year old, my family moved to New Jersey and then on to San Jose, California, where we remained until I was twelve.

My first love was baseball, but I also played and enjoyed soccer until I was about ten. But basically, I grew up with baseball. Even when I was a toddler, I loved to hit and throw a ball with my dad. I played all the time, hit baseballs all the time.

My father was really into baseball. He taught me everything about the sport, bought me a batting cage and also a pitching machine. Those things were part of my backyard equipment. Some days I would hit up to 200 balls a day. I would keep hitting until I could hardly hold a bat. But the next day I would be back for more.

I did a lot of dreaming of one day playing in Fenway Park in Boston like the player who was my all-time baseball idol, Ted Williams. Rod Carew, Rickey Henderson, Don Mattingly were three favorite players in my growing-up time. I just liked their tough and thorough approach to the game.

When our family moved to Tustin, California, I played in the San Jose Little League and enjoyed it very much. The big downer was that for two years in a row, the team I was on lost to the team that went on to Williamsport.

In high school I put the time and effort into baseball. There were scouts around from the start. I wound up during my senior year being a first team selection to the 1991 *USA Today* All-USA high school team. It was a big time for me. I also got a baseball scholarship to Stanford University. And Toronto drafted me as their first round pick. I was sixteenth overall in the nation.

Fortunately, I was able to work out an arrangement with the Blue Jays that allowed me to play ball in the summer and go to Stanford in the off-season. My signing bonus was one of the highest at that time, I gave a part of it to the Metropolitan Toronto Housing Authority Breakfast Club. It felt good to give back.

My first professional season was with the 1992 Dunedin Blue Jays of the Florida State League. I made the All-Star team. Toronto moved me up in 1993 to the Knoxville Smokies in double-A Southern League. But I only played in ninety-nine games — I broke my right thumb in early June. On September 23, 1993, I was called up to the majors by Toronto. It happened fast. I was just a twenty-year-old kid.

DARRYL HAMILTON

My dad was a high school baseball coach in Baton Rouge, Louisiana, where I was born on December 3, 1964. In all my growing-up time I was always around his players. I learned a lot doing from them. It was natural that I pick up the game.

My full name is Darryl Quinn Hamilton, but I have gone by my nickname of "Hambone" for quite a while, maybe as far back as Little League where I played shortstop. What I remember from Little League is that I was much too scared to swing the bat. I was always hoping to get a walk, to get on base.

I also played stickball a lot. We were only three or four guys playing, so you hit, you ran to second base, and you ran home. That was it. Just two bases. We pitched, but underhanded.

It's funny — looking back at those days, whenever there was a game rained out, we were upset. I can remember going out there and wanting to play all day long. I never thought I'd make a living doing it. That may be one of the reasons I made it — I never expected to make it, to become a major league player.

We didn't have a lot of people make it to big leagues where I was from. You couldn't turn on the TV and see someone from the neighborhood or the area playing. Those guys you saw were all from up north or California or Texas or whatever. So the big leagues and getting there wasn't something I counted on going through high school.

Back then football and basketball were the big deals. Everybody and his brother wanted to play them, and of course I played along with everyone else. But I didn't get a chance to play what I wanted to play most of all — and that was baseball. My high school didn't have a baseball team. I was lucky enough to play summer league American Legion ball all throughout high school.

In high school, I was a wide receiver. Nicholls State scouted and recruited me. But I didn't want to play football. So I talked to the baseball coach at Nicholls, and he said, "If you want to come out and try out, we'll give you a fair look." I did that, and I made the team.

The reason I liked baseball so much more than football was because I realized you couldn't get hurt as much playing baseball as compared to football. It wasn't a sport where one game, one play could be your last. And I also really enjoyed it. I really enjoyed baseball for the fun of it.

In my second year of college, five or six scouts began looking me over. By my junior year I started getting a pretty good number of guys coming out and watching what I was doing out on the baseball field. I was drafted by the Milwaukee Brewers in the eleventh round in June 1986.

I hit .328 with forty-two steals for class-A Stockton in 1987. The year before I had hit .391 in sixty-five games for class-A Helena. I was doing well and was content to play away in the minors. I didn't think I had a shot at the major leagues until the night I got called up. I never thought about it in the minor leagues, not even when I was playing triple-A and doing so well.

It was a surprise. It was one of those things where you don't expect it, and that's why it happens. When you start expecting things and they don't happen, you get crushed.

My first major league game was Milwaukee playing against California — back then it was the California Angels — June 3, 1988. I'll never forget that day. I got to the ballpark and into the clubhouse and saw Robin Yount, Paul Molitor, all these guys. I couldn't believe I was up in the big leagues.

In the seventh inning, Tom Trebelhorn, who was the Milwaukee manager then, told me to get loose — that I was going in for Robin Yount. I was scared to death. I didn't know what to do. I was shaking all the way going out to the outfield. Robin passed me as he headed towards the bench.

"Just relax and have fun with it," he said. "It's just like being in triple-A or double-A. Don't think about anything. Just do what you do best."

What he said made it a lot easier for me. I went in and took my position in centerfield. I got my first major league at bat in the eighth inning, got a base hit. And the rest has been a roller coaster.

MYRON "RED" HAYWORTH

$\mathcal{I}$ *was* *born* in Guilford County, North Carolina, on May 14, 1915. They say that is a long time ago, but it doesn't seem so to me. I was the youngest one in the family. We were raised on a dairy and tobacco farm. It wasn't but about thirty-three acres.

I had to get up at 4:30 every morning and milk ten cows. To tell you the truth, pulling those cow tits certainly helped my hands and forking hay really helped develop my arms. You'll find so many fellahs back then that worked on farms who could just get out and throw. And you believe me, they certainly could throw. They didn't baby their arms, and they developed a good strong grip.

We were five boys in the family, and we played baseball in the yard. We played with the same ball over and over again. When the cover came off, we'd put black tape on and play with it some more. That's the way it was. We didn't have the money to just go out and buy a lot of stuff. Louisville made the good bats and once in a while I was able to lay my hands on one of them. That was some feeling. But I never had a bat of my own or a glove of my own when I was growing up. I just had an old glove that my brothers passed on to me.

When I went on to high school, they had me play first base. I also pitched, and in one game I got to pitch a no-hitter. After high school, I wound up at Oak Ridge Military Institute, which turned out a lot of ballplayers. All my brothers went there. So did Wes Ferrell.

The institute was strictly for baseball. That's all we did there — we played. There weren't but about 250 students at that time. We played Duke and Carolina freshmen, and we played Marines and teams at Marine bases. We also played against other military schools in Virginia and North Carolina.

Colonel Holt was president of the institute and also the baseball coach. He was a big man, a big-eyed fellah, a first baseman, a wonderful instructor, and very graceful in everything he did. He always taught us to work on our weakness; that was the way he said that you improved.

My brother Ray was about twelve years older than me. Ray was a pitcher, could throw hard, threw overhand. The ball carried good, so the Colonel made a catcher out of him. My brother Chester was a third baseman, the only left-handed hitter in the family. The Colonel made a catcher out of him, too. When I got there, you know what happened. The Colonel said to me straight out, "Well, get a mitt, you're going to catch." He made a catcher out of me, too. All the Hayworth brothers were catchers of one kind or another.

When I was a teenager, Ray was catching for the Detroit Tigers. I went to Washington, D.C., to see Ray play, because that was the closest baseball city at the time to North Carolina where I lived. I met the players on the Tigers. They were a fine bunch of fellows and very nice to me.

Most of my school time I had a nice relationship with Tom McCann, a scout with the Yankees. He followed my progress. He was called "White Tie," because he always wore a lot of white ties. In 1936, he signed me with a $750 bonus and sent me out to Joplin, Missouri, to play C League ball. I was there with Johnny Lindell, who later made a nice splash with the New York Yankees.

When you signed a contract in those times, you wanted to be with the Yankees. But my brother Ray told me, "You get to a stage where somebody's looking at you at all times, and somebody else may want you and give you a chance to go, and that's exactly what happens."

That was exactly what happened. I was traded out of the Yankee organization in 1937 to Dallas in the Texas League. The next year I was off to a good start and got hit in the head with a bat. I didn't get to finish out that year. The next year, I came back and caught in 143 ballgames. The St. Louis Browns made a deal for me. They moved me to Toledo.

Finally, in 1944 I was in the major leagues. The Browns brought me up to spring training. World War II was on. Before the war the Browns had trained in California. Now because of the war they trained near Cape Girardeau near the Mississippi River, not too far from St. Louis.

I'll never forget seeing Sportsman's Park in St. Louis for the first time. It was out there near a big General Motors carburetor plant. I'll always remember walking along that street and then going into the stadium for the first time. My brother Ray had played there, but by this time he had retired from pro ball.

I got into ninety games with the 1944 Browns. The manager then was Luke Sewell. There were players on those teams like Sig Jakucki, Jack Kramer, Mike Kreevich, Chet Laabs, Frank Mancuso, Bob Muncrief, George McQuinn, Al Zarilla, and Sam Zoldak. Some had good careers and others did not. In 1944, I batted just .212, but I did get into the 1944 World Series against the Cardinals.

That 1944 season my parents came to Washington one time to see me play. They stayed around for three days. When I was a kid, it was a thrill for me to have seen my brother playing in a ballgame there in Griffith Stadium. It was even more of a thrill to come back there as a member of the St. Louis Browns and play in the old ballpark.

The next year, 1945, President Truman came out to the first game he attended as president of the United States. Oh, they made a fuss out of him — he was from Missouri, you know. And he threw out the first ball. In that scramble, I got it. The FBI man brought the ball to him, and he took his pen out. And then he did the greatest thing. He dated the ball, signed it, and gave it to me. I saved that ball for my boy.

My whole career was just 146 games for the St. Louis Browns, ninety games in 1944 and fifty-six in 1945. But I did get to play in the major leagues.

KEITH HERNANDEZ

$\mathcal{I}$ *was probably* around five when my dad sawed off a Little League bat and started throwing tennis balls to me in front of the garage. He sawed off the barrel of the bat to make it lighter and give me more control. My dad had been a minor league infielder for a decade, so there was all that baseball equipment in the house. It was Baseball 101.

I grew up in the Bay Area in the 1950s. We were baby boomers, tons of kids. But there was only one field in the neighborhood for all those kids. That put us in a position where we had to make up games.

A nunnery nearby owned some property with all this grazing land. It was just sitting there. So the parents went up there and talked the nuns into letting them build two ballfields on that property. It became an all-out community effort. With all of the homes being built in the area, people had equipment. One man had a grader that he brought home from work, and in the space of a weekend he graded the land. The parents literally sodded and watered the field. They raised money. The whole community chipped in a great deal because all these parents wanted their kids to play ball. The final result was an area that was almost like a minor league complex.

I played pickup baseball there every day. There were always enough kids. Sometimes we'd play half-field. The right-handed hitter would hit just from centerfield over.

My dad was a fireman who worked a twenty-four-hour shift and then was off for forty-eight hours. In the summer, he would call the parents and have them bring their kids down to the field. My dad would pick sides for two teams, and then he would pitch. Since my dad had been a first baseman, he taught us. We learned the scoop, how to work from the ground up. Catching a ground ball, he told us, you can always move your hand faster upward than you can downward. He used to throw tennis balls at us so we wouldn't be afraid to get hit. We were able to look intently at the ball, and if the ball took a bad hop and hit us in the face, it was no big deal.

It was just a tennis ball, and it didn't hurt. That was a great way to learn how to scoop when we were six, seven years old. Those games were a great learning experience for everybody.

The kids I grew up with, people I haven't seen in years, all have fond memories of that time and that experience. It was pretty much, you know, leave your kid, give him a little bit of money. My dad would chuck them on the truck and give them lunch, and the parents would come back down whenever they could to pick up their kids and bring them home.

My dad wanted me to become a major league player. He'd often tell me, "You know, at one time Willie Mays was an eight-year-old kid like you. Mickey Mantle was eight years old, and Stan Musial was eight years old. Look where they're at now. So why don't you make that you?" Thinking those baseball greats were once kids just like me kind of put it in perspective. I bought it hook, line, and sinker. I knew I wanted to be a major league ballplayer.

My first year in organized ball, I was in the minor league of Little League. The minor leaguers were eight or nine, and the major leaguers were ten, eleven, twelve. When I was nine, I was already in the majors. There were very few nine-year-olds who were good enough to play in the majors, but I did. My dad was the manager. My brother, Gary, who was two years older than me, played first base. I played centerfield. When Gary moved on to the Pony League, I went back to first base and pitched.

The games that stand out for me are the games that I pitched. I struck out a lot of people, but I lost the championship game 1–0 in a game that went extra innings. It was the only game I lost all year. Basically, in sixty innings I had struck out about 125 guys. I had a good fastball and a big curveball. I had a great arm. My dad was a left-handed pitcher, which is why I always hit left-handers good. I was weaned on left-handers.

Even though I enjoyed the pitching a lot more than the hitting part, I had big hitting games all the time. I was hitting .475, .490. Every game was a big day. I'm not taking any 0-fers there, you know.

When I was young, I liked the outfield. But when I got older, I saw there was a lot of action at first base. You can get bored in the outfield.

During World War II over in Pearl Harbor, my dad had played ball in the service on the navy team. He was on the same team as Stan Musial. So when Stan would come to San Francisco, he would leave tickets for us whenever the Cardinals played the Giants. I'd get to go in the clubhouse after the game. This was in the early sixties.

My favorite teams then were the Cardinals and the Yankees, because Mickey Mantle was my idol. When I got my first bubblegum baseball card of Mickey Mantle, I was very young. When I saw we were born on the same day, October 20, along with Juan Marichal, I was hooked. So that sold it. From then on I always had a 7 (Mantle's number) on the back of my jersey someway. I wouldn't wear *the* number 7, but my number always had to have a 7 in it. I wore 17, 27, and 37. I was 37 with the Cards and 17 was available with the Mets.

I loved baseball. In my Little League days, I couldn't get enough. But when I was thirteen or fourteen, it got to be too much. I actually didn't play one summer in between my junior and senior year of high school. I got into football instead. My dad handled it well. He said, "Okay, not a problem. I guarantee you you'll be ready to go again next year." He was right. I just needed a break.

Once I moved into situations that were out of his control and worked with another coach like I did with my high school team, my dad became very worried. He thought other coaches would ruin me. It became an obsession with him.

That's when it all became very difficult for me. Those high school years were tough. He'd sit up there in his blue Mustang and watch us practice football and baseball. It put pressure on me. I'm sure he talked to the coaches.

My favorite sport was basketball. He wasn't allowed to come to the gym to watch us, so that was the most fun. I was point guard. We had a fast-break offense, and I ran it. I was very quick. I was All-County point guard, first team, West Bay and San Jose, all the way up to San Francisco. That's a lot of schools. Three public school leagues and San Francisco proper. I got tons of assists. Our team was so good that the starters were always taken out of the game late in the third quarter, because we were beating the crap out of teams. I averaged a little less than twenty points, but if we'd had more competition, I probably would have averaged twenty-five a game.

I had a pretty good high school basketball career. My high school put me in their Hall of Fame for whatever reason. Still I never could have taken it to the college level except maybe at a small college. I knew I wasn't tall enough to play professionally.

After high school, I was picked by the Cardinals in the 1971 draft. It was amazing. I mean, you're up for grabs there, and you don't know who's going to draft you. I was very fortunate, very pleased. I was drafted low, the fortieth round because I had quit playing baseball my senior year due to a conflict with my coach. My junior year I hit either .500 or high .400s.

Every team in the world was scouting me. I quit and went and played semipro ball on weekends against guys that were much older than me. It was actually a pretty good learning experience. It was a difficult time, because they were throwing breaking balls, and I was playing against guys that were five, six, seven years older, grown men. That was during school.

Then I played in the summer in the Joe DiMaggio League. There I just burned it up. I hit .490. There wasn't any getting me out. The Cardinals said they just took a chance on me. If I had played baseball for my high school team in my senior year, I would have been someone's number one draft pick. But I think not playing and having that rift with my high school coach scared them off. They thought I was trouble.

In 1974, my first minor league season, I made it all the way to triple-A and won the American Association batting title.

My first major league game was in Candlestick Park on August 30 of 1974. I was twenty years old. I was called up late in the season to replace Joe Torre, who had gotten hurt.

I was back home, and I had to leave tons of passes, so that was very nerve-wracking. Here I was competing against Tom Seaver and Jerry Koosman — these are guys you were watching when you were in high school. And playing on the same team with Lou Brock and Bob Gibson.

I was thrown into a major, major, major pennant race. The Cardinals wound up losing the division to the Pirates on the final day of the season. I was oblivious to what was happening. I was numb. You get called up, and you're playing in a stretch drive, let alone starting.

In mid-1975 I became the regular first baseman for the Cardinals and a fixture on the major league scene for many seasons.

GLENN HOFFMAN

$\mathcal{I}$ *was born* July 7, 1958, in Orange, California, and grew up in Anaheim, where I played a lot of catch with Dad in the backyard. I loved the game, had the desire, and just took it from there. I really got my start in organized kid baseball in the Park Director Recreation League.

It seemed to me that Saturday afternoon games on television all came from Fenway Park. Maybe because of that, I became a fan of the Boston Red Sox. I saw a lot of Carl Yastrzemski, and he was my hero.

All through my growing-up years I was a shortstop, and I was good. At Savanna High School in Anaheim, I was All California, Southern California Player of the Year. So there was interest in me early on from quite a few scouts.

I was Boston's second-round selection in the June 1976 draft. Joe Stephenson of the Red Sox, who was a very well-known scout in California, came to the house to talk about my signing with Boston. My dad left it up to me. I had offers to go to college, but my dream was to play professional baseball and that was the route I took. I signed for $25,000 and a $7,500 signing bonus on top of it for each level and went on from there.

Day after graduation, while all my buddies were going to the river and having graduation parties, I was on an airplane flying 3,000 miles to Elmira, New York, my first stop in my professional baseball career. The manager there was Dick Bearnadino. They always say you remember your first and last manager. But I remember all of mine. Each one had an influence on me.

Our Elmira team won the league championship. I hit .285, had a solid year. Wade Boggs was on that team, John Tudor, Bobby Ojeda. Altogether about seven of us from that Elmira team made it up to the major leagues.

At triple-A Pawtucket in 1979, I hit .285, and the next year I was on the Red Sox. The first game I got into was in Milwaukee, the second day of the season. Butch Hobson couldn't play because it was real cold, about thirty degrees, and he had a bad elbow. Jack Brohamer was playing third base. In the second inning, a two hopper came, hit him in the head and knocked him out.

Don Zimmer had me out in the bullpen on the ready for late-inning defense. I was scared to death of him, the way he looked frightened me. But he was a baseball man, a no nonsense guy. Zimmer put me into the game.

First play: man on second base, ground ball to Burleson at short. I step on the bag at third and hand the ball to the umpire. "Safe." There was no force play. The guy scores making it 1–0. We scored two in the eighth inning and won the game 2–1.

I was twenty years old, and I was there with Carl Yastrzemski and all the other guys. It was a dream come true. Being in Fenway Park was like being in heaven.

FRANK HOWARD

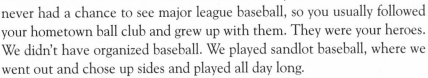

I grew up in Columbus, Ohio, where I followed the Columbus Redbirds. They were a triple-A affiliate of the St. Louis Cardinals. As a kid, you never had a chance to see major league baseball, so you usually followed your hometown ball club and grew up with them. They were your heroes. We didn't have organized baseball. We played sandlot baseball, where we went out and chose up sides and played all day long.

Today, you pass some beautifully manicured fields, parks, and there is nobody on them. The kids are all at the mall, they're playing Nintendo. When I was a kid, we played baseball all day long on a little playground or wherever we found a place to play. We didn't have good fields.

I grew to be big and strong and played all kinds of sports. At 6'7", I was an All American in basketball and baseball at Ohio State. I set a Big Ten tournament record with thirty-two rebounds one game. I still hold two Madison Square Garden Holiday Festival Tournament rebounding records.

I liked basketball a great deal and was drafted to play in the NBA. I thought about it, but finally with a $108,000 bonus on the table, I signed with the Los Angeles Dodgers.

I began in the minors at Green Bay of the class-B 3-I League in 1958 and did pretty well. I hit thirty-eight home runs. I got into a few games for the Dodgers at the end of the season. The next year I played for both Victoria in the Texas League and Spokane of the Pacific Coast League. I hit a combined forty-three homers and drove in 126 runs. I was fortunate to be named the 1959 Minor League Player of the Year by the *Sporting News*.

I began the 1960 season with Spokane, but that didn't last long. I soon joined the Dodgers. I guess it was there that I got the nickname "Hondo" after the John Wayne movie. I won the National League Rookie of the Year award in 1960 batting .268 with twenty-three home runs and seventy-seven RBIs in 117 games.

And it was on from there, on to a career of 1,895 major league games and a lot of time as a coach for different teams.

MONTE IRVIN

I was the seventh child born to Cupid Irvin and Mary Eliza Henderson in Haleburg, Alabama, on February 25, 1919.

I have just a few memories of Haleburg. I remember on Saturdays, when the farmers finished working, they would gather in the field and mark off a diamond and play baseball. These were spirited and highly competitive games. After the game, there would be lemonade, hamburgers, barbecued chicken, and so on, all of that would be served.

When I was seven years old, my family that included six boys and four girls migrated to Orange, New Jersey. There at the Park Avenue School, I joined the soccer team. I played soccer so well that my coach asked me to come out for the baseball team in the spring. I did and liked it very much. In fifth and sixth grade, I could throw so hard that the coach made me the pitcher when we had really tough games. For other games, I was the short-stop.

During that time we played softball in a playground. Later on, there was church league baseball. I played all the time, everywhere, every sport, wherever I could.

I was seriously interested in music then. I'm talking about Duke Ellington, Count Basie, and Cab Calloway. We used to go down to the theater and watch those guys perform. I wanted to become a saxophone player. So I asked my mother if she would loan me $5 so I could go down to the music store and pay down on the saxophone.

She said, "Five dollars is a lot of money. Are you sure you will work hard enough to pay me back?"

I said, "I will."

My mother gave me $5, and I started out for the music store. But before I got to the music store, I passed a Davegas Sporting Goods store, and in the window was this glove, a brown leather Spalding catcher's mitt, and it was only $5. So rather than paying down on the saxophone, I went into the store and bought the catcher's mitt outright.

I bought it so I could catch my brother, who I thought had a fastball like Satchel Paige. It turned out to be a good investment. Catching my brother in the long driveway of our house, I learned how to catch. That is really how I got started in baseball.

I graduated from grade school and got into high school where I became involved with a local team called the Orange Triangle that came out of a very popular athletic club. The team had some really great athletes; some of them were older guys who were out working in the world. Our team was all black, but we played white local teams, Essex County teams. To get money for balls and bats and to pay the umpire, we passed the hat. There were some blacks in the audience, but most were white people who came regularly. They really enjoyed the games.

That New Jersey area I grew up in is known for its great athletes. One of the greatest that New Jersey ever produced was Jesse Miller. He was the local hero and my baseball manager, the fellow who taught me how to play baseball. He motivated me and remained my hero until he died at the age of ninety in 1999.

But my heroes growing up in the early years were not the black players — it was the white major leaguers like the Gashouse Gang. They got all the publicity. The Negro Leagues did not get much publicity in the daily white papers. There would be just a line here or there saying who won or who lost. The *Afro-American*, the *Amsterdam News*, Chicago *Defender* would have more information — box scores, stories. But you would have to wait a week for that sometimes.

I aspired to play in the Negro Leagues. In those days I could have had no thought, no dream of ever playing in the major leagues. I remember in 1936 I was playing so well (I hit .666 in high school playing shortstop, first base, playing everywhere) that one of our teachers who was a friend of Horace Stoneham, the owner of the New York Giants, told him, "We've got a kid here who you should take a look at."

Sure enough they did. They took a look. But that was all they did. I learned later that a report came back: "Monte Irvin is everything you said he is, but the time is not yet right for him. There is no way we can sign him for the New York Giants. We will have to pass because we would not be able to get the other owners to go along."

That was the way of things. During my high school years I played on integrated teams. I did not feel prejudice outright, but there was that undercurrent. They wouldn't let more than two blacks play at one time on a high school football team. That was the procedure throughout the whole state of New Jersey.

The state back then had great athletic programs in the grade schools, in the high school. Some of the greatest athletes came out of the New Jersey area. Years later, I was honored as the greatest all-around athlete to ever come out of New Jersey. I lettered in four sports, set a state record for the javelin throw. I was All State in baseball, basketball, and football. I was a linebacker with a lot of speed and agility. But like many other New Jersey athletes, I did not go to a college in the state. Instead of ending up at Rutgers or Princeton, many went out west or to the Midwest. They wouldn't stay in New Jersey because they were black, and Princeton and Rutgers wouldn't recruit them. Many also enrolled at the black schools in the South and went on to become very famous.

Michigan offered me a football scholarship, but when I asked for $100 in expenses to get to Ann Arbor, they turned me down. Instead I got a four-year scholarship to Lincoln University in Pennsylvania. My coach there, Carl Siebert, tried to interest the Yankees and the Giants in signing me. No dice.

In 1937, I was still in college when I signed with Abe and Effa Manley's Newark Eagles in the Negro Leagues to play only on the road. I was not offered a bonus. Abe Manley said, "Bonuses only spoil players; if you work yourself up to a good salary, you'll appreciate it more."

I was still an undergraduate and played under the assumed name "Jimmy Nelson" to protect my amateur standing and that Lincoln University athletic scholarship. "Jimmy Nelson" was a white fellow, a catcher I used to play with and against. He had a great build, was a good friend, and a perfect model. I played 1937 through 1939 under the Jimmy Nelson name. When the Eagles played at home in Newark, I would work out, take a shower, and then go sit in the stands.

The Eagles had Hall of Famers to be: Ray Dandridge, Leon Day. Later on the team had Larry Doby and Don Newcombe. So we had a great team with a lot of wonderful people. We were a great force in the community. On a Sunday everybody would come down to Ruppert Stadium to watch us play. There would always be a full house which held about 22,000 people. Lena Horne or Ella Fitzgerald or somebody like that would throw out the first ball. It was just a great time for Newark, a great time for the Eagles, and a great time for us.

We were able to use Ruppert Stadium, the home of the Newark Bears, the top Yankee farm team, when the Bears were on the road. The Bears had the greatest minor league club ever. Mrs. Effa Manley wanted to have us play a series of games with the Bears. Her idea was that the money that came in would be donated to charity. But the Yankees refused to let us play the Bears, because they had too much to lose if we won. And we could have won.

After my sophomore year, I left Lincoln to play full-time with the Eagles. At the time the top salary was two hundred bucks a month, which was excellent because the average working man made only about fifteen or twenty dollars a week. So we used to say that playing baseball was better than working for a living. I loved it.

As a rookie in 1939 I made the All-League team. The word that was heard was that many Negro League owners felt I was the best qualified candidate to break the major league color line. I would go on to hit .400 or better three times in the Negro National League.

The talent that was in the Negro Leagues was just terrific. I played against Satchel Paige in the Puerto Rican Winter Leagues and also in the Negro Leagues. He was with the Kansas City Monarchs. I have never seen a better pitcher than him. He was real fast with real good control. I also never saw better hitters than Buck Leonard or Josh Gibson.

In 1942, I was drafted into the army. I was in the service for three years and came out with a medical problem. My nerves got a little shaky. It took me a couple of years to get back on track.

I returned to the Eagles after my hitch in the army. When the team disbanded, I nearly signed with the Dodgers' farm team in St. Paul. However, Mrs. Effa Manley said that I was still under contract to the Eagles. The Dodgers offered $2,500 for me. She turned them down. A year later she offered me to Bill Veeck of Cleveland for $1,000 in a package with Larry Doby. Veeck passed.

I spent time playing ball in the Mexican League, the 1948–49 winter playing baseball in Cuba. I had gone to high school with Giant executive Chub Feeney. It was he who recommended that the team sign me. The New York Giants paid Mrs. Manley $5,000 for my contract and assigned me to Jersey City in the International League. This was 1949.

I was batting .373 when the Giants told me to report. It was July 5, 1949. I came to the Polo Grounds along with Hank Thompson. We became the first black players on the Giants, making for a total of seven in the majors. We were greeted by Leo Durocher and shown around.

There were a couple of days when I just sat on the bench and watched. Then we played the Dodgers at Ebbets Field. Leo called on me to pinch hit against Joe Hatten. It was July 8, 1949.

Talk about "Growing Up Baseball." I was almost thirty-one years old at the time and had been through a great deal of baseball experience. Nevertheless, my knees started knocking as I got into the batter's box. And they wouldn't stop. I called time, stepped out. I felt better and stepped back in and worked the count to 3–2 and then walked. I ran all the way to first base. It was a great feeling just to get there. That was how it started for me in the majors.

It was not a time without incident. You'd walk into a room, and some people would walk out. You'd sit down on a train, and one person, maybe two, would get up and walk away. This was 1949 in the United States of America. I do believe that many of them who were prejudiced were sorry afterward that they behaved that way.

Again, I am so sorry that I did not get a chance to play major league baseball earlier. What happened to me should have happened to me ten years before it did. I was not half the ballplayer I was in 1949 that I was in 1939.

But then I say look at Josh Gibson. Look at Buck Leonard — all those fellows. Those guys were as good as any players who ever lived. They never got a chance. I am just grateful for the accomplishments that I did make, for the opportunities I did have.

You are not angry, but you are rueful.

GREGG JEFFERIES

There was a lot of hype about me even before I reached the major leagues. *Sports Illustrated* had a feature on how my father had trained me. When I was growing up, I did do unusual exercises such as swinging a bat underwater to build strength.

I was born in Burlingame, California, on August 1, 1966. I started playing baseball with Wiffle balls with my dad and my brother, Dean, when I was three years old. My dad was a schoolteacher, and all through Little League baseball and high school, he'd bring my brother and me to the school gymnasium at night and we'd hit tennis balls so we wouldn't break anything. It was a blast. On weekends, my dad would throw us hardballs.

Our backyard was grassy and that's where Dean and I used to play stickball. I was always the Dodgers, and Dean was always the Reds. In the back of the yard there was a big wall. If you hit a ball over the wall, it counted as a home run. There was a bush that figured in our game. If Dean pitched to me and I hit, I'd run to the bush. If he threw the ball and it hit the bush before I got there, I was out. If I got to the bush first, I was safe.

It was around that time that I learned how to switch-hit. I was emulating Reggie Smith and Rick Monday. I followed what they did; I followed all the left-handed hitters who were big in the major leagues then. I was a natural right-handed hitter, but I'd get a bat and actually hit left-handed. And I started hitting it pretty good.

Then Dean said, "Why don't you ask Dad to look at your left-handed swing?" So I did. "Yeah, you have a chance. Just work at it," he said.

It was hard at first. I found that I was pulling everything. It just wasn't as comfortable as hitting right-handed. But the more I did it, the more I got used to it.

Keith Hernandez was always around, because he lived in the same area. I knew his dad really well. In fact, my dad and his dad were pretty good friends. When Keith was in the big leagues, his dad would come around to the local high school once in a while. He'd see some kids working out and would give us advice and tips.

To tell the truth, football — and not baseball— was my favorite sport. I was a shortstop in baseball, but a cornerback and a quarterback in football and was actually a better football player than I was a baseball player. I figured I was going to play both in college. But all along, I knew in my heart that baseball, for someone my size, was the best option for me.

I was the New York Mets' first-round pick in the 1985 June draft. I was minor league Most Valuable Player each of my first three seasons. I came up at the end of 1987 and then in September 1988 batted .321 in twenty-nine games. I was twenty-one years old. I was a major leaguer from then on.

I just loved the game. While I never really thought about going all out after a major league career, somehow I just knew that eventually I would make it.

ADAM KENNEDY

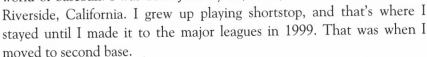

My dad was a high school baseball coach before I was even born, so right away I was in the
world of baseball. I was born January 10, 1976, in
Riverside, California. I grew up playing shortstop, and that's where I
stayed until I made it to the major leagues in 1999. That was when I
moved to second base.

I can remember messing around in the front yard as much as playing in
any game. I was never pressured into playing baseball. It was always a matter of keeping it fun. And that's why I never got tired of it.

It was learning by failing. I'm still going to fail, and I'm still going to
learn from failing. I really believe in that. My friends and I played with a
Wiffle ball, tennis ball — all that stuff. In Wiffle ball, we never ran the
bases; we'd play over the lines for bases. When we played with a tennis
ball and a metal bat, we would run the bases. We played wherever we
could, usually the front yard and the street. The neighbors probably got
sick of our asking to go in their backyard and get the ball. But that's how
it went. We played whenever we could get a game together. In California,
you don't have winter; you can be outside all year. That was great.

I grew up trying to imitate players. I wanted to be Ozzie Smith one day,
Cal Ripken Jr. the next. It was always a dream of mine to make the
major leagues, but it wasn't until my second year of college at Cal State-
Northridge that I started thinking about playing professionally realisti-
cally.

Even when I got to the minors, when I was in A ball and double-A, I
just wanted to prove myself, prove that I could go to the next level. The
major leagues was not something I thought of. It was not really until the
year I broke in that I started thinking about what I needed to do to play in
the big leagues.

My first major league game was August 21, 1999, in New York at Shea
Stadium, facing Kenny Rogers. My first at bat, he struck me out. I ended

up going 0-for-4 that day. But my parents flew out to see me play, and there were 50,000 people in the stands. It was just great.

I was more nervous on defense than I was on offense. When you're hitting, it's just you and the pitcher. But when I got out in the field, I looked up, and all of Shea just seemed so big to me that it took my breath away. The first ball that came to me was a double-play ball — 4-6-3 — and I turned it.

The next day I came back and had a couple hits, so I settled in just a little bit. The first was off Orel Hershiser. Since I grew up watching him pitching for the Los Angeles Dodgers, that made it a little more special.

But in this game, you don't have too much time to reflect on what you just did. You've got to think about what you're going to do tomorrow.

JOHN KENNEDY

I was born on May 29, 1941. I lived the first twelve years of my life approximately eleven blocks from White Sox Park, so the White Sox were my favorite team when I was a youth in Chicago. My favorite player at that time was the White Sox shortstop Chico Carrasquel. He was a good player, an infielder, and I just liked the way he played the game.

I didn't come from a baseball-oriented family, but I took to baseball early on. As a matter of fact when I was three years old in 1945 I was playing marbles on the living room floor while the family was listening to the description of President Roosevelt's funeral on the radio. My father asked, "Would you like to be president someday?"

I said, "No, Dad, I'm going to be a baseball player."

So from the age of three I knew what I wanted to do and was fortunate enough to be able to do it.

As a young kid I would go to bed with my glove and throw a ball into the glove over and over and dream of playing in the major leagues. I played mostly everywhere on the baseball field — all the infield and outfield positions, as pitcher. I played Little League, then Pony League, and then in high school. I didn't hit that much in high school, but I was told that I impressed everyone with my versatility.

Various teams came around to scout me. I also attended several tryout camps. It got serious when I was taken to Cleveland with a couple of other players from the Chicago area whom I had played with in the summertime. The Cleveland scout "Double Duty" Radcliff highly recommended me. His nickname came from the fact that when he had starred in the Negro Leagues, he often caught the first game and pitched the second game of a doubleheader.

I was set to sign with Cleveland, but "Double Duty" Radcliff was taken ill and couldn't come to my house. In the meantime a guy I was playing for in Chicago had become a bird-dog scout for the Washington Senators, a new expansion team. The old Senators had become the Twins.

I ended up signing for less money with the new Senators. I was going to get $5,000 from Cleveland. But I signed with Washington for $1,500 because I was told that if and when I got to the big leagues it would be faster playing in the farm system of the Senators as opposed to Cleveland.

I reported to Pensacola, Florida, in the Alabama-Florida League — class-D. It was the first time I was away from home for any length of time. Eddie Brinkman had been signed out of high school that year for about $60,000. I was signed for $1,500. I was the shortstop; Eddie played second base. He had never played on the right side of the infield before. When he got taken out on a double-play ball, he hurt his knee. The powers that be decided after it was wiser to put the $1,500 guy at second base and put the $60,000 guy back where he belonged at shortstop.

The next year both Brinkman and I were promoted to class-B ball in the Carolina League at Winston-Salem. In September, I was called up to Washington. I flew from North Carolina to D.C. Going up to the big leagues gave me the chills.

That Washington Senators team had a very interesting collection of players at the end of their time, many with big major league reputations. There was Jimmy Piersall, Gene Woodling, Dale Long, Danny O'Connell.

My first big league at bat was September 5, 1962. The Washington manager, Mickey Vernon, told me to get a bat and go out there and hit. We were playing the Minnesota Twins. I came in to face Dick Stigman, who had a no-hitter going through $6\frac{2}{3}$ innings.

In spring training that year the first pitcher I faced was Early Wynn, who was still around with the Chicago White Sox and as mean as ever. I took three strikes from him without swinging. So when I was called upon to pinch hit, I said to myself, I am not going to strike out taking pitches. If I strike out, it will be swinging.

The first pitch Stigman threw me bounced. I swung at it. The second pitch was inside and off the plate, and I hit it out. I ran around those bases as if it was an inside-the-park home run. I didn't trot. I ran. When I got into the dugout I could hardly breathe — not from running, but from being so excited. That was how it began in the majors for me.

John F. Kennedy was president and might have been at that game that day. We shared an eerie coincidence — the same name and the same birthday, May 29. I never did get to meet him, but I did vote for him. When I was in Washington at the start, there were a lot of articles written about the two John Kennedys.

At the start in every American League city I went to, reporters asked me about my practice of exchanging birthday cards with the president. They also wanted me to comment on the fact that we had the same birthday. No matter what the papers said, we never exchanged birthday cards.

Sadly, I do remember the time of the assassination — November 22, 1963. I was in the Instructional League in Tampa, Florida, and a game was in progress. After they announced what happened, the game was cancelled. Later I just sat in front of the television for days like everyone else.

RALPH KINER

$\mathcal{I}$ *was an only child.* I was born on
October 27, 1922, in Santa Rita, New Mexico.
My father died of a mastoid infection when I was four years
old, and my mother moved us to Alhambra, California, where she had
some friends.

Alhambra was a small town just outside of Los Angeles. The neighbors
across the street had a son, Robert Bodkin. He was about ten years older
than me, but nevertheless we became friends. That Bodkin family was involved a great deal with semipro baseball across the area. They had a Sunday morning team, all men. I became the batboy for the team and spent a
lot of time picking up tips and advice from them.

Robert's father used to pitch batting practice to him. I was the kid just
hanging around, shagging balls, trying to make myself useful. This went on
for a couple of years. Eventually I got tired of shagging balls. I spoke up
and said, "How about giving me a chance to hit?"

I was around ten or eleven by this time. So they let me hit, and of course
I enjoyed that more than shagging balls. I could hit a softball farther than
anyone I knew. It certainly wasn't strength or bulk muscle. I just happened
to have that kind of swing.

At the age of twelve, I was playing on the men's team. I was skinny and
fairly tall, about 5'10" or something like that. I kept hitting the ball better
and better. I sort of grew up around these men and the Sunday baseball
games. But of course, I also played a great deal of pickup baseball with kids
in the area. We'd choose up sides and get a game going every day after
school. We played a lot of softball, which was a big thing at that time
in the LA area. In grammar school, we had a lot of softball, too. There
wasn't too much hardball.

I was raised during the depression. There wasn't any money around at
all. One Christmas my mother bought me a glove. Somehow I got a hold
of a bat. The baseballs I played with were taped-up jobs. I was very adept

at taking balls that were ripped up, sewing them up, and making them like regular baseballs.

It was not until 1933 that I developed my first real interest in major league baseball. That year the New York Giants played in the World Series against the Washington Senators. I followed those games in much detail.

But the team I really cared about, my favorite team, was the Detroit Tigers. My idol back then was Hank Greenberg, and I picked the Tigers because of Hank, who was just starting to become one of the great hitters of the game.

In 1934, the Tigers played in the World Series against the St. Louis Cardinals. I was in the seventh grade. The Bodkin house was only an eighth of a mile from the school. I would look out the window of my class-room, and Mrs. Bodkin would come out and signal to me with her fingers the scores of the games. We worked out a really good system where I could get the scores inning by inning of that 1934 World Series.

I was interested in all sports, reading about them, getting information about what was happening. I listened to major league baseball games that were broadcast into the area by a guy named Sam Balter. It was re-created games over the tickertape every Saturday out of a network out of Texas. But actual big league ball wasn't played on the West Coast except during spring training.

The father of a pal of mine had been a minor league baseball pitcher. The father and the son were both named Harry Johnston. Mr. Johnston used to take us to see the Philadelphia Athletics, who trained in Anaheim. I saw the White Sox, who trained in Pasadena, which is a contiguous town to Alhambra. I also went to Pacific Coast League minor league games.

I was into sports, really into them. I was always one of the guys who was shagging balls, hitting balls, doing all of those things. When baseball sea-son was over, I'd play pickup football in the sandlot. I would play basket-ball, run track, play tennis. If there was a game with a ball, I was in it.

When we were about thirteen or fourteen, Harry Johnston Jr. — who was called "Lefty" because he was a left-handed pitcher — and I got on different teams, semipro teams in the area. Mr. Johnston used to haul me and "Lefty" around to games.

I was crazy about all sports, but especially crazy about playing baseball. Over the period of a year, I played somewhere around 250-some baseball games. It was baseball from early morning to very late in the day. Of course the weather was conducive to playing all year round in southern California.

My mother wasn't too happy that I was always playing some kind of sport. She never remarried, so she had to work to survive and to raise me. She was an office nurse for the Title Insurance Company in downtown Los Angeles. I did all the things that kids used to do to make some money at that time. Maybe, because my father was dead, I had to do a little more. I was out there mowing lawns. I had an *LA Times* paper route. I had to get up at three in the morning and get the papers delivered before I went to school. I had about forty customers, and I was able to make about $14 a month, which at that time was a pretty good amount of spending money. Of course, I had to give some of the money I made to my mother. I kept the rest — which wasn't much.

I also sold magazines around the area, door-to-door, which I hated to do because it took away from the time I could play sports and only gave me a profit of only a penny a magazine. I had to go and knock on doors and ask people if they wanted to buy *Colliers* or the *Saturday Evening Post* or *Ladies Home Journal* or whatever I was trying to get rid of. So I got real smart one time. The magazines sold for a nickel each and cost me four cents. I had to pay the guy who ran the route 80¢ for the week. I took the twenty magazines and buried them in the backyard. Then I went out and mowed a couple of lawns and gave the guy the money that he was due for the twenty magazines that I had to sell.

That worked out fine until my mother discovered what I was doing. She became very unhappy about that and wound up sending me to a military school in Long Beach, California. That took me away from all of the kids that I grew up with and knew. I lost all the free time when I could be playing ball. I hated it. Fortunately, after six months I was back in my old stamping grounds and able to make up for lost time.

I made the high school varsity baseball team, played a lot of different positions. When we didn't have a regularly scheduled game to play in the afternoon after school days, we'd just go out to a vacant lot, choose up sides and play, sometimes with five guys on a team, six guys on a team. The rule was you couldn't hit to the field where there was no position player.

All of that kept me busy during the week. But I was also involved playing baseball on the weekends. There were several major league clubs that sponsored teams around the area. On Saturday afternoons all through my high school days I played for the Yankee Juniors. The team was actually sponsored by the Yankees. We were given old uniforms that had been worn by players that had been passed on through the Yankee organization. We were also supplied with the bats and balls.

A fellow named Dan Krowley ran the Yankee Juniors team. But the one who was really in charge was the famous Yankee scout, Bill Essick, the man who signed up Joe DiMaggio. Of course, when Essick was around at the games, which was not often, it was a big thing. I'd say, "Well I hope I have a good day, because maybe the Yankees will try and sign me."

Baseball wasn't considered a great way to make a living at that time. Still I dreamed of a career playing ball. Kids were going to D ball out of high school and making $65 a month. Today that sounds like nothing, but during the depression, if you had a job, you had something better than anybody else.

On Sundays I played baseball with teams like the Alhambra Merchants, that were sponsored by the businesses and stores in town. I was about seventeen when I had the chance to bat against Satchel Paige. I was touching everybody up then. I touched him up, too.

There were scouts and other baseball people in the stands wherever we played in a lot of places. One of those who watched me and actually helped me a little bit was Casey Stengel, who was the manager of the Boston Braves then. He gave me a lot of tips about outfield play, was very interested in me, and talked a lot about signing me. I got to know him well.

Another scout that was around quite a bit was Hollis Thurston, who had been a major league pitcher. He scouted for the Pittsburgh Pirates. There was also Babe Herman, who had been such a great hitter. He was a scout for the Hollywood Stars, an independently owned Pacific Coast League team.

One of the offers I got was from Babe Herman. He wanted to give me fifty percent of whatever my sale price to the major leagues would be if I would sign with the Hollywood Stars. An interesting sidelight to all of that is the only time I ever met Babe Ruth was when Babe Herman took me down while they were filming the motion picture "Pride of the Yankees." Babe Herman was the guy who doubled for Gary Cooper in the movie in the hitting scenes.

In 1939, 1940, I had several offers from different clubs to sign up for a small amount of money. I was playing all around LA in ballparks like Griffith Park. People were becoming more interested in me because I was a good player, and the more I played the better I got.

Then in 1940, I graduated from high school and things came to a head. My mother wanted me to be a doctor, or a lawyer, a professional man. It was now a matter of whether I was going to sign and play minor league ball or go to college. My mother didn't want any part of my signing and going on to play baseball. At that time, baseball players didn't have any great reputation; certainly they didn't make a whole lot of money.

The Yankees came up with a good offer. They were prepared to pay me a good sum and a chance to play minor league ball. Then Hollis Thurston, representing the Pirates, came to our house. His nickname was "Sloppy." But he was anything but that. A meticulously dressed person, well educated, Hollis was a world-renowned baseball scout.

It finally came down where Hollis Thurston offered me $3,000 in cash in hand to sign with Pittsburgh and a contract in A ball. He also argued that if I signed with the Yankees, I'd be buried in their farm system for a period of seven years, which was about what it took most ballplayers to get through the minor leagues to the majors at that time.

Harry Johnston, who was a surrogate father to me along with Mr. Bodkin, was a milk company executive, so he knew something about business and negotiating. He more or less approved and helped clinch my deal.

I ended up signing up with Pittsburgh. Hollis Thurston also promised me, but it was not in writing, and technically it was illegal — that if I made the major leagues, I would get another $5,000. Well, at that time that kind of money was unheard of. Nobody had ever gotten a bonus that was that good. The money, I guess, swayed my mother, the $3,000 of cash in my hand and more to come. She went along and approved my signing up.

Another part of the deal that was appealing to me was that I was going to go to spring training with the Pirates in 1941. My high school graduation was June of 1940. I went to Pasadena Junior College in the winter of that year, which satisfied my mother. She wanted me to get a college education, and that was a beginning.

Pasadena Junior College had a pretty good athlete on campus named Jackie Robinson. I played softball against Jackie in Pasadena, but overall he didn't play a whole lot of baseball, although he was a really good player.

He concentrated on what he was renowned in — football, basketball, and track. He starred in all those sports.

Spring training of 1941 finally arrived. It was in San Bernardino, about sixty miles from my home in Alhambra. The first game I played was the first game of the spring training season. I was fortunate. I hit two home runs and went 4-for-5. That was how I began in professional baseball.

When spring training ended, the Pirates assigned me to Albany, New York, class-A in the Eastern League. It was a real tough pitchers' league with guys like Warren Spahn performing there. At that time, they had double-A, A-1, and A, so I started at the third-highest level. I played there in 1941, did fairly well. I went back again the next year to Albany and led the league in home runs with fourteen. Overall, I had hit twenty-seven home runs in two minor league seasons.

In 1941, right after Pearl Harbor, I signed up for the cadet program for the navy to become a pilot. I spent two years in the service, got my wings, and ended up as an officer. I was released from the service in 1945, in December.

Spring training 1946, I was there with the Pirates. I was twenty-three years old. I had a fantastic spring, hitting something like eleven home runs. Not too many recall that Frankie Frisch was the manger of the Pirates then; he was fired at the end of that season. Al Lopez caught for the team, Billy Cox played shortstop. Preacher Roe and Rip Sewell were a couple of pitchers I remember from that staff. I became Pittsburgh's starting leftfielder that 1946 season. Despite starting slowly, I hit twenty-three homers that year and became the first rookie in forty years to lead the league in that category. I was on my way as a major leaguer.

Looking back, I always think that if it were not for my two surrogate fathers, Mr. Bodkin and Mr. Johnston, I don't know what I would have ended up doing. They helped keep me around baseball all the time in my growing-up years. And they helped getting me started off as a professional.

MAX LANIER

I could have been a right-handed pitcher, but I became a left-hander because I broke my right arm twice when I was a child. I was born in 1915 and grew up in North Carolina, on the farm. We were poor, but we always had plenty to eat and never really wanted for anything.

I was very interested in baseball. My favorite player was Lou Gehrig. But there wasn't that much time to listen to games on the radio. I was either going to school or working in the fields. I plowed and pulled corn and hauled hay. I milked cows, too.

I learned to play baseball when I was in high school. Vernon Cashawd, the baseball coach, taught me and recognized my pitching ability. I won every game that I pitched. That was something else.

I signed a contract to play in the St. Louis Cardinals chain. But they didn't keep the promises they made to me, and so I got out of the contract. I went about playing semipro ball in Lexington, Kentucky, where I won sixteen games in a row.

Frank Rickey, the St. Louis scout who had signed me and Branch Rickey's brother, came by and asked me if I would be willing to go to spring training in 1937. I said, "On one condition: You have to pay me what I'm making now and a bonus." Somehow I wound up signing again. The bonus this time was for two bird dogs. Frank Rickey said they was both broken in. He said they were good dogs and ready to hunt.

I brought them home, and one of them got out that night. I have never seen him since. I've been told that I wasn't the only one that happened to. Maybe that dog was used over and over again, who knows?

I started to play with Columbus, Ohio, the St. Louis Cardinals farm club. It was my first year in professional baseball. I won ten games and lost four. I had a good curveball and a good fastball, too.

St. Louis promoted me to the major leagues the next year. That 1938 Cardinals team had Pepper Martin, Johnny Mize, Enos Slaughter, Paul

Dean, Bill DeLancey, Terry Moore, Mort Cooper, and Joe Medwick. Not too shabby a bunch of players.

Early on I was out in the bullpen, and I was called in to pitch. The starter was in trouble. I crossed through the outfield. Joe Medwick was there in leftfield. You know what he shouted out to me? "Now's your chance to go back to Columbus."

Wasn't that something to say to a young player? I hate to say it, but that's exactly what happened.

Frankie Frisch was the manager. He was a good manager, but he was tough on a young player. I had pitched that one season of double-A ball, the same as triple-A is now. Our Columbus team had played in the Little World Series. I pitched and won a game against the New York Yankees farm club. But the major leagues was another story. I threw wild. I just wasn't quite ready yet. They sent me down.

I came back up in 1939. I spent that season in the majors and minors. In 1940, I became a major leaguer for good. I spent fourteen years in the big leagues, not including the time I was suspended from baseball for three seasons when I jumped to the Mexican League. But that's another story.

DON LARSEN

Growing up was both a thrill and a struggle. I was born on July 7, 1929, in Michigan City, Indiana, basketball country.

I came from a middle class family. I had gloves, equipment. There wasn't much I didn't have in the way of sports. I just had one sister, and she was not really an athlete. I had no brothers. My dad played a little bit in American Legion and stuff like that, but he did not play with me a lot. Whatever sports I wanted to do, I did by myself or with other kids. We played everything.

I was worried about my own stuff, just playing and participating. I played all sports and all positions. I wasn't very good at anything at the start, couldn't run much until I started growing up a little bit. I played basketball a lot better than I did baseball.

As a kid making the big leagues is your goal. Why even start to dream if you don't have a goal? I had that goal. I started to dream.

I had no baseball idol, no basketball idol. I was not a Tigers fan, even though I was growing up in Michigan. I did follow the Chicago clubs a bit, although no players from those times stay with me. I never did get to a major league game as a kid. But whenever I could, I read newspaper accounts of games and listened to games on the radio.

I pitched in high school a little bit and played the outfield. There was no one person who shaped me or helped me. There is not really any coach or anybody who stays with me.

I guess that the first turning point for me after high school was going out to San Diego, California, and playing Sunday ball. There were a lot of scouts out there, and I figured I would do that rather than go on with my schooling.

I started my minor league time in the Northern League in 1947. The next year I was with Aberdeen. I played all over — places like Springfield, Miami, Wichita, and Wichita Falls.

The Korean War was on, and I went into the service in 1950. I grew up in the service. That helped me more than anything. I was also very lucky to have been able to play ball for two years in the service.

When I came out in 1953, I made the big league club of the St. Louis Browns in San Bernardino in spring training. I figured if I couldn't make it with the St. Louis Browns I couldn't make it with anybody. Marty Marion, the ex-Cardinal shortstop, was the manager. The players weren't all bad. They were big leaguers, you know, and a colorful bunch. A lot of them had been someplace else before — Harry Brecheen, Satchel Paige, Virgil Trucks, Vic Wertz. We finished eighth in an eight team league, winning fifty-four games and losing one hundred. I won seven games and lost twelve.

The Browns became the Orioles in 1954. I had a 3–21 record. No pitcher lost more games than me in the American League that year. But two of my wins came against the Yankees. That's probably why I came to them in the winter in an eighteen-player deal.

I have been asked a million times about the perfect game. I never dreamed about something like that happening. Everybody is entitled to a good day, and mine came at the right time. I pitched for fourteen years with eight different clubs, won only eighty-one games and lost ninety-one games. I wasn't anything special. Hey, I gave it my best shot. I tried.

I wish my record had been better. But I was very pleased to get into the World Series and pitch the perfect game. I guess that is what I will always be remembered for. And why not?

FRED LYNN

$\mathcal{I}$ $played$ all sports, not just baseball. But
Little League comes to mind when I think back
to my growing-up time. I was left-handed and remem-
ber struggling mightily against the first left-handed pitcher I ever saw. I
wondered if I would ever be able to hit a left-hander. In fact, the father of
one of my teammates used to call me "Kayo" for strikeout.

I was raised in the LA suburbs, but I was a Giants and not a Dodgers
fan. I loved the style of baseball the Giants played. I was not a fan of the
Koufax-Drysdale-Wills Dodgers, who in those days had a lot of pitching,
good team speed, and very little hitting. The Giants were thumpers with
Mays-McCovey and those players. Later, it became kind of a coincidence
that I played on teams who had a lot of thumpers on them.

My folks were divorced when I was thirteen. I lived with my dad
through high school. He liked sports and encouraged me to try everything.
That was why I played all sports and especially football, basketball, and
baseball.

Willie Mays and Roberto Clemente were my favorite baseball players.
They were the most fun to watch. It was clear to me even as a kid that
they didn't have any holes in their game. They did not do one special
thing. They could do everything on a baseball field. That was the way I
wanted to play. I didn't want to have any holes in my game.

I really wasn't pointing to playing baseball as a livelihood. It was just
something I did in the summer. In fact, it was my least favorite sport.
When I was pitching, it was okay. But when I played centerfield, it was
boring. In high school we had nice crowds coming out to watch the basketball games. There were always maybe a thousand in the gym plus the
band. To come from that to baseball where there might have been twenty
or thirty people watching us — it was not as exciting.

But we did have pretty good high school baseball teams, and I experienced a lot of success being a part of them. My junior season we got all the
way to the play-offs in southern California. We won our first game but lost
our second. That was it for us.

I remember one game when I was a sophomore. I pitched thirteen innings. My arm started up high and just got lower and lower as the game went on. But I had a gummy arm. I could throw forever.

My junior year in high school I was 11–1 with a 1.01 ERA. I had tons of strikeouts. My senior year I pitched some more and had a 6–5 record. My ERA was 0.5-something. Our school had graduated all those good players we had. I was a raw pitcher. No one really worked with me on technique, but I could throw hard, and I had good breaking stuff. I pitched all the time in high school, and I played centerfield when I wasn't pitching.

When I wasn't on the baseball field, I played offense and defense for the football team. I kicked and returned punts and kicks. I never came off the field unless I was hurt.

I know I was seriously scouted for baseball as early as my sophomore year. There were scouts around all the time. I was never flustered by that. It was pretty obvious. There weren't many people in the stands, and there'd be these guys with notepads who kept writing away. Even the pastor from the Lutheran church I belonged to got into the act as a scout for the St. Louis Cardinals.

A lot of clubs — I knew for a fact the Dodgers and the Orioles — were looking at me as a first-round draft choice out of high school. But we told them point blank that it would take a lot of money to keep me out of college. No one in my family had ever gone to college, and it was a pretty important goal for me. We scared a lot of people off, and I really didn't expect to be drafted.

But I was drafted anyway as a pitcher in the second round of the June 1970 draft by the Yankees. I was pretty shocked when a scout came to the house and offered some money.

I said, "Sorry, I'm going to college."

There were a lot of the administrators at my high school who had gone to USC. I am sure they made contact and said, "You ought to take a look at this kid Lynn."

In those days at USC they recruited athletes. It was athletes first, then it was training them to play football. I received a scholarship that switched over from football to baseball my sophomore year at USC. But I played both sports my first year. I really think if I had stayed in football I would have wound up as a free safety, because Lynn Swann and I were teammates. He was a flanker and I was a flanker.

John McKay was my football coach. Rod Dedeaux was the baseball coach. So I really had legends there. I had met Rod for the first time the summer after I graduated from high school. I was on an All-Star baseball team that was playing the USC team. A lot of us were high school seniors going to USC in the fall. We sort of comprised a tune-up squad for the USC team that was going to Omaha to play for the national championship. I remember facing Dave Kingman, who was a pitcher then. A 6'6" right-hander, he was the hardest thrower I had faced to that point in my life. He threw four balls in a row over my head. I was just happy to trot down to first base with a walk.

After the game Coach Dedeaux came up to me. "I liked the way you hung in there," he told me. I was thinking "hung in there?" I was just watching baseballs going over my head. Rod just had so much energy. He called everybody "Tiger." He exuded confidence, which was a good model for me because I was a pretty shy kid.

At USC, we had lots of guys on those baseball teams who went to the majors like Roy Smalley, Steve Kemp, Steve Busby. Basically I was the centerfielder and batted three, four, or five in the batting order. I played that position on three College World Series winners in three years, winning All-American honors in 1972 and 1973.

We played with wooden bats. What I accomplished, what we did, pales in comparison to what numbers are put up now. If you hit .300 back then in college, you were a good hitter — just as it was then in the big leagues. I hit .320, somewhere in there. I led the nation in home runs my sophomore year with fourteen. Today you would not even lead your team with fourteen.

Playing in the College World Series in Omaha was always on our schedule. We just printed it on there. "Save these dates," was the word. "And tell your parents."

We beat teams a lot of time because we knew and believed we could win. We played teams that had equal talent but they could never beat us in a big game. Never. The three years that I played at USC we never lost a game that meant something. We had talent, and we were well coached; we never made a mistake in a game to beat ourselves. In crunch time we would pull off plays that other players and teams would just dream about.

We never got flustered. In the 1973 College World Series we were facing Minnesota. Dave Winfield was pitching and dominating us. They had a 7–0 lead. Dave had a two-hitter going. He had struck out fifteen going into the ninth inning. Rod was telling us, "Stay with it. Stay with it."

We stayed with it. We scored eight in the bottom of the ninth to win.

Other teams used to hate us. We had some pretty good bench jockeys. We would not ride people when we were ahead, but when we were behind — that's when we got tough.

Since USC was a very visible team and played a lot of games, there were scouts around all the time at all our games. You don't even pay attention to them — you really don't. The Dodgers guys were always at our games. Coach Dedeaux had strong ties to the O'Malleys. I thought I was going to be picked in the June 1973 draft by the Dodgers, but they passed me up in the first round. I was stunned. They were set to pick me in the second round. Their pick was right behind Boston.

But Boston took me. I was shocked. The drafting was on the recommendation of scout Joe Stephenson, who was the Red Sox West Coast guy. He was one scout I never saw in college, high school, ever. The first time I saw him was when they drafted me.

It was a down and disappointing time for me. I could have been maybe the first or second pick in the nation as a sophomore. As a junior I didn't have as strong a season as I did in my sophomore year, but I was still the best collegiate player in the country. I played on USA teams, Pan Am teams, and I was the best player on those teams.

And for the scouts to put me there as the forty-first pick was a shocker. The Red Sox, no less. What? Who? Where are they? I was a West Coast guy.

I found out later that the reason I did not go as high in the draft as I thought I should was the feeling among some teams that I couldn't hit left-handed pitching. What did they know? But that dropped my value down.

Nevertheless, I signed for $40,000, which was a lot of money in those days. My first stop that summer of 1973 was double-A baseball, Bristol, Connecticut. I had been all over the country and many places in the world playing baseball but had not spent that much time in the East. It was culture shock.

Our ballpark, Muzzy Field in Bristol, was a great little park cut out of the woods. The backdrop was all pine trees. But we were just a terrible team. I had signed in July and had just come off a USA–Japan series. I had just been on a team that had won a national championship again.

To have just done all that and then to find myself on a team that was thirty games out of first place and thirty games under .500 was a downer. When I first joined Bristol, I still had a lot of adrenaline flowing and had a twenty-something hitting streak right away. I was hitting .360, .380.

But I had played a lot of games that year, and here I was on a team that really had no chance to win games. I just wore out. That's why I hit only .259 with six home runs. But even with those stats, there were flashes of my showing that I could handle the pitching in that league in the month and a half that I was there.

Jimmy Rice and I were teammates on that Bristol team. We became friends. We didn't even finish the season at Bristol because we were sent up together to triple-A Pawtucket for the play-offs. Now my juices started flowing. I was on a team that was battling to get into the Little World Series. As it turned out, I had a pretty good role in getting that to happen.

The opposition didn't know much about me, didn't have much of an idea of my capabilities. In the play-offs I did really well against the Pirates farm team, the Charleston Charlies. Then we moved into the finals against Tulsa, the St. Louis farm team. We beat them for the crown.

April 1974, I was back with Pawtucket, the International League. It was not a happy time. The team had lost players from the year before and was almost as bad as the Bristol team I had played for. Aside from the losing, what I especially remember are the bus rides. That was a killer.

I was used to flying everywhere when I was on USC. Now it was a fifteen-hour bus ride, getting off the bus and playing a game. I don't think I ever got used to that. I also never got used to the cold weather. It was freezing. I was used to playing in beautiful weather.

Rick Burleson was on that team with us. He got called up to the Red Sox in June or July. Jimmy Rice got called up in late August. I was called up in September.

Fenway Park was something special right from the first moment I saw it. The Green Monster looked like it was ten feet away. It's forty feet high. When I played in college, my rightfield wall was that way so I was used to playing caroms off the wall. The left side of the field looks very small but when you turn to the rightfield side, the park looks huge. Strange dimensions. I sat on the Sox bench. And sitting on that bench were Juan Marichal and Orlando Cepeda on the left and right of me. These were great stars I had watched as I grew up and rooted for the Giants.

September 5, 1974, was my major league debut. I pinch ran against the Tigers at Fenway. I was on third base. There was a bunt down the third base line. I tried to score. Aurelio Rodriguez was the third baseman. He had a cannon for an arm. He threw to Bill Freehan, who blocked the plate. I was out. That was my introduction to major league baseball.

My first at bat was a pinch hit attempt. I flied out. The next at bat was also a pinch hit attempt. It was a tough way to break in. I wouldn't do that to a youngster if I were a manager.

The first game I started was against Milwaukee, managed by Del Crandall, whom I always admired as a kid. Our team was struggling mightily. No one could hit. In batting practice I was knocking balls out of the park, so they had to put me in finally.

My first at bat as a starting player was against Jim Slaton. He threw me a fastball away, and I hit it down the leftfield line. It just went foul. But it had home run length. The next pitch, he threw me a curve, and I hit it out — home run to right. My next time up I hit a double. Then Crandall brought in a left-hander, and our manager, Darrell Johnson, took me out. I couldn't believe it. Guys were saying, "Nice game, kid, nice game." But I was out of the game.

Finally, after a couple of more starts where I continued to hit well, Johnson just left me in there against everybody. Against Detroit at our place, I went 4-for-5 with a couple of doubles off the wall. In fact, their catcher Bill Freehan, when I came up for my last at bat kidded, "Hey kid, don't tell the reporters that I told you what was coming." I hit .419 in fifteen games that September.

Marichal and Cepeda said nothing except maybe, "Good, keed." The relationships back then between veterans and rookies, especially call-up rookies, was not that great. They just looked at you as someone who had to prove himself before he became one of them. That didn't really happen for me until my first full year.

It was probably a very good thing that Jimmy Rice and I both came up together. We leaned on each other. They called us the "Gold Dust Twins." A lot of things happened to me that season of 1975. It was new, and it happened very fast. I really didn't enjoy everything that was happening until later.

It was wonderful and enjoyable that our ball club was winning and in first place almost the entire year. I came from a winning background at

USC and had success all my life in sports. But to have it at that level that quickly was Walter Mitty-an. Nobody had ever done it — ever.

There were moments that I would never forget. On June 18, 1975, I bombed the Tigers, slugging three home runs, driving in ten runs, and getting sixteen total bases in one game.

There was a doubleheader against the Yankees on August 1 in the heart of the pennant race. The first game was a real duel — Bill Lee against Catfish. Graig Nettles was hitting, and we played him to pull. I was in right center, maybe almost in right. Nettles crossed us up and drove a ball into left center. I had to run for what seemed like miles. I dove and tumbled and had a little snow cone at the end of my glove. Jimmy Rice was in left, and as I dove down, he leaped and jumped over me. That catch preserved that win. We won 1–0. We shut them out the second game of the double-header, and that pretty much knocked the Yankees out of the pennant race.

We came up against Oakland in the play-offs. They were a tough, veteran team who had won three World Series in a row. We were a very young team with the exception of a couple of guys. We blew them away. We were good and we could hurt you in a short series. Then we played the Reds in the World Series, but we were without Jimmy Rice, who had hurt his hand. We lost to them in seven games.

That was it. My first year in the majors was over. I won the Rookie of the Year award and Most Valuable Player award — an accomplishment that had not been done before or since. I was the first rookie to lead the league in slugging percentage. I was second in batting average, third in RBIs, and fourth in total bases. I also won the first of my four Gold Gloves.

As you climb the ladder in athletics, guys drop off for different reasons. A lot of it has nothing to do with baseball talent. It's just that living gets in the way a lot of times. I stayed with it all the time.

I wouldn't trade the time that I played for all the dollars you could make now. The country was just coming out of the sixties. Everybody was having a pretty good time. There was not the media as we know it now. And a guy like me who was pretty introverted could just hide, play baseball, play with reckless abandon.

SAM McDOWELL

From the time I was six or seven years old, it was a given that I was going to play baseball regardless of the weather and almost year-round. I was born on September 21, 1942, and grew up in Pittsburgh. I doubt there was a single day that I wasn't playing some sort of a sport.

My mother was athletic. My dad played every sport. In fact, he still holds the University of Pittsburgh football team record for the longest punt. My parents wanted us to play organized sports all the time. I played on three teams every summer.

In any sport I took up, my dad always had me play with guys who were a lot older than me. He felt that would motivate me, push me on, and help me to learn better and faster.

They all talk about how Pittsburgh was dingy with all the smokestacks in my growing-up time. I was kind of oblivious to all of that. I knew that my father worked in the steel mill, that we all wore hand-me-down clothes and did hand-me-down everything. I knew that my mother would do the shopping on Saturday for the whole week. I knew that during the week we would have only two meals of meat and all the rest were a combination thereof.

But I just lived day-to-day and tried to enjoy life, and that meant playing ball. I never got to that position like a lot of others where I talked about dreams of becoming a Mickey Mantle, a Willie Mays, or a Ralph Kiner, who was hitting a lot of home runs for the Pirates — which incidentally was not too good a team then.

Since we didn't have a television set in my early growing-up time, and since we were too caught up in playing sports all the time ourselves, we didn't have any time to follow any team. I never saw a professional baseball game or even heard one on the radio. The first professional game I ever saw was when I played in one myself.

I lived in the inner city. To get to a grass field on a fairgrounds was a three- to four-mile walk. That took away time from playing ball. So most of the time we played in a school yard that had a brick surface. I did not have much in the way of equipment. My glove was another hand-me-down. I remember I spent a lot of time black taping and re-taping a baseball with a ripped cover.

When I was about six or seven years old, I started out playing on my dad's baseball team. He was the manager. He raised the money and did everything so the kids in our neighborhood would at least have a baseball team. Most of the players were head and shoulders above me in ability, so at the start I sat on the bench and watched a good deal of the time.

When I was about eleven years old, I just got sick, tired, and angry about being on the bench. They gave me a chance to start out as a centerfielder and there were a few games where I was able to show off my arm. I threw runners out at home plate.

I think that power in my arm came about from my throwing rocks through people's windows. Mostly it was vacant houses that I threw at. The higher the floor, the more I took aim and the harder I threw. My parents got flack about that and I ultimately did, too.

I was switched to pitching because of my strong arm. When I was about twelve years old, my dad enrolled me in Little League in a suburb of Pittsburgh called Morningside. This was 1950, 1951. Our team got to Williamsport and the Little League World Series, where we were knocked out in the second round. It didn't really register that that was the World Series. I was just having fun.

After Little League, I went to Pony League in Johnstown, Pennsylvania. Again, we lost out in the second round. That was history repeating itself.

When I was fifteen and sixteen years old, I went out to the Colt League World Series to Ontario, California. Both years our team made it to the finals. Both times we came in second. I had done my best — the two games that I pitched in were both no-hitters.

I loved baseball, but I also loved all other sports and was good in whatever I played — basketball, football, swimming, track, tennis, you name it.

But I was not unusual in my family of four brothers and one sister. It was expected that we all would excel in athletics. All four brothers were superstars in one sport or another. One of my older brothers was an All-American pick in football, baseball, basketball. Then in his senior year he contracted polio, which paralyzed his right side.

During my high school years many baseball scouts periodically came around to look me over. In my senior year I was like 9–0 with six no-hitters. There were only three teams that scored off me — period. In the championship game I pitched a no-hitter, and I hit the home run that won the game. That was the only hit the opposing pitcher gave up. There were sixteen major league teams back then, and there were sixteen major league scouts in the stands.

I was signed by the Indians in 1960 straight out of Central Catholic High School in Pittsburgh for $70,000. I was the biggest bonus baby ever to that time for Cleveland. I was sixteen years old. The old ballplayer, Hoot Evers, was the scout. The rule that a bonus baby had to stay with a team for a year before you could send them to the minors was changed the year before I signed. So they sent me down to D ball.

I got off to a great minor league start striking out 100 hitters in 105 innings. The next year I was moved up to Salt Lake City in the Pacific Coast League. I was good and I was bad — I struck out 156 batters, but I also walked 152.

I was compared to Bob Feller all the time — it was a two-sided sword. He was a legend. He was nicknamed "Rapid Robert." I was given the name "Sudden Sam." That came about when some of the players said, "McDowell's ball gets up to the plate all of a sudden."

On September 15, 1961, I was given my first major league start. It was against the new Washington Senators. I was eighteen years old. I guess I tried to outdo what I could do. I had a three-hit shutout going into the seventh inning. I had gotten five strikeouts and walked five batters. Then I threw a pitch with all the strength I could get into it. Bingo! I fractured two of my ribs. It was back and forth to the majors until 1964 when I finally settled in.

CHUCK McELROY

$\mathcal{T}exans$ are really known for football. But I just wanted to play sport, and baseball just happened to be a sport I could play well. I was born on October 1, 1967, in Port Arthur, Texas, and I grew up there.

I started playing Little League baseball when I was five. You'd watch it on TV, and you'd try to be like your Reggie Jacksons, your Willie Stargells, Dave Parkers — all those guys. You'd try to be like them when you're a kid. You try to mark them and do the same thing they did when they were playing the game. And the next thing you know, you're wearing the same number jersey they wore.

You'd see Willie Stargell and Dave Parker hit those long home runs, especially the whole Pittsburgh team back in the seventies. I guess that is what made the Pirates my favorite team. I loved the players. I really loved the way they played together. Their theme song was "We Are Family," and they were a family. Even an outsider could tell they did a lot together. They just went out and played the game right and had fun. As a kid, you saw all the fun that they were having, but you didn't quite realize all the work that went into their excellence. It wasn't until later that I realized all the little things they did correctly.

I had someone around me in my growing-up time who had a lot of excellence about her and knew how to play the game. It was my aunt. She played a lot of coed softball where they traveled to different cities. Actually, she was like the Hank Aaron of softball. She was the one who showed me how to play baseball.

My aunt would take me in the backyard and play catch with me. We'd play "burnout," taking a baseball and throwing it as hard as we could to each other. On Saturdays and Sundays, I would go to watch her play in her tournaments. The next thing I knew, I'm eleven or twelve years old, and I'm playing in those tournaments.

It could be a hundred degrees outside in that Texas heat, but I would be out there with the other kids, playing away. We did all kinds of odd and unusual things playing ball in my growing-up years. We used to play stick-ball in the street barefoot. There would be four or five guys on each team. You'd have to hit the ball over a wire for a home run. You'd get a broom-stick and a tennis ball, and just hit it. The fielder would throw it to the base. We didn't have first base, second base, third base. We just had one base. That was it. But it was fun.

In Little League, I played first base, outfield, and catcher. I was a left-handed catcher and the only left-handed hitter on the team. When I was playing centerfield, I had a lot of fun throwing guys out at first base. I fired the ball on a line. One time I broke our first baseman's tooth.

I think that was what made them think it might not be a bad idea to get me to try pitching. The only way I developed control as a pitcher and learned how to throw strikes was through something my Little League coach did. He put a guy on either side of the plate. I was too scared to hit anyone. So where could I throw the ball? Right down the middle. I guess it was a good way for a kid to learn something about pitching.

In high school I was an All American my freshman year and on up. We would practice on an elementary school field. It was unusual, you know, but that's all the school could afford. You're hitting home runs in batting practice, so you'd have to see that no cars are coming.

Back then I couldn't throw any breaking balls like guys do now. I just threw fastballs. I threw about 85, 86 miles per hour. I was only about 150 pounds soaking wet. But it was fun. I had two no-hitters. One time an-other pitcher and I were hooked up in a seven-inning game that lasted just an hour and five minutes. I was responsible for the only run of the game — an opposite-field home run.

My senior year, in 96 innings I had 238 strikeouts. Seventeen or eigh-teen a game — these were seven-inning games. We played twenty games that year, twice a week, and I pitched eighteen of them.

But with all of that, football was actually my favorite sport. I was the quarterback on our high school team. I had about fifty football scholarship offers, and a hundred baseball scholarship offers. Once I found out that five or six professional baseball teams wanted me — including the Angels, the Rangers, the Dodgers, and the Phillies — I chose baseball. When I graduated from high school in 1986, I signed with the Phillies.

My first game in the major leagues was on September 4, 1989. It was a point that you've worked hard all through the minors to get to. I was shaking from the time I got called up, from the time that I drove to the stadium, and from the start of the game to the end of the game.

We were playing the Pirates. The call went out to the bullpen. Wow! I was excited. I just couldn't believe it. I was so nervous. The first and only batter I faced that night was Barry Bonds. He lined out.

To this day, I'll get caught up in certain things and not enjoy the game. Then I realize, I'm a man playing a kid's game, and I enjoy it. As a kid, you'd pick up the baseball cards. Then all of a sudden, you're picking up your own baseball card. You don't realize until you get one of your own that you've made it.

SAM MELE

My given name was Sabath Anthony Mele. That is why I was called S.A.M. I was born on January 21, 1922, and grew up in Astoria, Queens. Two of my mother's brothers, Al and Tony Cuccinello, were major leaguers. Tony played for the Dodgers, Braves, Giants and coached for the Indians. Al played for the Cardinals and Giants.

We were poor, really poor. But I would never, never, never exchange those days for anything. My parents were Italian immigrants. There was seven in our family — four boys, three girls. My older brother was the only one of the kids who was fortunate enough to have his own bed because he was the only one old enough to work.

My father made about $14 a week working for the Consolidated Gas Company, and he had to walk at least two miles to get to his job. My mother made meals out of nothing. But, brother, we never starved.

The neighborhood I grew up in had a lot of empty lots all over the place. We played in those a lot. But my favorite spot was Queens Park, just around the corner from my home. I would go out in the morning and play and play. My mother would have to send my brothers out looking for me to bring me back home.

Most of the time I was playing ball, I was more interested in basketball than baseball. I had watched my brothers play basketball. Sometimes I got lucky, and they threw me in when they needed a man.

The greatest thing operating for me was my two uncles. When the major league baseball season was over, they would come home and teach me how to do this, how to do that. My Uncle Tony would bring over the great Al Lopez, who taught me a lot about hitting. He also gave me tips for catching, even though I never thought of becoming one.

I was way ahead of the other kids fundamental-wise because I was taught by guys who were darn good in their profession. My Uncle Tony would bring over a glove now and then, a bat, and some balls.

Strangely enough, all the time I was a kid growing up in New York with the Dodgers, Yankees, and Giants to follow, I never went to Yankee Stadium or Ebbets Field. I only got to go to the Polo Grounds when the Braves played the Giants, because my Uncle Tony was a coach for the Braves.

I was not a fan of any of the New York teams. I followed the Detroit Tigers. I don't know why. Maybe it was because I just liked Schoolboy Rowe, Charlie Gehringer, and Barney McCoskey.

It was when I got to my late teens that I got interested in playing baseball in earnest. I played some sandlot ball. In one doubleheader I got about eight or nine hits. In the second doubleheader I was 0-for-13. Disgusted.

I came home and threw my uniform on the floor. My mother gave it to me. "You can't quit," and this and that. Then she told her brothers, and one by one they chewed me out. Tony was over at the house, and he had a lot to say, too.

"What are you worried about? You went 0-for-13? I went 0-for-17 in the big leagues. There's always a game tomorrow."

Boy, was I taught an awful lesson about not quitting.

As things worked out, and in life they never really work out the way you think they are going to work out, I was awarded a basketball scholarship to New York University. Bill McCarthy was the basketball coach there. I got to be pretty friendly with him. He introduced me to Neil Mahoney, who was the baseball coach, and I started to play a little baseball. Mahoney had a lot of contacts with the Red Sox and used to drive me up to Fenway Park on weekends just to work out.

One of those weekends I was in the batting cage. I let a pitch go by. A voice called out from the stands.

"What was wrong with that pitch?"

"I thought it was outside."

"Well, it was but it was high enough for a strike."

I thought it was some wise guy heckling me. So when I finished taking my cuts, I walked out of the cage and went to take a look at who it was.

It was Ted Williams. "It was good you laid off that pitch," he said. "There really wasn't anything you could have done with it."

Uncle Tony, who was still coaching for the Braves, found out that I was working out at Fenway Park. He said, "You've got to do me a favor and work out with the Braves. They won't be able to pay you a bonus like the Red Sox, but you are a relative and it will look bad if you don't give them a chance to make an offer."

I did as he said. The Braves offered me something, but it was not nearly as much as what I had heard the Red Sox were going to offer. One day Neil Mahoney took me into Manhattan to the Commodore Hotel. A meeting with Mr. Yawkey, the owner of the Red Sox, was in the works.

Mr. Yawkey was sitting behind a desk. He wore a white shirt and a nice tie. He was very vibrant with a very engaging smile. He got up and reached out to shake my hand, and it seemed like it was the genuine thing. This was not a put-on by a big man with a lot of money.

It was 1942. I was going to go into the service. Mr. Yawkey offered me $2,500 right then and there and promised me another $2,500 when I came out of the service. I didn't sign a thing — it was just a handshake. On faith.

I came out of the service on February 4, 1946, and four days later went to spring training with Boston. They sent me down to Scranton for the whole year.

I started my major league career in 1947, and it lasted ten years and one day. I recall my first game. It was against the Philadelphia Athletics. I walked my first time at bat. Then I doubled off the leftfield wall. Next I singled, and then I walked again. I had a 2-for-2 day in Fenway Park. I don't recall who started, but Tom Ferrick came in to relieve.

I was just so thrilled to be in an outfield in Boston with Dominic DiMaggio in center, Ted Williams in left, and me in right. When I tried to talk to Williams about fielding, he said, "Hey, you go talk to that little guy in centerfield. If you want to know about hitting, you come to me." Boy, did I have good teachers in Dom and Ted.

My parents came to see me play my first game in Yankee Stadium. I hit a home run, my first in the majors. The traveling secretary went and got that ball from the fan who caught it and gave him a new ball. The ball I hit, I signed for my mother. I hit .302 that rookie season.

BRIAN MOEHLER

$\mathcal{I}$ *grew up* in Rockingham, North Carolina, where I was born on December 13, 1971. I started playing T-ball when I was five or six, and I've played baseball one way or another ever since.

My dad used to play catch with me or throw me ground balls. And I'd play with my brother, who was five years older than me. We used to play games in the backyard with a tennis ball or a Wiffle ball and a wooden bat. We had this huge, green bush about a hundred feet away that we used to call the Dark Green Monster. You had to clear it for a home run. If you hit off a building, it was a triple. A double was anything past the pitcher, and anything into the woods was an out. You were basically just pulling everything.

Competing against someone who was older helped me along. When you play against your brother, you want to win. He won most of the time, but then I had my fair share, too.

When I was nine or ten, I started playing with a team called the Civitans, which was named for the men's club that sponsored us. I played every position except catcher. I loved playing the outfield. But in baseball you have to stand around a lot; there's a lot of downtime. That's why my favorite sport was basketball. When you're a kid, you like to move around a lot. I'd play small forward and guard, and center sometimes, too.

My favorite team was the Braves. I followed them so intently, I loved watching them play. My favorite player was Dale Murphy. I kept a poster of him above my bed. He just seemed like the nicest guy in the world. When I went down and got his autograph in Atlanta, it was one of the biggest thrills of my life to that point in time.

I honestly, truly believed that I would make the major leagues some day. I threw curveballs when I was eleven and twelve years old. That didn't mean much, but I imagined what it would be like to be doing that on the big league stage.

I've been fortunate to get the chance. I wasn't really scouted that much in high school. I was kind of a late bloomer, but I had a good fastball and an above average breaking ball.

I went to college at North Carolina at Greensboro, and I was drafted by Detroit in the sixth round of the 1993 free-agent draft.

I got called up in 1996 at the end of the season when one of their pitchers got hurt. Our season had ended by then, and I was already home in Georgia. I went to Milwaukee and made a start. The date was September 22, 1996. Then I made a start in Detroit. It was a lot of fun. I'll never forget it. I had a no-decision and a loss, but I pitched pretty well both games. What I did at the tail end of 1996 was good enough to get into the starting rotation in 1997.

BOB MONTGOMERY

It was my parents who made baseball available and accessible to me and for me, who made sure I was able to get to all my practices and games. I played baseball almost from the start in our neighborhood park league or for a Babe Ruth League team.

I was born on April 16, 1944, and grew up in Nashville, Tennessee. It was hot, but we never took heed of that. It was so good to be playing and doing something we had a lot of fun with.

I had no particular idols in the big leagues because down in Nashville we did not have real close proximity to the majors. But during the years that CBS owned the Yankees, every Saturday there was a baseball game on TV. It seemed like the Yankees were always on. I had a chance to watch Mickey Mantle quite a bit. That was a treat. But I spent more time playing games than watching games.

The Nashville team in the Southern League was a farm club of the Cincinnati Reds. I had the chance to see quite a few good players come through there and play, people like Jim O'Toole, Jim Maloney, John Edwards. I also was impressed seeing Harmon Killebrew and Bob Allison playing for Chattanooga.

The ball park in Nashville was a dandy. It was called Sulfur Dell and was located on the north side of Nashville next to a big coal yard. What was especially unique about the ballpark was a hill built all around the outfield. I was amazed at how many players actually played up on top of the hill to get themselves in proper defensive position to run down the hill to get a batted ball.

Rightfield was known as "the Dump." It was only 265 down the right-field line, but the wall was really high because of the hill and there was a screen built on top of that. A guy named Bob Lennon, who was a real strong left-handed pull hitter, hit about sixty-eight home runs one year in that Southern League. They said a good deal of his home runs were hit in Sulfur Dell.

The Southern League back in the fifties was a train league. Teams traveled by train. Oftentimes they would play two games on Sunday and have Monday off for travel. My father, who had been a pretty good amateur baseball player and had a strong interest in the game, would take me to the park on those warm Sunday afternoons. We would sit there and enjoy the doubleheaders together. Every time I went with my dad to Sulfur Dell, I dreamed of becoming a major leaguer. I was probably about fifteen years old when I got to pitch in that park on a Babe Ruth League team. I struck out fourteen batters in eleven innings.

In high school, I was a pitcher and shortstop. I was All State in three states. I was All City for probably all four years. There were about four clubs — the Orioles, the Pirates, the Twins, the Mets — interested in me.

Then out of the blue, the day after graduation, this scout from the Red Sox, George Digby, called me up. I learned later that he did his work on a quiet basis. He asked me if I had signed with any team.

"No, not yet," I told him.

"Please," he said, "don't sign with anyone else until I have an opportunity to get together with you and make an offer."

I was set to play a game that eventually got rained out. Ellis Clary of the Twins was on his way to see me play. Probably had that game not gotten rained out, I would have signed with Minnesota. But it was, and George Digby showed up.

In 1962, there was no draft. It was auction signing. Players had the option of picking the team that they felt most comfortable with and the one that offered the most money. In both cases that happened to be the Red Sox. It all happened so very fast. I graduated from high school on a Friday. I spoke with George Digby on a Monday. My signing bonus was $8,000. I was in Olean, New York, on Thursday — my first professional baseball experience and the first time I was away from home.

The manager was Hal Halland. He was very strict, I thought, but maybe he had to be. He seemed to expect too much from first and second year players. But then again who was I to judge? I hit maybe .275. I didn't play a lot because at the time Olean was trying to hide some of their better players so they would not lose them in the draft. At the end of the season our third baseman was injured, and I took over for him. Even though I never played the third base position before, I did well there.

I was assigned to Waterloo, Iowa, in 1963 and proceeded to lead that league in errors real quick. I had a tremendous throwing arm but not much quickness. Lynn Okrie was the manager. He was a tall, thin guy who had been a catcher for the Red Sox and also for Detroit for a time. He suggested that I become a catcher.

I balked at first. He kept insisting. He said that if I had a chance to get to the big leagues it was going to be as a catcher. By the end of that year, I was catching a game or two after having spent half a season learning how to handle the position.

I liked catching when I got into it. It was running the whole show, and I enjoyed doing that. I was nineteen, and I had never caught before. But there was probably a plus side to that. When I learned to catch, I was taught by Lynn Okrie the proper way. I did not have any bad habits to break.

The next year, my third year in the minors, I went back to Waterloo as a catcher. I was really enjoying catching now. I made the All-Star team. The first game that my parents saw me play professionally took place in Davenport, Iowa. The first time up I hit a double off the wall. The second time up I hit a home run. Talk about family pride.

In 1965, I started my fourth year as a minor leaguer with Winston-Salem, North Carolina. In 1966, I played for Pittsfield, Massachusetts, in double-A in the Eastern League. The last month of that season I was moved up to Toronto in the International League and played for Dick Williams.

In 1967, I went back to Toronto, played for Eddie Kasko. The next three seasons — 1968, 1969, 1970 — I played for Louisville, Kentucky. The last four years in the minors I was glad that most of the traveling was by airplane. I had a particularly good time in Louisville the last two years I played there. We had good ball clubs and good conditions. At the end of 1970, I was hitting .324 and had fourteen home runs. Those stats finally got me a shot at the big leagues. I was promoted to Boston.

All the minor league bus rides — I took quite a few. Each year was a new adventure — one year closer to my goal of getting to the big leagues. I never got frustrated.

I was twenty-seven years old when I finally came up to the Red Sox. I had never been to Fenway Park before. When I first walked into the dugout, I couldn't believe how high the wall was in leftfield. It looked like it just engulfed you. I had also never been in a ballpark where the lights were so bright. My manager from Toronto in 1967, Eddie Kasko, was the Boston manager.

When I first got to the majors, I wasn't sure that I belonged. I saw guys hit the ball so very hard so consistently and they still made outs. This impressed me. That was one of the biggest differences between the minors and the majors.

I wasn't a very good player. I was a 50–50 player. I didn't hurt anybody, and I didn't help anybody. I was up in the majors for about nine and a half years, almost the same amount of time as my minor league career.

Some say my story is one of incredible fortitude, determination. All I ever wanted to do was play. I never had any thought of not giving it every chance for me to get to the big leagues.

MANNY MOTA

I played the game of baseball almost all my life and enjoyed playing it. I was born on February 18, 1938, in Santo Domingo, Dominican Republic. I was out there playing baseball from my early days on. At that time of your life, you just play any way that you can using any kind of ball, any kind of bat. We made baseballs out of newspapers. We made a glove from cardboard cartons.

Most of the players from my country came from poor families like I did. But I was proud to be raised by a Catholic family. You know, what you get from your family in your home, you take with you for the rest of your life.

As a kid, I pitched, I used to catch, I used to play the outfield. It was kind of difficult for me to get close to any professional ballplayers. I did not know anyone of them and had to do things on my own and play my own way. I really did not have any professional coaching. But I was fortunate to play in a big tournament when I was almost fourteen years old. I won the batting title there. Those were the great days.

When I started getting a little older, I followed the league in Cuba and read about major league baseball. I would always try to go and see the championship tournaments in the Dominican. I would watch and remind myself of my dream to be a professional ballplayer when I grew up.

Felipe Alou was one of the first of the Dominicans to sign a major league baseball contract. Mid 1950s. He opened the door for us, for the other generations. He was a guide by letting us know about the culture of the United States and what to expect if and when we got the chance to play in the major leagues.

I moved on to play for the Dominican Air Force team. At that time there were not many scouts around, but there was one from the New York Giants who liked the way I played and followed me around. He offered a contract. I signed.

In 1962, I made it up to the big leagues after spending six years in the

Giants' minor league organization. My first major league at bat was against Sandy Koufax. I struck out.

But I have been around the major leagues ever since. I have been happy and pleased to accomplish what I have accomplished with my limited abilities. I cannot compare to today's players.

JOHN "RED" MURFF

My full name is John Robert Murff. I was
that fifth child, the middle child of nine. The
big ones worked on me, and I worked on the little ones. I was
born on the first day of April 1921 in Burlington, Texas.

My dad, Louis Ellison Murff, was the umpire and the main player in my
growing-up years. Daddy loved the game, and surely passed that love on
to me.

We made our own baseball equipment. He had been a carpenter, so he
knew his way with wood. We found an old bat that had been thrown away,
and he fixed it up.

Momma would make the baseballs. She would put a little rubber ball in
the middle and just unravel a woolen sock and wind it back upon that ball
and sew it every three or four layers of string. We called it the string ball,
and we learned to play with that. You couldn't get hurt with that. You
could catch it bare-handed. Momma also made me my first glove out of
old cloth and stuffed it with all kinds of soft cotton.

Playing baseball really got into my blood early. If someone was not playing it right, I would get so mad that I'd just start crying almost. Dad
worked for the railroad, and all the rest of us were sharecroppers living in
a farmhouse. Daddy was the farm manager, and the landowners liked to
rent land to him because the word was known that he had a family that
could work it right.

We tried to listen to major league baseball games on those little crystal
radios. I would hear part of a game, and then it would fade. The crystal
would give out. Radio was pretty new to us. We didn't have electricity. We
lived like all the farmers lived in the twenties and thirties, without indoor
plumbing and electricity.

Every town had a town team. Ours was called the Burlington Bearcats.
My three uncles and my dad played on that team. There was always a lot
of tough competition. That was about the only organized, for want of a
better word, baseball I saw in those early years. There was a team for adult

beer-drinking men that played in what was called the "beer league." I never did see them play. That team was something my dad did not want me to go see.

I also didn't get to play baseball on Sunday because of the strict religious belief that my Baptist father had that baseball was not the right thing to do on a Sunday.

My dad told me that when he was growing up he had played amateur baseball against the great Tris Speaker. Both of them were about the same age. I had no idea who Tris Speaker was. But every time I would make a catch, my dad would say, "That's just the way Tris Speaker catches them, son." Then he would hit me another one.

When all of the kids in my family were out there playing, we used an open place between our house and the barn. We had a stock tank, a water storage tank for cattle. If you hit the ball against it, you were automatically out.

I continued my baseball playing at the elementary school in Burlington. We would get there Monday morning and choose sides. We would start playing before school started and have a fifteen-minute recess at ten o'clock and go right back to where we were. If you had a strike, two strikes on you, whatever, we would pick up the game from there. We kept playing that ball game all week long. It was a continuous baseball game.

You graduated from the seventh grade in Burlington Elementary and entered Rosebud, just like the flower, High School. But I didn't play high school baseball. There was no baseball team in my high school. Football and basketball were the only sports they played there.

When I graduated from high school, there were sixty or seventy in my graduating class. There was a lot of farm work to do. That was what I had to concentrate on. I worked hard and started to grow from the 127 pounds I weighed at the time of my high school graduation.

After a time I left to get a job in Freeport, Texas, where they were building the Dow Chemical Plant. I was tall and the boss, foreman, or whoever was hiring that day could see me easily. "Hey, slim, come on in here," the guy yelled. I was in the labor gang there for about six or seven months until I decided that I would rather go to school.

I enrolled in an aircraft and sheet metal school. I really wanted to fly an airplane, but first I wanted to know something about it. I had no dream whatsoever of playing pro baseball at that time.

Then I wound up working for Union Carbide until 1943 and then was in the service for three years and one month. I flew trainer airplanes and played on the Cadets baseball team in Maxwell Field, Alabama. It was kind of an embarrassing experience being on that team, because all of the other guys there had experience playing organized baseball. As I said, I never did play anywhere organized before, not even in high school.

I came out of the service and was a civilian again working for a living. But being on that service baseball team gave me a yen to find out if I was any good. I was thirty years old in 1950 when I started playing in the minor leagues. My first stop was Baton Rouge, Louisiana, in the Evangeline League, class-C then, single-A today. I was a pitcher and outfielder. There were all these young kids and me. But I could play the game. As a pitcher I went 17–3. I won three more games in the play-offs. I ended up hitting .334 in 100 ball games. I made just one error the whole season. I was a baseball player. I was on my way. Better late than never.

The next year I went to Florida for spring training in double-A ball with Nashville, Tennessee. The manager came up to me and said, "You've got to make a decision."

"What decision should I make?"

"You've got to decide whether you want to pitch or play the outfield."

I said, "I believe that's your job, not mine. You are the manager."

"You choose," he said.

I chose pitching.

In 1952, I was on the roster of the Tyler East Texans in the Big State League. I had a good year. I was 27–11. I got shut out four games in a row. After that last shutout, I wasn't too well mannered because I took a lead bat and broke every bat in the dugout. I moved on up to Dallas in the Texas League in 1953 and had more wins than any other pitcher in that league.

In 1954, I won my first three games pitching for the Dallas Eagles. Then I was in a serious automobile accident. I hurt my back and wound up having my only losing year.

Back with Dallas in 1955, I won twenty-seven and lost eleven. You might say I was stuck on those numbers. I was honored as Minor League Player of the Year by the *Sporting News.* Everything was going right.

I am sure all of that convinced the Milwaukee Braves to purchase my contract and slot me in to play for them in 1956. Earl Halstead was the scout involved in the deal. He told me this story later on.

"Dick Burnet, the owner of the Dallas team, wanted three major league ballplayers off our Milwaukee club for you, Red, and $100,000. Milwaukee offered three ballplayers and $40,000. They argued back and forth, back and forth.

"Finally," Earl told me, "I played a gin rummy game against Burnet, who thought he was something special at the game. But I beat him, I beat the damned guy. And, Red, I got you for Milwaukee's price."

So I was a pawn in a gin rummy game. But I was also going to the major leagues.

I was thirty-five years old in 1956. That first day of spring training I walked into that clubhouse of the Milwaukee Braves like I was a rookie. I was a rookie, but a seasoned one. You talk about your growing up baseball. I was starting in the majors at an age when most players have retired.

We came through New Orleans after spring training, and my dad and mother were there to watch me. I came in and relieved against the Brooklyn Dodgers. We were barnstorming north with them. My dad asked me later, "When you came in to relieve, were you afraid of Duke Snider?"

I said, "No. I have this game figured out, Dad. He was afraid of me, because I was an untried rookie. He had never seen me, and he wasn't going to let me hit him in the head or hurt him. In fact, he gave me the time at bat. I made one pitch to him, and he hit into a double play."

Duke Snider had his job. He wasn't trying to make the ball club. I was.

Opening Day in Milwaukee in 1956, County Stadium. We played Cincinnati. "Jolly Cholly" Grimm was the manager. He put me in to relieve Lew Burdette. The tying run was on third base; the winning run was on first base. It was the ninth inning. The score was 3–2 Milwaukee.

Was I nervous? I just didn't know my name. The batter was supposed to be Wally Post, a right-handed batter. But Bob Thurman, a left-handed batter pinch hit for him. I got him to pop up to Eddie Mathews at third base. Eddie walked over and handed me the ball and said, "That's the way to go. Now all you have to do is get Ted Kluzewski out, and we can go home."

I had just been reading about Ted Kluzewski, who had those bulging biceps. Here I was facing the blacksmith on the coldest day of the year, of any year to that point, for me. It was about thirty-three degrees and almost sleeting. I pitched — and I think I tried to do something that I was not capable of doing. Ted got all that baseball. He hit it down the line to right-field. The wind was thick with mist and sleet, blowing off of the lake twenty-five miles an hour.

Henry Aaron didn't get interested in the ball at first because it looked like it was out. Then it went straight up and came down, and Henry caught it for the third out. Two Hall of Famers helped me out — Eddie Mathews and Henry Aaron.

Warren Spahn won his ball game, so our team was 2–0 going into St. Louis. I read the *Post Dispatch,* and the probable starting pitcher listed for the Milwaukee Braves was named John "Red" Murff. This was the third game of the season. I thought the paper had a misprint.

That St. Louis team had a lot of fine ballplayers, including Stan Musial. I ruptured a disc in my back in the third inning of that game. I did not lose the game, but I lost my baseball life, because I never did have my power after that. I knew how to do most things on the mound, but I lacked the ability to put the stinger in the fastball.

I got my dream. I was on the 1957 Milwaukee Braves, who played for the world's championship against New York. The Yanks came over to Milwaukee and called us "Hickville" and "Bushville." So we just went out there and showed the Yankees some skill and expertise. We won the World Series. I was a member of that championship team with two wins and two saves.

My major league career was much too brief, but I could not help that. I started late and left early. I have often thought I would like to come back again and play again as Nolan Ryan.

CHOLLY NARANJO

$\mathcal{I}$ *was born* November 25, 1934, at three o'clock in the afternoon in Havana, Cuba, and had the given name — Lazaro Ramon Gonzalo Naranjo.

Baseball was a Cuban thing then and still is now. Baseball then saw the politicians give out pictures of famous players to win the support of the people and get their vote.

In my beginning days with baseball, I used to play with the other kids on the neighborhood corner. Cigarette boxes then were made of cardboard. We would go around and collect them. We would break them in half, get a piece of paper, put a stone inside and wrap it up in the cigarette packaging. We would play baseball using our hands as bats. We did not have real bases, so we used the four corners of the street as bases. We played at night, when it was cooler, under the lights of the poles. As we kids grew up, we played soft pitch, then hardball with the older guys on the sandlots.

I attended a private Catholic school. It was a wonderful experience in every way and especially as far as baseball was concerned. The brothers organized our baseball team. The brothers supplied us with bats, balls, and uniforms. We had a beautiful field, too.

My favorite position was shortstop, but the team already had a good shortstop. So the brothers tried me out as a pitcher. They liked what they saw. They switched me over to pitching. I pitched our team to the high school baseball championship of Cuba in 1949 and 1950. That earned me the honor of being chosen the best high school player in Cuba.

Most of the knowledge and all the good tips about baseball, I got from reading newspapers. I concentrated on the sports pages and the funnies. My favorite player was Joe DiMaggio, because he was something special. I was able to get a lot of playing tips in the papers from Dazzy Vance and Bucky Walters, Melvin Ott and Marty Marion.

By 1954, I had something of a reputation as a baseball player and was invited, along with some other Cuban players, by the Washington Senators to Orlando, Florida. We were worked out and checked out in hopes of being able to make the team. Connie Marrero, Camilo Pascual, and I were the only Cubans left on the Senators when spring training ended.

Washington owner Calvin Griffith called me to his room in the hotel just before we were breaking camp and heading north. He signed me to a major league contract — what was called a retroactive one. If I made the team I was to make the limit salary. If I was cut out by May 15, I was to make $600. I was nineteen years old, and I was so happy. It seemed like a wonderful deal.

Opening Day 1954. The Yankees against the Senators in Washington, D.C.'s Griffith Stadium. The custom back then was for the president of the United States to throw out the first ball for a game between Washington and another American League team. The next day all the other major league teams started playing.

After I threw batting practice, the Senators manager, Bucky Harris, came over and told me I was assigned to sit with the president while the game was going on. "You carry your glove, and you guard him," that is what I was told. The president was Dwight D. Eisenhower.

I started to walk over to the box seat where Eisenhower was. He waved at me like he wanted to throw a ball to me. Then he threw the ball to me. I waved to him, like nice throw.

He shouted, "Throw the ball back."

We played catch. Everyone got a kick out of that. When the game started, I sat with the president for a while. He gave me an autographed baseball and talked to me just as if we knew each other all our lives. He asked me where I was born, what school I went to, what my father did. Then after a while he told me I could go back to the bench. He had a glove that Mr. Griffith gave him. He said, "With this, I think I can take care of myself."

I got back to the dugout and sat down; the other ballplayers started kidding me: "You got benched already." After the game was over, all the newspaper people interviewed me. Everyone made a big fuss over me. Unfortunately, that very same day I was shipped out to the minor leagues, to Chattanooga. That was my only day with the Senators. But what a day it was.

I made it back to the major leagues in 1956 with the Pittsburgh Pirates. Bobby Bragan was the manager. Even though I had been with the Senators a couple of years before, I was never officially on their roster. I joined the Pirates on July 1, and my official major league debut was July 8, 1956. I was with the team for eighty-nine days. I pitched in seventeen games, started three of them. I had a record of 1–2. That was my big league career.

CLAUDE OSTEEN

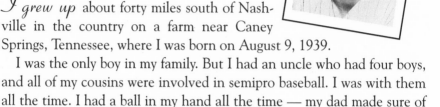

I grew up about forty miles south of Nashville in the country on a farm near Caney
Springs, Tennessee, where I was born on August 9, 1939.

I was the only boy in my family. But I had an uncle who had four boys,
and all of my cousins were involved in semipro baseball. I was with them
all the time. I had a ball in my hand all the time — my dad made sure of
that. I was not without the game at any time.

I had stats in my mind. I had pictures of all the current baseball stars on
my bedroom wall — Ted Williams. Jimmy Piersall, Jackie Jensen. I knew a
lot about all the stars on every team.

I was an outstanding pitcher in high school — especially my senior year.
Our team lost the first game of the season and went undefeated thereafter
all the way to the state championship, which we won. My high school
baseball coach was a Dodgers scout, Don Mohr. At that time there was a
rule that if you received more than $4,000 they had to keep you as a bonus
baby on the major league roster for two years. The scouts discouraged,
young kids from doing that naturally, because they didn't want to pay the
money. They also claimed it hampered a young player's development sitting around on a bench in the majors.

All the offers really boiled down to a choice between the Reds or the
Dodgers. I chose the Reds because they gave me a major league contract.
I went directly from Reading High School in Ohio to the major leagues
with Cincinnati at age seventeen in 1957. I knew I didn't belong there
with the Reds, but they had a spot for me.

I spent my first month out of high school with Cincinnati. I pitched in
three games. My first appearance was at Crosley Field on July 6, 1957. I
also pitched in Ebbets Field and St. Louis. They told me, "If you get in the
game against the Cardinals and have to face Stan Musial, just give him
your best stuff and hope and pray it stays inside the park."

After that one month with the Reds I was sent down to the minor
leagues to serve my apprenticeship for three years. I consider what I did a

wise move, because I was under a major league contract. I got a $3,100 signing bonus and $300 a month for the remainder of that first season — the maximum.

My first minor league season was at Nashville, double-A. It was a little high and probably too competitive for me, but there were only three months left in the season. A day for me was staged at the Sulfur Dell ballpark in Nashville, a park I had gone to many times as a kid to watch baseball. It seemed all the people who knew me in my growing-up years — Little League, Teener League, so on and so on — showed up to see me pitch. Thirteen busloads came down from my hometown of Caney Springs — a forty-mile trip. It was an incredible moment in my life.

I went out and I pitched. I was wild, walking people. I got knocked out in the first inning. I deserved to be taken out. I more or less just served out my time at Nashville, not pitching a lot. The Nashville club was going for the pennant, and I did not belong in the rotation.

Little did I know back then that destiny had an eighteen-year major league pitching career in store for me.

JIM PALMER

I was born in New York City in 1945. I was an orphan. When I was two days old, I was legally adopted by Polly and Moe Weisen. My first nine years were split living in New York City and on an estate in Westchester.

We moved to California when I was nine years old. Just before I turned twelve, Moe Weisen died. My mother remarried to the Hollywood character actor Max Palmer, and we lived in Beverly Hills. I wanted to keep the name Weisen, and that was okay with Max.

As a boy, I was always interested in sports. But I didn't really get started playing baseball until we moved to California. I used to play Wiffle ball against the handball courts in Beverly Hills, on a blacktop surface. We used a square on the wall as a strike zone. We'd play all Saturday afternoon, and every day in the summer. You could make the ball do anything. But I think it helped more for my developing hitting skills than pitching ability.

I don't believe I would have ever played organized baseball had we not moved to California. Once there, I didn't go to camp in the summer, so I got involved in Little League instead. I played in the Golden State Little League, all positions — pitched, played rightfield, leftfield, whatever they wanted me to play. I enjoyed Little League baseball very much and pitched six straight no-hitters and made the All-Star team. Still, our team never played the play-offs. But I had good coaches. They taught us how to play.

It was Little League baseball that helped bring Max and myself together. We would play catch in the backyard. During my last year in Little League, Max spent a lot of time with me taking me to the games and watching me play.

There was a postseason Little League banquet in Beverly Hills in the late 1950s when the league president shocked Max with an announcement: "Graduating from the Yankees is James Alvin Palmer." I had told the league president to call me Palmer, not Weisen.

Interestingly enough, there still is a record of Jim Weisen having played in the California Little League. One year Jim Weisen led the league in home runs. The next year, this new kid in town, Jim Palmer, ended up as a good pitcher and a good hitter.

I played Little League, Pony League, and Babe Ruth League as a kid. Some coaches were very good, and some knew nothing about what they were doing. I don't remember anybody ever telling me how to throw a baseball. I don't think I learned the Jim Palmer windup until I got to pro ball. But I was a natural athlete, so that made up for a lot of things.

Back then, nobody had the sophistication or the knowledge to really be able to teach at the level to prepare you for a major league career. You know, I never had a Jim Palmer telling me what is a good windup and what is not.

It really wasn't until I got together with a coach named Bob Brown in Pony League that I finally learned more about the game. He knew his stuff. I played most positions and was usually the best hitter and the best pitcher.

Later, as I grew into my teens, our family moved to Scottsdale, Arizona, where I played sports all the time — especially football, basketball, and baseball. At Scottsdale High I was a three sport, All-State athlete.

I averaged twenty-five points a game as a senior and led all basketball scorers in Arizona. I was offered a basketball scholarship to UCLA by Coach John Wooden. But I turned it down. As a senior I was a wide receiver in football. In one game I caught four balls for touchdown receptions. I played centerfield and pitched in baseball. Besides being the All-State starting pitcher, I batted .483.

There were a lot of major league teams interested in me. I chose Baltimore. In August of 1963, I signed for a $60,000 bonus. My first pro season was spent in South Dakota with Aberdeen in the Northern League. I was lucky enough to pitch a no-hitter there. But I was very wild, walking 130 in 129 innings. I was basically the only high school player in that league, but nobody ever worked on my windup. I was left basically to my own devices.

I had a year in A ball and then was in the Instructional League. There I came into contact with pitching coach George Bamberger, who helped me a lot with mechanics and with my windup. He made me go down and actually shadow pitch even on the days that I wasn't throwing.

In 1965, I was promoted to Baltimore. I had spent just one year in the minors. I was nineteen years old. I got into my first game in April. Little did I dream that would be the first of 558 major league games and a lot of history all spent pitching for the Baltimore Orioles — twenty-one seasons.

MEL PARNELL

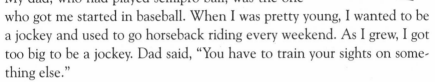

I have lived most of my life in New Orleans, Louisiana, where I was born on June 13, 1922. My dad, who had played semipro ball, was the one who got me started in baseball. When I was pretty young, I wanted to be a jockey and used to go horseback riding every weekend. As I grew, I got too big to be a jockey. Dad said, "You have to train your sights on something else."

That something else was baseball, which I had always liked as well. I played baseball daily. There was terrible heat all the time, but we got used to it, built up an immunity. During the summer months, my mother would get after me constantly to come home for lunch. I would tell her, "Mama, I don't have time to eat lunch. I'm playing ball."

Our family was of average means. My father was the head machinist for the Illinois Central Railroad in charge of the million-dollar train — the Panama Limited that ran from New Orleans to Chicago. He was in charge of the train on the New Orleans side. I rode on that train that was his pride and joy many times.

The train brought me close to my dad and so did baseball. I used to go with him to Heineman Park, which later became named Pelican Park. It was the first ballpark I saw professional baseball in. Even though the park was only about three miles from my home, my dad and I would go there by streetcar because there wasn't very much parking space.

The park seated about ten to twelve thousand, but usually when the Cardinals and Indians played exhibition games, there was an overflow crowd. They would then let the people stand out on the field in a roped-off section. I recall one day when my dad and I were part of the overflow crowd just outside of first base in foul territory. Big Hal Trotsky, a first baseman for Cleveland, hit a line drive. The ball came right at me. I had nowhere to go, because we were jam packed into the crowd, so I tried to defend myself by trying to catch the ball. It hit off the palm of my hand.

Later, I was given the ball because I had stopped it. They said I had prevented damage to others.

My baseball hero as a kid was Mel Ott, who was a great hitter and also a great person. He came from a town named Gretna just across the river from New Orleans. I knew everything about him since he was such a famous baseball player. When I got to meet him, we became great friends. We did a lot of things together. Mel took a liking to me, and I liked and idolized him. Off-season was the time he came back to Louisiana after starring for the New York Giants. That was when we would get together.

He and I used to go into the "Bad Boy Home" and play baseball with the kids who were in trouble. Mel would play on one team, and I would play on the other. We would talk with the kids and try to let baseball convert them from their bad habits. This all took place way back when I was in my early teens.

Carl Hubbell was another fellow I idolized quite a bit. He was another New York Giant. The Cleveland Indians and the Giants played spring training games in New Orleans, and almost every Sunday there was a classic duel between Bob Feller and Carl Hubbell. I was just agog seeing Carl Hubbell making the game seem so much easier than most pitchers. Bob Feller was out there grunting and groaning on every pitch, throwing as hard as he could. Here's Hubbell out there throwing a screwball, making it look so easy. His style was so impressive, and I like to think some of that rubbed off on me.

New Orleans was always an area for baseball talent. I grew up with some of those players and also played with some of them. There was Dr. Bobby Brown, who played for the Yankees; Connie Ryan, who played for the Braves; Putsy Caballero, who played for the Phillies; and Charlie Gilbert, who played for the Phillies and Dodgers.

There was Howie Pollett, who went on to pitch for the St. Louis Cardinals, and Larry LaSalle, who got a shot with Pittsburgh. Howie, Larry, and I were left-handed pitchers. Howie was a next-door neighbor. I played first base on our neighborhood team and Howie was always the pitcher.

Coming up, first base was my position. I didn't pitch at all except some batting practice when I was in high school. However, whenever I did that, everybody used to claim that my pitch was very much alive.

One day we were a little short of pitching. My coach asked if I would like to pitch. I said, "I'll do anything. I just want to play baseball." There were scouts from the Red Sox, Detroit, and St. Louis in the stands. They had come to see our leftfielder — a fellow by the name of Red Lavigne, a great looking prospect.

I pitched. I struck out seventeen.

My performance got the interest of the scouts and the organizations they represented. Herb Pennock, who had been a great pitcher and was a scout for the Red Sox, would come out to my house to talk to my dad. A very personable fellow, Pennock sat and talked baseball and expanded on his career. Branch Rickey, the general manager of the Cardinals, came over. He brought along Ray Blades, who was the manager of the ballclub, and Wid Mathews, who was his right-hand man. All three talked to me.

I wound up pitching batting practice to the New Orleans ball club, a Cardinals farm team. Blades gave me and two others who were on the high school team the "loan" of his tan Oldsmobile, which always had a full tank of gas. We were told to use the automobile carefully and at our discretion. The only thing we had to do was remember to drop it off at the ballpark the next morning.

The other two fellows signed with the Cardinals. One was a right-handed pitcher by the name of Ray Yochim. The other was the outfielder Red Lavigne. The Cardinals and the car probably didn't impress me as much as it did the other fellows.

St. Louis was very much interested in me, but the feeling was not mutual. I had been told that the Cardinals were loaded with ballplayers. They had two triple-A and two double-A teams in their farm system. It was said that you were more or less a number and not a name in that organization, because of all the players they had.

I was told that the Red Sox were another story. Herb Pennock brought along Ed Montague, who was the area scout. I signed for a $5,000 bonus and $125 a month in salary in the minors. I was seventeen years old. My father was very impressed and happy, too, hoping that I would now be able to fulfil my wish to become a professional baseball player.

I was sent in 1942 to Owensburg, Kentucky, to a team managed by Hugh Wyatt, who had been a catcher for the Braves. I was just a scrawny kid of 130 pounds when I reported. Wyatt looked at me and asked, "What are you supposed to do?"

I said, "Sir, I am supposed to pitch."

"I have four left-handed pitchers, and I certainly don't need a fifth," he said.

I was sent to Centerville, Maryland, in the Eastern Shore League, class-D. That team was short of outfielders, so one day early on I was put in rightfield and got two hits and drove in two runs. That made me as happy as a lark, because I thought I'd be playing every day after that. But word came down from the office of the Boston Red Sox: "Get that little skinny kid on the mound. He is a pitcher."

At first it was strange to be so young and away from home for the first time. But it got to be old hat. A ball club in the minor leagues then was very much like family, a bunch of young kids thrown together, there for one purpose — to play ball, to make a career for ourselves.

From Centerville, Maryland, I went to Canton, Ohio, and led the league in earned run average. Then I went into the Air Force and stayed there just short of four years.

When I came out of the service, I made contact with the Red Sox again. This was 1946. The Red Sox had so many ball players after the war that they did not know where to send us all. So they split us up. Half went to Scranton, Pennsylvania, in the Eastern League, and half went to Louisville, a triple-A team. I was assigned to Scranton in a real tough class-A.

Our Scranton team was outstanding. We had top players like Sam Mele, Don Johnson, Maury McDermott. It was said that we had enough talent to even beat Louisville, the triple-A ball cub. We finished in first place — nineteen games ahead of our closest competition. I led the league in earned run average.

The next year, 1947, I went to spring training at Sarasota, Florida, with the Red Sox. There were two spots open on the pitching staff, but there were six of us vying. I was aware all spring that I had to pitch as good as I could to have a chance to make the big league roster. Harry Dorish got one of the pitching spots. I got the other.

It was a thrill coming into Boston, which was similar to New Orleans in that it was a city that was small and had a lot of old history. I am Irish, as Irish as one can be. So I was a natural fit for the Red Sox and Boston. Yes, indeed, I fit in beautifully.

When I came into Fenway Park and saw that leftfield fence, I thought maybe I made a mistake and went to the wrong ballpark. But it helped me work on making a change in my pitching style. I came up as a fastball pitcher, but when I got into Fenway I realized I would have to use a lot more breaking stuff.

We had a very friendly ball club and got along very well together. I was treated fine, even though I was just a raw rookie. Baseball was quite different in those days than it is today. We traveled by train, and on a train there was nothing really to do other than eat your dinner, sit down, and talk baseball. We would talk about the opposition, about various situations that would occur.

I sure do recall my first major league game. It was April 20, 1947, against the old Washington Senators. Frankie Hayes, an old veteran player, was my catcher. I lost that game, 3–2, to Walter Masterson on a passed ball. I guess that's why I remember Frankie.

My first win in the big leagues was in Detroit. Hal Newhouser was pitching against us that day, and he was a great pitcher. He had a nine game winning streak going for him. I guess the Red Sox figured that Newhouser would collect his tenth victory that day. I was a rookie and they figured they'd throw me out there and try and get an idea of what I could do. It wound up that we beat Hal Newhouser 4–1.

Those two games, my first game, my first win, really stay with me through all the years. You don't forget them and many others.

The Red Sox owner, Mr. Yawkey, was like a father to all of us, we being young kids. He and Mrs. Yawkey were just fine people. It truly impressed me as a rookie kid to see Mr. Yawkey quite often come out on the field and take batting practice with us. He was a pretty heavy man at the time and was trying to shed some weight. The kids who worked around the ballpark would shag flies for him. When he was done, he would give each one a twenty-dollar bill.

To this day I never regretted anything that happened with me and the Red Sox. I enjoyed being able to play for Mr. Yawkey, who was a great owner. I enjoyed playing for Boston, a great baseball city. It was something special beginning a career with one team and staying with it through all those seasons.

JOHNNY PESKY

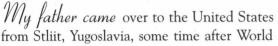

My father came over to the United States from Stliit, Yugoslavia, some time after World War I. He was with a bunch of guys who emigrated to America so they could get jobs to feed their families. The grandfather of the old Tigers pitcher, Mickey Lolich, was one of the guys in that group.

The route my father took was into New York, a stop in St. Louis, and then on to Oregon, because the logging camps were hiring people out there for the saw mills. My father got a job, along with a number of his cronies that he came over with.

I was born in 1919 in Portland, Oregon, which was a booming city of about 400,000 at the time. There were eight high schools. When we were kids growing up and going to school, we were considered Austrians. Later on we were considered Croatians. My Christian given name was John Michael Paveskovich.

"Pesky" was the nickname the kids came up with for me and called me. I went by that. It was kind of catchy, and it caught on. There was a writer in the Portland area by the name of Gregory, who said, "With a name like Paveskovich, you're going to have a tough time getting it into box scores." That also helped convince me that "Pesky" was the name to use.

I had a wonderful time as a kid. My parents were good, not overly strict. When things had to be done, they let you know where you stood. I had great brothers and sisters, and they all helped out.

The school furnished us with bats. We got books and read about the major league players. The first glove I had was a catcher's glove, even though I was a small guy and couldn't be a catcher. My favorite player became the great catcher Mickey Cochrane, because of the catcher's glove. I had a poster of him. Eventually, I got around to playing the infield and just played ball all the time. I started reading a lot about Charlie Gehringer, who was an infielder. Then I got a poster of him, and he became my favorite player.

I had read about superstitions and rituals players had. Quite a few of the kids I played with had some of those habits, too. But I never had anything serious like a lot of guys. Only small things. Like if our team's dugout was on the first base side, I would make sure I stepped on first base coming off the field from my shortstop position.

I never had a big dream of trying to make the major leagues. At that time the Pacific Coast League was close by. It really was quite the league. I thought that it would just be fine if I could make it there. But the more I played baseball, the more I dreamed of playing in the major leagues.

I played a little American Legion first. Then in high school I did all right. I made a couple of high school teams. I can't even remember being an All Star, but they tell me that I was.

When I was in high school, I was the clubhouse boy for a number of years for the Portland Beavers in the Pacific Coast League. The great Yankee pitcher Spud Chandler was on the team on a rehab, and I got to know him pretty well. He would tell me stories about the Yankees and the big league cities, and that whetted my appetite for the majors even more. Four guys who I liked a lot played in the Pacific Coast League — the three DiMaggio brothers and Bobby Doerr. Little did I dream that I would be on the Red Sox with two of those guys later on.

A few of those high school summers I played semipro baseball. One year I went up to Bend, Oregon. Another summer I stayed in a lumber camp in Silverton and played for the Silverton Red Sox. We competed against teams in a couple of leagues. A guy by the name of Bill McGinnis was the general manager of the camp and also the sponsor of that semipro team. He took good care of all of us, even though we were a mixed crew with kids like me out of high school, a couple out of college, and a couple of veteran players.

In Silverton, I earned a little extra money working as a groundskeeper. I was out there early fixing up the batter's box getting it ready for the six o'clock game of a tournament. My team was playing in the game after that. I was stripped down to my waist marking off home plate when this well-dressed guy came over.

"When does the Silverton club play?"

"They're playing the second game," I told him.

I just continued to fix the box, but he just stood there and continued to talk.

"I represent the St. Louis Browns," he said. "Do you play ball?"

"Yes, I do." I was really trying to get the batter's box ready for the game and didn't have that much time to talk. But the guy continued to ask questions about how much I liked baseball, what position I played, what my name was.

When I gave him the name, "Johnny Pesky," that did it.

"Jeez," he said, "I'm here to check you out."

And he did. He was just one of a lot of them who came to look me and others over. There were a lot of scouts out there from different teams.

My father did not know anything about baseball. He knew about bocci. A mixture of Italians and Slavs played it with him. He spoke very little English. He read the Slav papers but could not decipher the English ones. My brothers and sisters helped him out. When the scouts came to talk to my parents about me, either my older sister or brother would sit there and would more or less interpret for them.

Ernie Johnson, from the Babe Ruth era, was a scout with the Red Sox. He impressed me. He spent a lot of time in my home talking with my parents. He made an offer.

The guy from St. Louis who came to see me play at Silverton where I was the groundskeeper also came around. He offered more money than the Red Sox did.

But my mother said, "Mr. Johnson, Boston, is where you are going, John." She was impressed with him and the Red Sox. She really picked my ball club for me. I was given $500 to sign. This was late thirties, early forties. There was no money around, so that was good money.

The Red Sox paid me $150 a month for my first year in the minor leagues. The contract I signed said that if I stayed in the organization for two years I would get another thousand dollars. But they were nice. After the first year, they gave me the thousand dollars.

After I signed as a pro, I had a pretty good year my first season with Rocky Mount in 1940 in the old Piedmont League. The old outfielder Heinie Manush, who had played seventeen seasons in the majors, was my manager. It was Heinie who had a great influence on how I played the game. He was a great guy to be around who knew his baseball. He did a couple of corrections with me.

The next year, 1941, I went to Louisville. The next year I was with

Boston in spring training in Sarasota. Eddie Pellagrini, who had played in San Diego in 1941, and I battled for the shortstop job.

Manager Joe Cronin played Eddie one day, and he played me the next. He gave us the same opportunity. I was doing pretty well. Eddie was doing okay, too. Finally, cut-down time was coming. Joe sent Pelly to Louisville. But he never did tell me I had made the ball club.

We were in Kentucky playing an exhibition game because we played exhibition games coming north. We played against Cincinnati. Johnny Vander Meer was pitching. I hit a ball to right-centerfield for a triple. Cronin came over to me, and he said, "Kid, you just made the ball club."

I got to play. Joe let me play. That was how it all started in 1942.

Being in Boston, being in Fenway was just wonderful. We played the old Boston Braves, a city series. It was one game at Fenway and one game at the old Braves Field. We played one of the games on a Sunday. The season was going to open on a Tuesday. The day was cold and rainy and snowy. This was in the middle of April. I made four errors and felt just terrible about it. I thought Cronin was going to call me in the next day and send me to either Scranton or Louisville.

But he didn't say anything to me. The season started. I hit behind Dominic DiMaggio and in front of Ted Williams. I hung on Ted and Dominic's coattails. I was at shortstop. I made sure I got in front of every ball and tried to catch or knock it down. I think I went about eighteen games before I made an error.

My first major league game was April 14, 1942. My first hit in the big leagues was a single off Phil Marchildon, a pitcher with the Athletics who won seventeen games that year.

The first time I saw Fenway Park it was dark and dreary. That was for the exhibition game against the Braves. I didn't even look around much. I was mainly concerned about playing as well as I could and about keeping warm.

But Opening Day was when I saw it, in a matter of speaking, for the first time. It was a beautiful day. I came up the runway up the three steps and looked out from the dugout. It felt I was going into paradise. It was an old park even at that time, but it was very well kept, clean and nice. And right in the middle of the city.

That rookie season of 1942 I finished one-two with Williams in the batting title race. But no contest there. He was such a great hitter. I hit .331. He hit .356. I wasn't even close, even though it was still one-two. I led the American League in hits with 205 — the first of three straight years that I did that. The guys called me "Needlenose." They said that was an affectionate nickname. They could have called me whatever they wanted. It was just wonderful being in the majors.

TODD PRATT

$\mathcal{I}$ *was born in* Bellevue, Nebraska, in 1967, but my parents got divorced when I was five, and my mom moved me out to San Diego. My mother used to teach me how to play baseball in the backyard. When I was old enough to sign up for Little League, she's the one who said, "OK, it's time. Do you want to play Little League?"

I said, "Yeah."

I played shortstop, pitched, played outfield. Wherever they needed me, I played. I wasn't very good at the ages of seven, eight, or nine. I remember I would be striking out all the time. Of course, I broke down crying. I always used to cry when I struck out.

There were times I would be trying to catch a fly ball in the outfield, and I would get hit right in the face with the ball. I remember my mom taking me home saying, "You're going to be all right, just keep playing."

As soon as I reached ten years of age, I suddenly got better. My talents started being noticed. I was always the best player on the team after that. There was this kid on our team that threw so hard that nobody wanted to catch him. I said, "I'll try." All I had to do was catch the ball. It hurt my hand, but I wasn't afraid. From then on, I was a catcher. I was eleven years old.

I played all sports, really excelling in football and basketball. Football, not baseball, was my favorite sport. Baseball takes so much time and so much practice to get really good, whereas in football you just put on the gear and play aggressive. But as time marched along, I played baseball more and more, got more interested in the game. I think playing all sports helped me with baseball.

While other kids were going to the malls or checking out a matinee, I was out there on those summer days from eight o'clock in the morning until eight o'clock at night playing baseball. There was a park next to the baseball fields. We were a bunch of kids who would just meet at the park and have seven-on-seven pickup games. There was a trailer all the way in the back of the park. We would use that as a target in deep centerfield.

Oh, yes, those were the great days of baseball — the camaraderie, the friends. Obviously, you couldn't have a catcher suited up. You couldn't have batting practice. But we did have soft throw. Boy, we also did get into the game and whacked that ball. There were times when we would have to dodge picnickers and barbecue grills. But that didn't seem to bother anyone. It seemed like the adults loved watching the kids play out there. It was a great time in my life.

A lot of my playing also took place out in my street. I'd play "Stickball Out" using a tape-ball and a Wiffle ball bat. The curb addresses would be bases. There were also days when I'd grab a 4x8 piece of plywood and set it up in my front yard against the fence. I'd paint a square on it for a strike zone. Then I'd throw a tennis ball for an hour or two and just play a game by myself. I'd pretend that Steve Garvey was up. There were a lot of times that I'd play by myself.

I liked the Padres, but the Dodgers were winning back then, in the late 1970s, so that was the team I grew up watching. I remember the duels against the Yankees. But I didn't watch much baseball because I was out playing it.

I used to play with eighteen-year-olds when I was fifteen in a summer pickup league. I still remember playing when I was sixteen years old with Kevin Mitchell, who was already in the Mets organization. It was the guys who were good in junior high school and high school against the minor leaguers. We'd also play against college players, too. I remember scouts talking to me there.

By my senior year at Hilltop High School in Chula Vista, I had a good feeling that I would be drafted. There were a lot of college scouts that were watching me, too. There would be ten or twelve scouts at every game that I'd play in. There were a few scouts that said I was a potential first-, second-, or third-round pick.

I was selected by the Boston Red Sox organization in the sixth round of the free-agent draft on June 3, 1985. I think I was the fiftieth high school player taken. When Ray Boone, the signing scout, called and said I was drafted by the Boston Red Sox, it was a great experience for me and my mom.

But getting to the majors was a very long haul — seven years in the minors. I finally made my major league debut, not with the Red Sox but with the Philadelphia Phillies, in July of 1992. They threw me in there right away. I got called up. The next day I started against Sid Fernandez of the Mets. I had a lot of butterflies. It was a day game in the middle of summer, so Veterans Stadium was packed. I went 0-for-3, but I played good defensively. It was just an incredible feeling being a major league baseball player at last.

JEFF REED

My favorite team growing up was the Baltimore Orioles, back when they had that great pitching staff in the 1970s. Believe it or not, the reason I picked them was I liked their uniforms. They were a good team back then, too. They were always in the play-offs and the World Series. The Big Red Machine — I liked them, too, with Pete Rose, Johnny Bench, and Tony Perez.

I grew up outside Chicago, so I also liked the White Sox. My buddies were all Cubs fans, so I had to go for the South-siders. They had some good teams back then, too.

I grew up in Joliet, Illinois, where I was born on November 12, 1962. I started playing baseball in the backyard when I was four or five with my dad and my brother, who was a little older than me. I was fortunate to have an older brother to play with, to learn from. My dad would pitch to me. My brother would shag. I'd shag for my brother. My dad would hit us ground balls by the hour. We played a lot of pepper in the backyard.

When I was nine, I started playing Little League. I was put out into the outfield because I was one of the younger players on the team. I wasn't one of the best players right away. I wasn't that strong. I also played a little bit of third base. The coach practiced us a lot, and we were out there all the time. Our team was really good, and we won it all that year.

My brother, Curt, was twelve years old and one of the better players on the team. He wound up playing minor league ball for nine or ten years and got all the way up to triple-A. In my growing-up years, Curt was a big help to me. I always played on his teams. Since he was a lot better than me, that pushed me to become better.

My dad was really into baseball, not only with coaching, which he did a lot. He was also very much into equipment. He got us a batting cage and a pitching machine when I was maybe twelve. We'd go back there and hit every day. That sort of fueled the fire right there, because you want to play.

We would have games where we'd hit for distance. We had a hedge around our yard, and we made up baseball rules to fit it. A ball hit over the hedge was a home run. We'd play maybe six, seven, eight kids on a team. We just kind of rotated hitting and pitching and fielding. It was baseball, baseball, baseball.

When I got to high school, my brother was the shortstop on the varsity team, so I played first base as a freshman. When he graduated, I moved to shortstop and pitcher. My senior year was the first year I caught.

Our high school team had some pretty good ballplayers. There were all kinds of scouts watching my brother. When I was a freshman, Bill Gullickson was a senior. The scouts came to see him, but they also were watching me. They wrote my name down. Then there were a lot who came back to watch me when I was a junior and senior.

When I was a kid, I always dreamed of being drafted by a major league team. You can dream, but you don't really believe it can happen to you until you see somebody else in your area get drafted. My brother was drafted in the twelfth round. When that happened, I thought there was a great chance that I could be. I really got hungry for it. I really started working very hard.

The Minnesota Twins wound up drafting me in the first round, twelfth pick overall, of the 1980 free-agent draft. It was unbelievable. I was fortunate — I went in the first round. It was the best dream come true, having the opportunity to play pro ball and getting drafted in the first round. I got a little bit of a bonus.

I began my pro career with a rookie league affiliate for the Minnesota Twins in 1980. From there, a lot of stops along the way — Wisconsin Rapids, Visalia, Orlando, Toledo, Indianapolis, Nashville, San Jose. It took me ten years before I played a full season in the major leagues.

BILLY ROGELL

The name I was born with way back in 1904 on November 24 was William George Rogell. But as I grew, everybody called me "Billy." My professional baseball playing career began in 1923 with Coffeyville, Kansas, in the Southwestern League. That team released me after just six weeks.

That was all right with me. I went to Chicago and lived with my sister for the rest of that season. In 1924, I was back in the Southwestern League, this time with Salina. I batted .317. The Boston Red Sox purchased my contract and in spring training of 1925, I hit almost .400. Manager Lee Fohl kept me. They paid me three hundred bucks a month my rookie season in the big leagues, but it was the big leagues. I wore number 7. I always wore lucky number 7.

I live in Florida now. I was glad to be around at age ninety-six as the world saw the year 2000 come in. I have a lot of baseball memories, a lot of all kinds of memories.

AL ROSEN

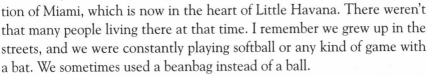

$\mathcal{I}$ *was born in* Spartanburg, South Carolina, but my family moved to the Miami area when I was three years old. I grew up in the southwest sec-tion of Miami, which is now in the heart of Little Havana. There weren't that many people living there at that time. I remember we grew up in the streets, and we were constantly playing softball or any kind of game with a bat. We sometimes used a beanbag instead of a ball.

In those days you didn't get much baseball information except through the newspapers. There were two papers — the *Miami Herald* and the *Miami Daily News*. Box scores were a very real part of my growing up. Looking at the box scores in the paper, the line scores, all of that was al-ways very fascinating to me. The baseball news and box scores were dom-inated by the Yankees. My earliest memory was that everybody became a Yankee fan because of all of the terrific teams they had and players like Babe Ruth, Lou Gehrig, and all the other greats.

I had two favorite players: Lou Gehrig and Hank Greenberg. I probably liked Greenberg because I was Jewish and he was Jewish. Why else would I have picked Hank Greenberg and not Babe Ruth? But Gehrig? He was and is my all-time favorite.

I grew up without a father and was raised by three women: my grand-mother, my mother, and my aunt. My grandmother stayed home with my brother and I, and my mother and aunt worked all the time, as did my brother and I.

On my twelfth birthday, I can remember that I was given two choices for a present by my grandmother — a baseball glove or a guitar. I picked the baseball glove. It was my first glove, and it cost $15.

I was an asthmatic as a child. In those days, they didn't have the things they do today to treat asthmatics. The doctor said that the best thing for me was to be outside in the fresh air as much as possible. So my mother and my grandmother and aunt were always pushing me to compete. They didn't have to push very hard, because I was always a much better athlete than I was a student.

Growing up, I was fortunate that I could compete with anybody in whatever sport I played. I played just about every sport. My first exposure to any kind of a baseball league was the American Legion. There was a junior program for kids ten to twelve years old. At thirteen, you'd move on to the American Legion program. Primarily, I played softball until I got to play in the junior American Legion. It was all the times I pitched in softball games on Miami's sandlots that I earned the nickname "Flip." That was because I did a lot of quick wrist snapping.

I went to Miami Senior High. One day early in my freshman year after football practice, a bunch of us kids, all friends, jumped into the car of the assistant coach. The plan was for one after another of us to peel off as the car got to near where a kid lived. I was sitting on the knees of a friend in the back. There were six of us in the back and three in the front.

The coach turned around and looked at me. "Rosen, what are you doing going out for football?"

It was sort of a startling question. But I had a ready answer: "Because I love it."

"I didn't think you Jew boys liked contact," he snapped back.

I could not believe what I had heard. I didn't understand it then, and I don't understand it now. Some of my friends took such great exception. They were really furious about the whole thing, because in south Florida at that time, other than Miami Beach, where there were signs that said "No Jews or Dogs Allowed," the southwest section of Miami was just working class people. In fact, there were no Jewish kids in our neighborhood, which was made up primarily of people of Greek descent, Irish descent.

I won't get into what I felt like doing to that assistant coach. However, I let the whole thing pass. But for the first time, I truly became aware of how some people felt about Jews.

Despite what he said, I played football all through high school. I played football, basketball, baseball, and I boxed. In my junior and senior years, I went to Florida Military Academy in St. Petersburg on a scholarship. There I began to box even more. All the boxing I did probably added to my image as a tough guy. I don't know how tough I was. I do know as an amateur boxer, I had my nose broken eleven times.

But the sport I really loved and did well in was baseball. I had an over-whelming desire to continue on in life in a baseball career. In my senior year at Florida Military Academy, I occasionally dated this girl. Her father was a golf professional from Ohio who had some baseball connections. He got me a tryout with the Cleveland Indians Wilkes-Barre farm club. The only problem was the team was training in Sumpter, South Carolina.

During spring break in 1941, I got on a train and traveled all night to Sumpter. I played shortstop at that time and worked out at that position the next day with the Wilkes-Barre team. Then I played for them in a doubleheader. I went 0-for-8.

Surprisingly, I was offered a contract for $75 a month. I turned that down. I wanted to go back to school. I also knew, along with everyone else, that the United States would be at war and that when that happened I was going to either enlist or be drafted.

I attended the University of Florida in the September session of 1941–42. I boxed there, played basketball and baseball. I decided then that I really wanted to make a career for myself in pro baseball.

I paid my own way going to a Boston Red Sox farm club in Virginia that was under the auspices of Herb Pennock, the former great left-handed pitcher for the Red Sox, who was their farm director. After I had worked out three or four days, the manager of the team called me into his hotel room.

"Young man," he said, "you're never going to be a baseball player. You better go on home and get a lunch pail. I mean it."

I was crushed. I went back to my room and told the fellow I was room-ing with what the manager had said. "That's crazy," my roomie said. "You can play. You know, there is a scout, Frank Stein, who runs the YMCA here. He told me that he has been watching you play, and he really likes you."

I met with Frank Stein and learned that the third baseman on the Thomasville, North Carolina, team in the North Carolina State League had broken his leg. I went down there on a long bus trip and was told to find Jimmy Gruzdis, the manager of the team. Some way or other I found him. I drove down with him to a gas station. While Gruzdis was getting gasoline, he opened up the glove compartment and got out a contract. I signed right then and there for $90 a month. Amazing! I wound up going to the same town, the same league, that Cleveland wanted to send me to the year before for $75 a month, so my holdout netted me $15 a month more.

I played one half season at Thomasville and then went into the navy. There I played more baseball and did some boxing. When I came out of the service, I was under contract to Cleveland, which had a working agreement with Thomasville, the team I played for before I went into the navy.

The Indians assigned me to a spring training base. I reported in full dress uniform and signed a contract to play for Pittsfield, Massachusetts, in the Canadian-American League. That was the beginning of my trek to the big leagues.

I went from Pittsfield to Oklahoma City. At the end of that season, I was invited up to the big leagues. I joined the Cleveland Indians in New York in September of 1947. My first major league at bat was against the lefty Joe Page. I pinch hit. I struck out on three pitches.

But it was not until 1950, after what seemed like forever in the minors for me, that my time finally came. I became a regular for Cleveland. I hit thirty-seven home runs my rookie season, a record for rookies until Mark McGwire came along and broke it thirty-seven years later.

All through the climb to the big leagues, my aunt Sari kept a scrapbook of every game I ever played in starting in North Carolina. She was a great booster, as was my mother who remarried and lived in New York. She would come to all of the games I played at Yankee Stadium and kvell that her boy had made it.

NOLAN RYAN

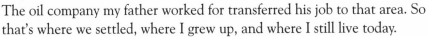

I was born in Refugio, Texas, on January 31, 1947, the youngest of six children. When I was only six weeks old, the family moved east to Alvin. The oil company my father worked for transferred his job to that area. So that's where we settled, where I grew up, and where I still live today.

My brother, Robert, was something of a hero to me, being a few years older and more advanced in athletics. I'd hang around with Robert and his friends, shag flies for them, sometimes get into a game when they were shy a player. I'd practice a lot with Robert in our backyard. We would pitch to each other. He'd catch me, and I'd catch him.

Some people claim that I developed my arm throwing the *Houston Post*. That was not the case. It was a short throw from a car, and I made the throw backhanded with my left hand while I steered my 1952 Chevy with my right. But I did develop the knack of being able to roll and tie fifty newspapers in just about five minutes, and that probably helped me develop strong fingers and wrists.

We got our first TV set, a Philco, in 1953, and I remember watching the "Game of the Week" with Dizzy Dean. He was colorful. That was the only baseball we got except what you heard on the radio. Major league baseball was far removed. The only team you could pick up was the St. Louis Cardinals on KMOX.

But when major league baseball came to Houston later on, I really got into the habit of following Colt .45 games. And I would lie in bed on those hot summer nights, listening to the radio and picturing the action. My favorite players at that time, though, were not on Houston and not pitchers. They were outfielders. Hank Aaron was one of them. I admired him because of his power and his durability. I also especially liked Roberto Clemente. He was what I thought an athlete should be. He was driven and put every bit of himself into what he was doing.

My first organized sports experience was in Little League. The first field in Alvin was cleared and built by my dad and the other fathers of the kids in the program. I played Little League from the time I was nine years old until I was thirteen. Some of my fondest memories of baseball come from those years.

I had heard that my dad was a pretty fair ballplayer in his time during the depression. As a Little League parent, he was always there when I needed him. My dad was just interested in my having a good organized sports experience.

Making the Little League team was a thrill for all us kids in Alvin. When we got our caps and uniforms, we'd be so proud we'd wear the caps to school. That was a big deal. We played our games in the Texas heat in those old heavy flannel uniforms, but no one seemed to pay the weather any heed.

I was a good player, not a great player, although I did pitch a no-hitter in Little League and was on the All Star-team as an eleven- and twelve-year-old. I didn't develop great pitching velocity until my sophomore year in high school.

One year after our Little League team had been eliminated from tournament play, I remember standing on the field for the closing ceremony. The man who was presenting the awards gave a little talk. "One day," he said, "one of you Little Leaguers will go on to play in the major leagues."

When I heard what he said, it was like a bell went off in my head. I got home and told my mom about the ceremony and what the man said. "Mom," I said, "that man was talking about me."

"What do you mean?" she asked.

"It's me that he meant, Mom. I'm sure it was me he was talking about."

There were under six hundred kids in my high school, and you knew almost everyone. All I thought about in high school was basketball, not baseball. I was 6'2", but I was the center on the team because I was a good jumper.

In baseball, they said I could throw a ball through a wall, but I had a lot of problems with control. I was so tall and skinny and raw that I didn't pay much attention to being scouted. I had no idea that I could ever play in the big leagues.

One Sunday between my junior and senior years in high school, we went to see the Houston Colt .45s play the Los Angeles Dodgers. Sandy Koufax was pitching, and I was a big Koufax fan. It was the first time I had a box seat and the first time I had ever seen Sandy pitch. I was truly amazed at how fast he was and how good a curveball he had. I think he was the most overpowering pitcher I have ever seen.

My senior year in high school, 1965, I went to the Astrodome. It was the year it opened. I watched these major leaguers play. They were so much older and more polished than I was. I never considered myself on their level.

Throughout high school I was in my own world, having fun on Friday and Saturday nights playing ball. Going to the majors was not a big item as far as I was concerned. Scouts came through and checked me out and didn't have the interest. There were no radar guns — I didn't know how fast I was. I was so wild. I was just a kid with a great arm. I didn't know what I had.

No one did — only Red Murff, who was a scout for the New York Mets then. I was selected in the eighth round of the 1965 free-agent draft, the 295th player taken. I was pretty disappointed. It was like they were sending me a message that 294 high school players had a better chance of making the majors than I did.

My first stop in organized baseball was Marion, Virginia, in the Appalachian Rookie League. I was eighteen years old and had never been away from home. Some of our trips on those old broken-down buses lasted almost eight hours, and the conditions in some of those ball parks — awful — rough fields, poor lighting, no showers.

The season there began very late so that high school and college players signed after graduation would have a place to play. That summer of 1965, more than seventy players passed through the Marion roster. I lasted the whole season. Pitching in thirteen games, I won three and lost six and struck out 115 batters in seventy-eight innings. In the dim light, to a lot of nervous kids, I guess I was a little dangerous to hit against. I gave up fifty-six walks and hit eight batters.

The following spring, 1966, I was assigned to Greenville, South Carolina, in the Western Carolina League. I earned $600 a month there, $100 more than the year before. The conditions were a bit primitive, cramped, and there were dirty dressing rooms, bus road trips every other day. My wildness was still with me, and the word was out that I frightened some batters and catchers alike with my velocity. I wound up with 272 strikeouts, 127 walks, and seventeen wins — all league highs. I had a great year, losing just two games, the least in the league.

When the season ended, I was promoted to Williamsport, Pennsylvania, in the double-A Eastern League. It was only ten days, but a lot happened. I struck out thirty-five batters in nineteen innings. On September 1, 1966, I had the greatest game of my career up to that point in time — striking out nineteen batters in nine innings against Pawtucket. I wound up with twenty-one strikeouts in ten innings but lost the game 2–1.

I was very excited about what I had accomplished in the minors, but I was even more excited by the thought of pitching in the majors, throwing against major league hitters. I'd been told that I would join the Mets after September 1 — the date major league teams called up prospects from the minors for the final month of the season — and I was looking forward to trying out my fastball against top hitters.

In my last start for Williamsport, I was scheduled to pitch just four innings and then get on a plane and fly to LaGuardia Airport to join the New York Mets. I had a no-hitter going through four.

When I returned to the dugout, my manager, Bill Virdon, said, "You've got to be going to report to the Mets, but you've given up no hits. Do you want to continue pitching in this game and go for the no-hitter?"

"Mr. Virdon," I told him, "if it's all right with you, I'd just as soon move on to New York City."

I was excited to be in New York City but also a bit awed by the whole thing. I had come all the way from A ball to the major leagues in one season and had attracted a lot of fanfare. Players would say, "Wait till you see this kid Ryan pitch. Wait till you see his arm." And I felt I had to go out there and show everybody how hard I could throw. It was the mentality of the gunfighter, the fastest gun in the West.

I guess it was easy for Wes Westrum, the manager of the Mets, to pick all of that up. He told me, "Nolan, you're up here just for us to take a look at you. Your major league future does not depend on how you do. Just do the best you can."

His words helped me relax a little, but only a little. Shea Stadium was a noisy place with jets always roaring overhead from LaGuardia Airport. That was unsettling. The Mets drew about 25,000 a game — five times more people than lived in my hometown of Alvin. When the games began, I would sit out in the bullpen with the extra catchers and relief pitch-ers. Sometimes my mind would drift back to thoughts of home.

My first major league appearance was on September 11, 1966, against the Braves. I had a big case of stage fright walking out of the bullpen and stepping on the mound knowing I would be pitching to players like Hank Aaron, Eddie Mathews, and Joe Torre.

But I got through it, giving up a home run to Joe Torre — but also get-ting my first major league strikeout. The batter was Pat Jarvis, a rookie pitcher for Atlanta.

That first time on a major league mound was a big learning experience for me. Hank Aaron said I had one of the best fastballs he had ever seen. But one of the best fastballs I'd ever thrown was hit for a home run by Joe Torre. I learned the hard way that it would not be possible to get by in the major leagues with just a fastball, no matter how hard it was thrown.

RON SANTO

My father was born in Italy, my mother was born in Sweden, and I was born in Seattle, Washington, in a neighborhood called Gurley Gulch, on February 25, 1940. My father was a merchant marine and an alcoholic. He and my mother got divorced when I was six years old.

After the divorce, my father picked me up for about three straight weekends. Then he stopped. I did not see him again until I was nineteen. He had been a kind of a sandlot type player and was the first one to put a glove in my hand. The only reason I know this is that I have a picture from the time I was two years old with the glove he got me.

By the age of seven I knew that I was good in baseball. I did not know how good I was, but I knew I was good. At that time you could not start Little League until the age of eight, but my mom lied for me. I started playing at the age of seven — shortstop and pitcher for the Italian club. That was a kick. Ironically, Joey Jay was the first player out of Little League to make the major leagues. I was the second.

All through those early years, my brother and I would play a lot of baseball in the garage in the building where we lived. He would throw as hard as he could to me at the end of the garage. In order to get a base hit, you had to hit line drives out of the garage. You couldn't touch the garage. That was a way for me very early on to develop a batting stroke. I was always concerned with quickness with the bat.

At the age of twelve, when most kids are still in Little League, I was playing in the Babe Ruth League. I moved to American Legion at age fourteen.

We had triple-A baseball, not major league baseball, in our area. I followed the Seattle Rainiers, a Cincinnati farm team. I grew up around their ballpark first as an usher and then as a batboy for the team from my freshman year in high school on. I also worked on the grounds crew.

My favorite player probably was Mickey Mantle because he was on the Yankees, and they were always winning the World Series. I watched the

"Game of the Week" on TV — National League on Saturday, American League on Sunday.

While I attended Franklin High School, there was a bird-dog scout for the Cubs, Dave Kochher, who was always looking me over. He was a spastic, slurred his words, was in a wheelchair. But he was a great guy and knew his baseball. We became good friends.

"Son," he told me when I was a sophomore in high school, "one day you will be playing in the big leagues in Wrigley Field."

I had a very good high school athletic career — was All City in baseball and football. A lot of scouts were coming around from both sports. But baseball was my first love and so were the Cubs. I jumped at the chance to sign a contract with them — as a catcher. Some clubs offered me three or four times what the Cubs offered. But back then, some teams had fifteen to twenty minor league teams. You could spend an entire career trying to get a shot at the majors without getting noticed. Dave Kochher told me I could get there fastest with the Cubs.

Right out of high school, I went to a three-week rookie camp. Then I was with the Cubs for my first spring training in 1959. I couldn't believe it. There were seven other prospective catchers around at that time all looking to make it with the Cubs. Third baseman Alvin Dark was nearing the end of his career, so Cubs manager Bob Scheffing suggested that I switch to third base, a position I had played a lot of in high school. I agreed. They sent me down to double-A ball in 1959 where I hit .324 with some ninety RBIs.

That next year I went to spring training as a non-roster player. Manager Cholly Grimm told me that I had made the club. But then the Cubs made a late spring trade for Don Zimmer from the Dodgers, and I was sent out. I was very upset. I was nineteen years old, and I was going to quit baseball. That was how angry I was. But I was talked out of it.

Mid-season, I was called up by the new manager of the Cubs, Lou Boudreau, who went from the broadcast booth to the field. The day he became manager, he brought me up.

My first game was June 26, 1960, at Forbes Field. It was a doubleheader against Bob Friend in the first game and Vern Law in the second. I was hitting sixth. I walked to the plate. I was so nervous. There were 40,000 people in the stands. The first pitch was a breaking ball. I kind of backed off. It was called a strike on the inside corner of the plate. Smokey Burgess was the catcher for the Pirates. As he threw the ball back to Friend, he looked at me and said, "That's a big league curveball."

I stepped back. I was so nervous that my hands were shaking. Then Friend threw me a fastball. I hit it right up the middle — a line drive past his ear for a base hit. Getting to first base was like the whole world and its weight just fell off my shoulders. I went 4-for-7, drove in five runs. We swept the doubleheader.

At age twenty, I was poised to be a starter on the Cubs. It went through my mind that Vada Pinson had been a top player for Seattle in my home town, that I had shined his shoes in the clubhouse. He left for the major leagues in 1958. Now I had gone from shining his shoes to playing against him in the major leagues.

MIKE SCIOSCIA

$\mathcal{I}$ *grew up in* Philadelphia, where I was born on November 27, 1958. I was eight years old the first time I played organized baseball. It was called the farm league. We played in blue jeans and a T-shirt — that was the uniform.

I played nonstop baseball through so many summers. This was from the time I was eight years old until I was seventeen. We would play with a tennis ball in our driveway, three guys on a side. Our driveway had some power wires over and across it, and there were some on the other side of the street, too. If you cleared ours, it was a double. If you cleared the wires on the other side of the street, it was a home run. If a ground ball didn't get past a certain point, it was an out. Those were intricate rules for kids and sometimes led to big arguments.

I was a Phillies fan. Willie Montanez was my favorite player. The Phillies weren't playing very well at that time, but Willie Montanez was one bright, shining spot on the club. He had a good following. It seemed to me that he just had a flair. He hit like twenty-nine or thirty home runs, and everybody in the city liked him.

I remember when I was ten, my dad said, if you want to play baseball — he wasn't thinking professionally, he was talking about Little League, high school, or wherever — the best chance you have to play is catcher.

So I started catching. I didn't have a lot of range, I couldn't play the infield, I couldn't play the outfield. With catching, I was quick and I had a good arm, so it was a good position for me. I loved it.

Any youngster who plays Little League, the dream is to play on TV, play in the big leagues. I know that when I was Little League age, we all said, "Yeah, we're going to play in the big leagues."

I wasn't the best player on our team. I couldn't run very fast. I could hit a little bit. I had a good arm. But I certainly wasn't the best athlete. Probably when I was about fifteen, my body became more coordinated. I grew into my body a little bit, and I started to be a guy who was reaching his potential. I was more of a late bloomer.

At that time I started to play in a couple of men's leagues and a semipro league. In those leagues there were a lot of college players and a lot of guys in their mid-twenties. I was playing in three leagues in the summer. That's when I started to move up ahead of some guys I had grown up with.

Throughout high school I was scouted. I was very much aware of that. In 1976, at age seventeen, I was drafted by the Dodgers. I didn't really understand the system that well as far as scouting, signing, drafting — all that. But I understood that there were some big decisions to make.

I was offered a scholarship to go to Clemson University. I had the Dodgers and the future they were offering. I had to choose which direction I wanted to go in. I decided that if I wanted to give professional baseball a crack, I wanted to get into it as early as I could. The Dodgers also agreed to pay for my education, so I figured it was the best of both worlds.

I played four and a half years in the minor leagues. In 1980, in spring training I was the last player cut. I was sent to triple-A Albuquerque. But then two weeks later I was recalled.

I was twenty-one years old. I got a double my first at bat on April 20, 1980, scored a run, and we won 4–3. It's a realization of a dream, but you also realize that it's just the beginning. A lot of people get called up to the big leagues, but to stay and play, it's a different story.

CHUCK STEVENS

There was no major league baseball back then in California when I grew up. You're talking way back. I was born in Long Beach, July 10, 1918.

I can vividly recall playing baseball in grammar school, intramural. Number one, we were fans of the game, and we did everything possible to represent the game to the best of our ability and integrity. My idols as a kid were the people who salvaged the game — Babe Ruth and Commissioner Landis. People might disagree with me, but I feel the game would have been in shambles if not for them. I also had a first base idol, Lou Gehrig. I followed what he did on the baseball field very closely.

As I said, there was no major league baseball around when I was a kid growing up in Long Beach. I heard baseball on the radio occasionally. But come World Series time the *Long Beach Press Telegram* or the *Long Beach Sun* — I can't remember which one — had this massive scoreboard, I'd say it was two stories high. On it was a big magnetic board with a baseball diamond. The direct ticker tape from the World Series would come in. And the game would be replayed on that magnetic board. There would be literally hundreds of people seated or standing around watching this "ballgame." For many, that was the next best thing to being at the World Series.

I had it in my mind that I would someday like to play in the World Series and have these hundreds watching me on that big board or in the ballpark. But that was every kid's dream, not only the dream of Chuck Stevens.

Long Beach was a hotbed of baseball. At one time out of that town of 165,000, there were eleven people who went up to the major leagues. During my growing-up years alone there were probably seven or eight in the major leagues. It was an inspiration to me.

In Long Beach we were fortunate in having two guys, both bachelors, who devoted their entire lives to kids. One was Mike Romero; the other was Bob Hughes. Both had minor league backgrounds and gave us sophisticated teaching that was not available in high school. They developed fifty or sixty people — Bob Lemon, the Hall of Famer; Vern Stephens, who should be in the Hall of Fame; Bobby Grich; Bob Bailey; and so on.

Players who had been trained by Romero and Hughes also gave back to the community. When they were getting ready for pro ball spring training, they were good enough to take time off to talk to us kids and coach us. You couldn't put a dollar value on all of the information we got from these seasoned players. We also worked out together with them.

Although we were all depression people, we had state-of-the-art equipment for that time. It's laughable, but looking back — my first baseman's glove was the best one available. It was about a quarter of the size of the present-day glove. The main body was solid. This was all way before the claws and the fancy webbings that later developed. But with that small Reach glove, I was able to earn a reputation all over Long Beach as a pretty good fielder.

My high school days were in the thirties. From my high school starting nine, six of us went on to pro ball. I played first base for our team. Vern Stephens, a shortstop, was at second base because he couldn't beat out a guy named Bob Sturgeon, who later played six, seven years with the Cubs. We had a third baseman who played triple-A ball in the Dodger organization. Probably the best prospect in the bunch was a centerfielder named Dick Lang, but he was injured in the war and was never able to compete later on. Jack Brewer was a pitcher with the Giants for several years.

Out of high school, I attended Cal-Berkeley briefly. The opportunity to sign a bonus contract with the St. Louis Browns came up. I was eighteen. I snapped at the chance, becoming the first bonus player to come out of Long Beach.

I spent my first minor league baseball season in North Carolina. Each year I moved up in classification. I gave myself a limit of four years to make the majors when I first signed. At the end of the fourth year, my contract was purchased by the Browns.

I got in a year in the majors. Then the war was on. I lost three or four years to the military. No excuses. I was lucky considering the alternative. But my time away from baseball may have taken a little of the bloom off. I was never real successful in the major leagues. I never really achieved what I thought I was capable of.

It was the worst of times. It was the best of times. It was the worst of times because it was the depression and there were few ball clubs to play for. It was the best of times because those of us who were privileged to play before the war, during the war, and shortly after the war all remained very good friends.

Those are my reflections of growing up in the game. I only played in 211 major league games and batted .251. But I was in the game itself for sixty years plus.

BOB TEWKSBURY

I came into the American dream through baseball. Materialistically, it gave me everything I have. I was born November 30, 1960, and grew up in the small town of Salisbury in New Hampshire.

In the very early spring when I was growing up, I would force my brother to go out with me and play catch in the snow. I still have memories of waiting for spring to finally bloom, of chasing balls through the snow banks. I still have memories of wet baseballs.

You tried to play as much as you could. I did a lot on my own like throwing balls against the school-yard walls and hitting rocks into the woods up in the country. That was baseball for me.

I lived with my family in an apartment for a time. Then we lived in town for a while in a single trailer. There were three kids, and all of us slept in one corner of the trailer. My dad was an auto mechanic. My mom was kind of a baby sitter for some local moms. It was kind of hand-to-mouth existence. A common theme in my family was: "We don't have the money for that."

Never a new car, always a fixed-up car, a used car. We went through bankruptcy a couple of times. We eventually moved to a double trailer in the same spot that the single trailer had been on. There was talk and dreams of having a finished basement, but all that went by the wayside because of lack of money.

So we lived in that double trailer without a basement. It was just on blocks. My brother and I slept down below against the concrete walls. It got pretty cold in the winter, but it was nice in the summer. My father then finagled someone to put a concrete foundation in. We added portable electric heaters. That gave us warmth. But in the spring we would have water come in and join us.

I never had the trendy clothes that other kids wore, but no one ever made fun of me or what I wore. There were a lot of kids like me that I grew up with. But there were other kids who were fortunate to have better things. I remember going to a guy's house. He had red Puma sneakers. I loved them. They were about a year old, but I couldn't afford them. I traded some electric football players to him for them. I was probably twelve or thirteen. This was early seventies.

Around that time I went on a town trip to Fenway Park. I did not really have any baseball idols, but I liked Reggie Smith. He was my favorite player on the Red Sox.

What stays with me from that first time I went to Fenway was how I felt going through the tunnel and coming out and seeing the Green Monster. The Sox were playing the Senators. I still don't think I have seen anything as colorful as that day. The whites were as white as could be; the reds so brilliant. It had such an impact on me that I tried to walk up a ramp in all future visits to Fenway to get a full view of the ballpark to bring back those childhood memories.

The dream of becoming a major league player probably started for me when I was six or seven years old. When I was about twelve or thirteen, it was something I started to talk about. I started following baseball in detail. I had success at the Little League level and knew that I was better than some kids. I also had a plan. My motto was: Have a dream, have a plan, do the work.

My dream was to be a ballplayer. My plan was to go to college. I ended up doing the work. I knew it was hard to make it from New Hampshire. But I also heard that a lot of teams recruit New England guys because they like the traditional work ethic that has characterized people from the region. I never had any idiosyncrasies or superstitions except for when I played for the Salisbury Little League team. Our ritual was to always walk the same way to the ballpark and always look out for a good luck blackbird on the power line.

When I was in high school, the season came very quickly and left us very quickly. It was New Hampshire weather. Our annual schedule was just fourteen games, weather permitting. I played a little outfield, but essentially I was a pitcher. I was overpowering in high school. I threw in the low nineties.

April Fool's Day, going into my senior year, the local paper, the *Concord Monitor* did a mock trade. I was shipped to Concord High School for three hockey players. People were all up in arms about it. It was just a joke, but it showed the impact I had in the area.

We were undefeated during my senior year and were the favorites to win everything. I was the superstar. The last game I pitched in high school was in the first round of the play-offs. In the top of the seventh inning, we had a 1–0 lead. I got the first batter. Then two guys reached base on two errors. With guys on first and second, I gave up a clean base hit to leftfield. The ball went through the leftfielder's legs. We lost the game 2-1. The year before our team had also lost in the finals, but I remember this game the most. It was a game we were supposed to win.

Graduating from high school, I had a chance to sign a contract with the Red Sox. Everyone wanted me to grab the Red Sox offer, which was for $10,000. My parents put pressure on me to sign, because we didn't have any money. But my mentors said, "It's not enough money, $10,000. You can go to college, and that will be worth $30,000."

I went to Rutgers University for a short time and then dropped out, came back, and worked at a mail-order birdseed factory for about two months. I ended up going to St. Leo College about thirty miles north of Tampa, Florida, and was drafted in the nineteenth round by the Yankees in 1981.

I didn't think nineteenth was low — fortieth round was low. I thought I was kind of a middle-round guy. I was just excited to get drafted and especially by the Yankees. I got $5,000 to sign and after taxes it was probably about $4,300. I bought a used car and a couple of things, and it was gone.

In 1982, I led the Florida State League in wins, ERA, and shutouts pitching for Fort Lauderdale. It took me four years, but on April 11, 1986, I made my major league debut. As a rookie for the Yankees in 1986, I was 9–5. I was a major leaguer.

Injuries cut into what I could have been, but I really have no regrets. I pitched in the All-Star Game, won 110 major league games and lost 102 — that's better than .500. Growing up, I always wanted to be a professional baseball player. I realized my dream.

BOBBY THOMSON

Even though they called me the "Flying Scott" and I was born in Glasgow, Scotland, I have no memories of growing up there, for we left when I was two years old. The family unit was my mother and father, four sisters, and a brother.

I grew up in Staten Island. You name it, I grew up in all different sections of the island. We never owned a home. For whatever reason, we just rented them. My father was a cabinet maker for a construction company. Over in Scotland, he was a soccer man, but over here in the United States he became a big baseball fan, a Brooklyn Dodgers fan. But he did not play baseball with me. I guess he was too busy.

I was lucky that I had an older brother who was a pretty good first baseman. He was nine years older than me, and he was my mentor. We played a lot of catch together, mostly in the backyard. My brother often told me how graceful I looked playing ball. He especially liked the way I would go after a fly ball. That gave me confidence. He really had a lot to do with my growing up to be a baseball player.

I was always athletic from the start. In grammar school I was fast and would always win races. As a little kid of seven or eight, I walked miles on a Sunday with my brother just to see a ball game. Maybe it wasn't miles, but it seemed like miles. I was probably ten years old when I got my first baseball glove. My brother brought it home for me from Sears Roebuck where he worked.

When I was a freshman at Curtis High School, I went out for the baseball team. I lasted until the last uniform was given out. The coach said, "Sorry, son, we don't have a uniform for you. Show up next year."

He didn't have to tell me to show up next year. I was going to anyway. I came back and made the team as a sophomore. I made my share of errors, but I was on the team — the Curtis Warriors.

The coach, Harry O'Brien, ultimately turned out to be a good friend of mine. He was a well-known sportsman on Staten Island and coached basketball and baseball. He was an old Vermonter and would be out there pitching batting practice with a corn cob pipe in his mouth. He was quite a guy.

In high school I started to become interested a bit more in major league baseball, rooting for the New York Giants and players like Mel Ott and Harry Danning.

In my senior year I started to play for a Staten Island semipro team, the Gulf Oilers, a kind of industrial league outfit. They had a much older group of guys. Some of them worked for Gulf Oil and got paid for playing ball on Sundays. I was just a young high school kid, the youngest guy there.

One day George Mack, a scout from the New York Giants, came around to take a look at our big outfielder. He liked what he saw. The big outfielder told me, "Mack said, 'You will come up to the Polo Grounds and bring that kid shortstop Thomson along with you.'"

I never saw the Polo Grounds until I was invited there to work out. I don't remember how we got there from Staten Island. But we had to take a bus to the ferry and the ferry to the subway and the subway up. It took at least a couple of hours. I was sixteen, seventeen years old.

I really didn't get much into the history of baseball, so going into what people called the "fabled" Polo Grounds didn't have that much of an effect on me. I do not remember much about the tryout, but I would like to think that the glove my brother bought me from Sears Roebuck was long gone by that time. I do remember working out and walking around on that big league ballfield and thinking it was like walking on air.

I got into the batter's box. I took my swings. Then a coach with a loud voice started giving me the devil. "Get the hell out of there," he shouted. "Get out."

"I'm not done," I protested.

"You've had your five swings."

I didn't know you were supposed to get out after five swings. I got out. That's about the only thing I remember clearly from that tryout time.

Ironically, it turned out the Dodgers showed more interest in me than the Giants. Somehow, I don't know how it happened, the Dodgers made contact with me. I showed up at Ebbets Field for a workout before a game. I changed my clothes in the Dodgers locker room where Pee Wee Reese and some other players were sitting around playing cards. I was amazed. Here there was a game about to be played, and these guys were so relaxed they were playing cards.

I probably did very well at the workout, because I was put on the Dodgers rookie team. We played at different parks all over New York City. I don't even know how I got to those games. I probably was taking the bus, the train, a boat, and everything else.

The time finally came. I was getting ready to graduate from high school and had made up my mind that I was going to sign with some team. The Dodgers told me not to sign with anyone unless I checked with them. They also told me that they would top any offer, especially if it came from the Giants. An offer did come from the Giants. I was a Giant fan. I ended up signing with them Giants for one hundred bucks a month.

My mother and one of my sisters took me to Manhattan and put me on a bus to go down to Bristol, Virginia. That was how it all began. The time was 1942, August.

I was a pretty scared kid who never had been away from home. Half the season was over when I got down to Bristol. They had a pretty good ball club. I was being groomed as a third baseman, but I didn't play very much. I didn't like it there too much. There was a big fat lady who used to holler at the players and scare the hell out of us. It seemed she was always focusing on me. The old New York Giants legend, Bill Terry, was in the front office, and he wanted me to play. About that time Rocky Mount, North Carolina, needed a young guy. World War II was on, and guys were leaving. So I was sent there.

The first night I joined Rocky Mount for a game, the team bus stopped off for us to get a bite to eat in some little place out in the country. I went into the bathroom. When I came out, the bus had taken off without me. There was a trooper sitting there. "You know," he said to me, "I thought there was still one of you players left." He took me into his police car, and we went out chasing the bus and caught up with it.

After a time I got a chance to play all the time when the regular Rocky Mount third baseman was called into the service. Our team made the play-offs, and I hit a home run in one of the games. They passed a hat around, and I got about $13, which to me was really a lot considering what I was making.

I never read the *Sporting News* or any of those baseball type papers. But that fall friends of mine showed me a clipping from the *Sporting News* that referred to me as "the young kid with significant sloping shoulders a la Pie Traynor," who was one of the great third basemen. So the home run in those play-offs got me noticed. Later on someone said that homer fore-shadowed a home run that I was to hit in another play-off game.

From 1943 to 1945, I was a bombardier in the Air Corps. I was released out in California and was able to play ball on weekends. I worked in a steel factory all week. There was talk of my playing for the San Francisco Seals, an independent and powerhouse team in the Pacific Coast League. But the Giants still owned my contract.

In 1946, the Giants took all the returning servicemen down to a huge spring training camp. I went there figuring I would have to go back down to class-D at Bristol, which I didn't look forward to. I didn't want to have to contend with that big fat lady's hollering.

I did not realize it, but I was the shining star for the New York Giants in spring training. My older brother was home living with my mother. I wasn't writing letters or saying too much. That was the kind of kid I was. So finally my brother got frustrated not hearing from me or knowing what I was doing with the Giants. He went over to Jersey City and went through all the Jersey City *Journals* right from the start of spring training. He came across this article which said I was "the diamond in the rough." Apparently, I was the head of the camp and didn't realize it.

Opening Day 1946, I played for the Jersey City Giants. I played in the same game Jackie Robinson played in. He was with the Montreal Royals. I had a pretty good year, hitting a lot of home runs. The Giants brought me up the end of the season.

I slept at home. It was a mile from my home to the Roosevelt Stadium ballpark in Jersey City. I took the Hudson Avenue bus to the Bayonne Ferry and took another bus and I was there. I would get home at two o'clock in the morning. It was a wonderful experience, because I did have my friends and relatives around as a cheering section.

I was brought up to the Giants at the end of 1946. Mel Ott was the manager. Bill Rigney was there. Snozz Lombardi was there. I hit a couple of home runs and hit about .315. I played third base.

Scottish people are very low-keyed. I was brought up not to push. That probably hurt me more than anything in my major league career. I did not have much cockiness. I guess I should have been more outgoing. But the way we were brought up was to be seen and not heard — to stay in the background.

That was impossible after October 3, 1951 — when I hit what they called "the Shot Heard 'Round the World," the home run in the play-offs to beat the Dodgers to put our Giants team into the World Series.

Everybody associates me with the Giants, but I also played for the Milwaukee Braves, Chicago Cubs, Boston Red Sox, and Baltimore Orioles. I had a good career.

MO VAUGHN

I grew up in Norwalk, Connecticut, where I was born on December 15, 1967. We used to play in the backyard of my friend's house, and we'd hit this ball over the centerfield rock way off in the woods. That's what we did all day. Tape-ball, baseball, all types of things like that.

We used to play in an old tennis cage in this other neighborhood. The poles were out. There were no nets; we'd play with a tennis ball. We'd run the bases, and hit home runs over the wall. We'd play off sides of houses and break windows. We'd play off a shed, and we'd try to yell real loud at the same time the ball would make contact so nobody could hear it in the house.

I played all sports: football, basketball, and baseball. But baseball was my favorite game. There was always something different to me in baseball. I was always able to make that different kind of contact — the ball traveled pretty well for me. When I was a little kid, I played catcher. Then I played shortstop all through high school.

I was a Yankees fan. In Norwalk, we'd get WPIX, which carried the Yankees. We were only twenty minutes from the Bronx. We were all Yankees fans. I went to boarding school, Trinity Pawling Prep, in Pawling, New York, where I had an outstanding time there playing baseball.

The Philadelphia Phillies drafted me out of high school in the third round, but I never signed. I felt that if I was going to be a third-round pick out of high school, I could work on my game and be a first-round pick after college. I ended up like that. I was All American all three seasons I played at Seton Hall and named Big East Conference's Player of the Decade.

The Boston Red Sox selected me in the first round, the twenty-third pick overall in the free-agent draft on June 9, 1989. I was excited, because I knew once I got to the big leagues with the Red Sox, I would be close to home in Connecticut. That was the greatest thing of all about it.

People have dreams and aspirations to play in the major leagues, but it takes a lot of things to go right to get that opportunity. It was always a dream for me to make the major leagues. But there were so many steps that had to be taken to get to that level. I think once I got to the minor leagues, triple-A baseball, and I was so close, that's when I started thinking I had an honest shot.

My first game in the major leagues was at Memorial Stadium in Baltimore on June 27, 1991. I was really nervous. The whole moment was very intimidating. I was pretty much in awe of the whole situation. I got my first hit off Jeff Robinson. Once I got that first hit, I thought I was golden, but there was still so much to learn.

I got sent back down to the minors. I came up in 1992, and was sent back down again. I didn't start playing every day until 1993. I really had to reinvent my style completely to have success up in the major leagues.

I emulated Chris Chambliss and Reggie Jackson, because they were left-handed hitters. I tried to set my stance like their stance. It was unbelievable to be able to meet those guys — guys that I pretty much idolized. I had an opportunity to play with Roger Clemens, Tony Pena, Andre Dawson — guys like that. I came up right at the end of a great era – George Brett, Don Mattingly, Kent Hrbek, Kirby Puckett, Robin Yount, Paul Molitor. So I got a taste of that era, when baseball was really a solid, solid game.

BILLY WILLIAMS

$\mathcal{I}$ *grew up in* Whistler, Alabama, about two and a half miles from Mobile, Alabama. I was born June 15, 1938. Alabama was hot then and is still hot. We were right on the Gulf of Mexico, so it was not only the heat, there was the humidity. On a real hot day we would go swimming early in the morning in the creek and come back around ten or eleven o'clock and play baseball. We would listen to games after we finished the first session. Then we would go swimming again in the creek, which was only six or seven blocks from my home. In the late afternoon, we would start playing baseball again. As a kid, my position was third base. I wanted to get in the action.

My father had played a lot of baseball. I had three older brothers who played a lot of baseball. I saw them play, and so I wanted to do it, too. I became a Brooklyn Dodgers fan as a kid. That was mostly because of Jackie Robinson playing on that team. When that color line was broken — that gave hope not only to myself but to a lot of guys who had played in the Negro Leagues and had not had a chance at the majors. It gave you hope that if your talent was good enough, the opportunity was out there now for you.

I played for a semipro team named the Mobile Black Bears, an all-black team. Henry Aaron's brother, Tommy, was on that team. There was a scout from the Chicago Cubs named Ivy Griffin, who followed our team through five or six cities: Jackson, Mississippi; Biloxi; and so on. It did not mean that much to me. I was not too impressive as a baseball player. I enjoyed the game, but I thought the scout was there because of Tommy Aaron. The scout continued to follow us from city to city. Then we were in a town and Tommy Aaron wasn't with us, but the scout was. I got the impression then that Ivy Griffin was looking at me. Four or five days later he came to my house and started to talk to my father about my playing professional baseball.

I was signed out of high school in 1956. At the time, the highest bonuses were from about $4,000 to $10,000. But I was so anxious to play baseball, I just put my name on the dotted line. The money involved was $1,500. My father got a cigar. I got a bus ticket to Ponca City. Two days after I finished high school, I was on my way to Oklahoma and the Sooner State League, class-D.

When I first began, I was not given a chance to travel on the road with the team. In town, I was not housed at the hotel but instead in a private home. There was always a fear of something happening that year of 1956.

In 1957, I was still this little skinny kid from Alabama, but I played the entire season with Ponca City and batted over .300. Things were beginning to look up. I hit over .300 in 1958, and the following year with a double-A team in San Antonio, Texas, I was hitting over .300 again.

The Cubs called me up in July. I didn't get a chance to play. I just sat on the bench and observed. That was what they told me to do. I got my first major league at bat on August 6, 1959. I don't remember the circumstances. In all, I got into parts of eighteen games.

In 1960, I again batted over .300 in the minors and again had a brief trial in Chicago, forty-seven at bats. But the year was mainly another year spent in the minors. I was not despairing, but I was getting a bit restless.

Rogers Hornsby, a roving batting instructor for the Cubs, spent a lot of time with me in Arizona in spring training through those years. Hornsby was known to say about rookies: "They are not worth my time."

But it seemed he always found time for me. I was not aware of all the baseball history connected with him. I did know that he was a Hall of Famer and had been a good hitter. That was all. Hornsby befriended me and taught me a lot about hitting. He spoke a lot about the strike zone, about getting a good ball to hit, about zoning in and making the most of every at bat, about driving the ball.

It was on his recommendation that I was given the chance to make the Chicago Cubs. After almost four full minor league seasons, I was on the big league roster once again. This was 1961. I struggled. My batting average was below .150 for much of the first two months of that season. I was often benched, but I kept on plugging on.

On June 15, I celebrated my twenty-third birthday with a grand slam homer in a 10–6 win over the Giants. I then got ten hits in my next nineteen at bats. It started to all come together. I finished the season very strong and was voted National League Rookie of the Year. I was on my way.

ED YARNALL

I kind of started late in baseball. I was about eight or nine. My dad really had to convince me to do it. I wasn't too interested in the sport. He decided he was going to coach a team and wanted me to go out and play and get involved in some kind of sport. As a kid, it is always good to get into some kind of organized sport, that was what I was told. "It teaches you a lot of values and stuff in life." That was the line I remember.

I was born on December 4, 1975, in Lima, Pennsylvania, right outside of Philadelphia. Our family moved to south Florida when I was about nine years old. That is when baseball started to become a big part of my life. It was not only fun but also a good way to meet kids your own age.

I started out as an outfielder. I was happy to be out there. Then there was this game my dad was coaching. Something happened to the other pitchers, and my dad had to really, really push me to get on the mound. I'd never pitched before. "We need a pitcher," my dad said, "someone to throw in this particular game. That is you, Ed."

Once I got out there, it was pretty much a natural thing for me. I just liked the confrontation — me against each batter. I started pitching more often and also shifted about that time to playing a little first base.

When I was ten, I was on a Little League team with ten-, eleven-, and twelve-year-olds. I didn't play much because I was the youngest kid, and they had a bunch of older guys. We had a real good team. Our record was 21–1 or something like that.

Then something happened. One of our pitchers had worked the day before. There was a rule that you couldn't pitch two days in a row. So they needed someone to start the county championship game. That someone was me. I think I pitched five or six innings. I hit a three-run homer. We won that game. That was probably the most memorable of my Little League experiences.

I liked to watch baseball a lot when I was twelve, thirteen, fourteen. Will Clark was one of my big guys, my favorites. I used to have posters of him and collected all his baseball cards. Mostly it was hitters I liked to watch, more than pitchers. I don't know why, I guess everyone has a lot more fun hitting than pitching, especially when you're little. No one really wants to say, "Hey, I want to go out there and pitch."

I was probably about fourteen when I started playing baseball pretty good. I'd played on a couple of Junior Olympic teams and started to figure I would have a chance to make the majors. Then all through my time at St. Thomas Aquinas High School in Fort Lauderdale I made making the majors my goal.

I received a baseball scholarship to LSU. That was the first time I met my boyhood favorite, Will Clark. It was probably 1994 or 1995. Clark is from the New Orleans area and came over as a guest speaker. It was pretty exciting to meet a guy that you idolized and looked up to. I told him I used to collect all his cards and was a real big fan of him, growing up. I thought, as I talked to him, one day some kid might have the same conversation with me.

In June of 1996, I was selected by the New York Mets organization in the third round of the free-agent draft. In my first season of pro ball in 1997, I pitched at all three levels of the Mets minor league system.

I began the 1998 season at double-A Binghamton. There I was really on. I went 7–0 with a 0.39 ERA. What happened? The Mets traded me to the Florida Marlins, who then traded me to the Yankees. At Columbus, I was the International League Pitcher of the Year. My record was 13–4 when the Yankees called me up. My major league debut was July 15, 1999. A year later I was traded to Cincinnati. It has been a choppy beginning — four major league teams in four years. Go figure!

EDDIE YOST

I grew up in the Ozone Park neighborhood of Queens, New York, in the thirties. I was born in Brooklyn, New York, in 1926. At that time we had the New York Giants, Brooklyn Dodgers, and New York Yankees. But I had no favorite team. However, Lou Gehrig was my favorite player in those years. One thing I always liked about him was they called him the "Quiet Hero."

When I was a six-year-old, my brother went to a game at Yankee Stadium, and during batting practice he got a ball. For some reason, I used to put that ball under my pillow every night and sleep on it. My dad had played some baseball when he was young and won some medals. Those medals were under my pillow, too.

Baseball was something I enjoyed as a young man. Growing up in Queens, we didn't have a lot of fields to play on, so we played many of the activities that led up to skills involved in baseball: punchball, stoopball, stickball, palmball. We had all kinds of games that we played at different times. Prior to that, I remember using a broomstick, picking up pebbles and little stones, and hitting them as far as I could. There was no measuring involved, but it did help hand-eye coordination.

I went to a few major league baseball games with the CYO (Catholic Youth Organization). We would sit way out in no-man's-land. My dad took me to a World Series game, and I think Lou Gehrig may have been in this game. We left at six o'clock in the morning. We took the bus and the subway to Yankee Stadium and stood in line for I don't know how many hours to get into the seats in the bleachers. I was seven, eight years old, something like that.

My dad never gave me any instruction or extra encouragement or anything. He'd play catch with me. But nothing like you see these fathers doing today with their youngsters. I remember a catcher's glove that my dad had gotten for me somehow. That was the only glove I remember from my real early years. When I was twelve or thirteen, I got a Lonnie Frey glove. That glove had a big webbing.

During the summer, there was organized playing of baseball just on weekends. I belonged to the church team in CYO. The rest of the week you had to do whatever you could to continue in the game to develop your skills. There were about three or four guys in the neighborhood who hung around together. We'd go down to the open lots in our area, and we'd play what we'd call "Lazy Man's Baseball." That was because we didn't have enough players.

You had a pitcher, a batter, a shortstop, a third baseman, and a left-fielder. Or if the guy was a left-handed hitter, you would turn it around the other way. You hit the ball. If it was caught either in the air or on the ground it was an out. If it went through the infield, it would be a single. If it landed in certain areas beyond that, you'd get a double, a triple, or a home run.

We'd start out with a baseball that had the regular stitching on it. You know how they wear out in no time at all. Then we would take the cover off, and buy a roll of adhesive tape for 10¢. We got so good and experienced that we would turn that work into an art. We learned how to do it where you could do it just right and you'd cover the whole ball, and you'd be surprised how long that would last us. Our bats were nailed and screwed and glued.

We also engaged in very small-time betting that linked up with our interests in baseball. There was always one guy around the neighborhood who gave us an opportunity if we had a nickel to make 15¢. If you bet a nickel and picked three players to get five or six hits on a given day — if your pick was correct — you would get back 15¢. If I did put up a nickel, I'd look very, very carefully at the box scores the next day to see if I'd won.

In school, I was in the Rapid Advance program. That meant you skipped a year. I skipped, but I was so small a fellow when I went to Shimer Junior High School in Queens, I actually did not try out for any of the teams there. So I didn't play sports in junior high school at all. I moved on to John Adams High School. My first chance to play there came when I was a senior. I played third base and batted in the bottom of the lineup. That was because there were players on that team much better than myself. There were five or six guys who signed professional contracts. Our team won the Queens championship.

After I graduated from high school in 1943, I played in what they called the Queens Alliance. I was sixteen. The Queens Alliance was a very good league in those days. It had a number of players who had played minor league baseball, didn't make it, and came back to play in this league.

The playing schedule was limited just to doubleheaders on Sundays. I used to get $4 for each doubleheader I played. I got paid with an envelope filled with change, which the organizers had gotten from the people in the stands. No admission was charged. A hat was passed round, and people would fill the hat with whatever they could spare.

I was scouted by the famous Yankees scout Paul Krichel. He offered me a class-D contract. The pay was maybe $150 a month or something like that. I told the Yankees that I wasn't interested because I might go to college. Truth is, I wasn't pleased with what they offered. That is why I didn't accept the contract.

I went to New York University, and I played shortstop on the baseball team. Our main pitcher was Ralph Branca. While I was a student at NYU, I also got paid to play semipro ball. I played on Long Island and in East Orange, New Jersey. We played against very good Negro League teams.

Playing baseball to me was most important. I played enthusiastically and with all my heart, which was something the scouts who came around appreciated. I was scouted by a fellow from the Washington Senators, Joe Cambria. He had signed Mickey Vernon before me and Walter Masterson, who was a fine pitcher for many years. The day Cambria came to look me over, I went 5-for-5 playing shortstop. I also had eight or ten assists. It was a long time ago, but I still remember the team we played against in that game — it was the great Homestead Grays.

Cambria approached me shortly after that, and he said he'd like to sign me. We got together with my folks, and I went down to Washington to sign. My dad went with me, because I wasn't old enough to sign a contract by myself. We signed in the owner Clark Griffith's office. I got a $1,500 signing bonus and a contract for $600 a month.

My dad was very happy about it, because it was something that he told me he would have liked to have done — be a baseball player. My mother was a little hesitant and sad about the fact that I would be leaving home.

The Senators were playing in Chicago, so the next day I packed a bag, got on a train, and reported to the Del Prado Hotel in Chicago at 2:15. It was the first hotel I ever stayed in, and the furthest I'd ever been away from New York City.

The next day I got my uniform. If I recall right, the number was 28.

During batting practice, they put me out at shortstop. For almost the whole time, they hit ground balls to me. I guess they were just seeing whether I could catch a ball or not. I was maybe 155, 160 pounds. I had a glove. I had spikes. I just felt that I was there playing baseball. It didn't make too much difference to me that I was on a major league field. The first game I played in was on August 16, 1944. I got into seven games, but mainly I rode the bench until the end of the season.

The next year, 1945, I was drafted. I served in the navy for a year and a half. I was stationed at a big naval base in upstate New York where they brought in recruits. Having been a phys ed major my first year in college and having played baseball, those in charge made me a physical instructor.

In 1946, I came back to the Senators. Washington had a shortstop named Johnny Sullivan, who at the time wasn't going too good. They gave me a shot. I think it was the second game of a doubleheader against the Yankees, in Washington. I can recall that situation, playing in front of the hometown people. It was moving.

I played in my first spring training in 1947, a game here and a game there. They wanted to send me to the minor leagues because they felt I didn't have enough experience. But I was a returning veteran. There was a policy that any returning veteran had to have the same job back as the one he had when he left. This didn't apply to only baseball; it applied to everything in society. In my case, it was a job with the Washington Senators. Mr. Griffith asked me to write a letter to Commissioner Happy Chandler, asking that they make an exception in my case, so that I could get some experience in the minor leagues. But Commissioner Chandler said, "We cannot make any exceptions. He's got to stay with your ballclub."

I stayed. A month into the season, I got a chance to get into a game. I did well, better than Washington, which finished seventh in an eight-team league. I wound up playing in 115 games and became the regular third baseman for the Senators.

I earned the nickname "The Walking Man" because of the career 1,614 bases on balls I received and the fact I led the American League in walks six times. A lot of people made a big deal about my batting eye. There was the line that I could even draw a walk in a pepper game. I don't know about any of that. I do know that all those times as a kid swinging a broomstick did a lot to help my eye-hand coordination.

TODD ZEILE

$\mathcal{I}$ *was born in* Van Nuys, California, on the
same day that Sandy Koufax pitched a perfect
game, September 9, 1965. I grew up outside LA. We had
bats and balls in our hands from the time we were two or three years old.
My dad was an avid baseball fan and played at a relatively high level when
he was younger. My brother and myself certainly developed our interest
and our passion in baseball from our dad. Unfortunately, he had to be in
the workforce at an early age, so he never played professional baseball.

Growing up in California gives you a lot of time outside, a lot of decent
weather, and a lot of sunshine, so we were outside playing baseball, football, riding bikes, or swimming.

We were an active family. My brother and I played with soft, Wiffle-type
balls around the house. We would play a lot of tape-ball. I actually went
through the ritual of cutting down a dowel and creating a handle for it,
even marking it so it looked like a real bat. We would then take Wiffle
balls and tape them with electrical tape to give them a little extra weight.
We hung a tarp with a strike zone on it over the front of the garage. And
we played out in the front. A ground ball past the pitcher was a single. If
it hit across the street in the air it was a double. We'd use the house across
the street as a home run porch. You didn't have to hit the ball over the
house for a home run. We didn't want to have extra motivation for losing
the ball over the back of the house. We were satisfied if it just hit the
house.

It was great having a brother with an interest in baseball. We wouldn't
have to have the neighbor kids over. We could play at night, in the morning. We always had each other to go out and throw with and get some kind
of game going. We'd also play one-on-one-on-one — three-man rotation
with a pitcher, a hitter, and an outfielder.

Where I grew up we had a thing called Boy's Baseball — now Pony
League Baseball. It's not Little League, it's actually regular major league-

type rules from the time you're eight. So there's leading off, stealing, and all of those things. I played all through that system, which was called Pinto-Mustang-Bronco-Pony, up to age fourteen. Pinto was eight years old, Mustang was nine and ten, Bronco was eleven and twelve, and Pony was thirteen and fourteen. By my second year of Pony, I was on the freshman team in high school, so those crossed over.

I had some fun games, but unfortunately some of the memories that I have as a kid were disappointments, because we were a game away from the Pony Baseball World Series on two different occasions. This was the national tournament in St. Joseph, Missouri. It was good competition. I even faced guys that I later competed against in college.

Just about everybody who makes it to the major leagues pitched at one point in their Little League careers. It's almost unheard of not to. That's where they stick the guys that excel at that age. When I wasn't pitching, I was catching. I pitched because I had a strong arm for my age. After that it was catching straight through the minor leagues and up into the big leagues.

The Dodgers were my favorite team growing up, although I wasn't a huge sports fan. I've never been a card collector or avid follower of any particular sports team or sport in general, and that's primarily because in California, if I could be watching, I could be participating. I'd watch a couple of innings and then go out and play. If I could watch any part of a football game, I'd be out at the park playing football with my buddies the next hour. I'd rather participate than watch. But I was a big Dodgers fan, primarily because my dad was a huge Dodgers fan. He went to the first game ever at Dodger Stadium. The era that I grew up was the team with Steve Garvey, Davey Lopes, Bill Russell, Ron Cey, Dusty Baker, and Rick Monday. I really liked Garvey as far as his style of hitting. I emulated that to some degree as a kid, and I think I've taken a little of that with me all the way along — the upright approach, and being a very handsy hitter, using the whole field. As far as my catching, Johnny Bench was the premier catcher of that era, so he was somebody else that I followed.

I had a big growth spurt after my junior year. I had some baby fat my sophomore year, and then I sprouted up and filled out a little bit my junior year. So I was scouted late in high school. In my senior year, I got recruited a fair amount from college teams but only had major league interest after playing well for a California All-Star team in a tournament. I got scouted there and drafted by the Kansas City Royals out of high school.

But there was no way I was going to sign professionally. I wasn't ready. I wasn't physically ready, and I wasn't mentally prepared to go out and do that. Plus, I was a 4.0 student. I had every aspiration of going to school and continuing my education. I was certainly a realist. I didn't feel there was a realistic chance for me to become a major league baseball player.

My dad was good about letting me know the odds of making it. I figured if I could get my education paid for by excelling in high school, then I'm one step ahead of the game. I thought a major league career was out of reach.

I decided to go on to UCLA instead. I was really shocked when the Cardinals in June of 1986 drafted me out of college. At that point, I had talked to a couple of other teams and fully expected I'd get drafted by the Angels. It just so happened that my dad did a lot of business in St. Louis, and so he was very familiar with the Cardinals. He went to a lot of Cardinals games in Busch Stadium and knew the city very well. He was certainly pleasantly surprised. It didn't take long for me to get worked up about the organization.

They said I was one of the organization's most highly touted prospects. In 1989, *USA Today* named me Minor League Player of the Year. My first big league game was August of 1989 in Cincinnati. I remember getting to the clubhouse and seeing guys that I had gone to spring training with. I was the only rookie on that team. It was a very, very veteran team in the middle of a pennant race.

That first night was a doubleheader interrupted by a rain delay. Tony Pena caught the first game. I started the second game, which didn't get going until after midnight. So my first at bat ended up the next day — August 18, 1989. I had two hits, had a decent showing. My family was in town. I remember it being an exciting time, even though it got over at 2:40 in the morning. That was how I started in the major leagues.

DON ZIMMER

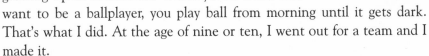

My dad put a glove on my hand, and I started playing baseball. I was eight years old, I guess, growing up in Cincinnati. When you're a kid and want to be a ballplayer, you play ball from morning until it gets dark. That's what I did. At the age of nine or ten, I went out for a team and I made it.

My elementary school didn't have anything. There was no baseball field, no basketball court. Across the street was a rock pile where we tried to play. And since we had no baseballs, we made do with rocks. Two blocks away was a Catholic school, which had everything including a football league and a basketball league. After school let out, I'd run down there and sneak in. I knew all of the guys and would play with them for fifteen, twenty minutes until the priest came by. He'd come in one door, and I'd go out the other, running like hell. I was scared to death of him.

I was a shortstop from day one, so was my dad. I learned how to play from my dad and Pete Rose's dad. They were great friends. At the age of thirteen, I was playing on the same team as my father and Pete Rose's dad. They knew how to play, and if you made a mistake, they corrected you. That's where it started.

I was lucky to get on a great American Legion team while I was still a student at Western Hills High School. We played for the American Legion midwest championship against Cedar Rapids, Iowa. I hit a triple into right center, and we wound up winning the game and going on to win the national championship. That was 1947. It was some time.

The Cincinnati team catered to me during my high school years. The Reds would invite me down to the park to work out, do batting practice and stuff like that. I'd be taken to dinner and lunch a couple of times a week. It was getting exciting.

Cincinnati was always known to be a very cheap outfit. At that time — it was 1949 — they had the bonus rule in effect. If you got $4,000 or more to sign, you had to stay on the parent club for two full years.

Then along came Cliff Alexander, a football coach at Cincinnati's Woodward High School, who was a bird-dog scout for the Brooklyn Dodgers. I would have loved to sign with my hometown team, but when Cliff Alexander came to me and offered to take my dad, mom, and me to Brooklyn to work out, my father said, "I think you should go."

He had a business; he couldn't go. But my mom and I, together with Cliff Alexander, went to Brooklyn. The people in Cincinnati found out and were angry. I said, "I'm not going to sign there. I'm not signing in Brooklyn. I'm coming back here to work out with you people."

Brooklyn was exciting. We stayed at the old St. George Hotel. They took us to Coney Island, things like that. I was a little guy from Cincinnati, Ohio. It was thrilling to go to Ebbets Field and work out there. The Dodgers offered me $3,950.

So I came back to Cincinnati, I got down to work out with the Reds, and one of the guys in the front office said, "Well, what did they offer you up there?"

Well, I could have said, "They didn't make me an offer. What do you want to do?"

But I told them. I didn't know any different; I was a young kid. I said, "They offered me 3,950."

"Oh," he says, "we can't pay you that kind of money. But what we can do is, we can give you $2,000. But we'll start you out in class-B."

I said, "No. I'm going to the Dodgers."

So I went — to the minors of the Dodgers. I made $140 a month when I started. Oh, those road trips. I recall once leaving the class-A league ballpark in Hornell, New York, at midnight. That was a trip. We arrived in Hamilton, Ontario, at 3:30 the next afternoon. And that was in a little yellow school bus with worn-out shock absorbers. We didn't check into the hotel until after the game. So I really don't understand it now when a guy making $8 million a year complains.

I was leading the American Association with twenty-three home runs and sixty-three runs batted in. The date was July 7, 1953. Then I was hit in the head by a fastball thrown by Jim Kirk. That was some hit. I was unconscious and near death for almost two weeks. I lost my speech for six and lost forty-four pounds. They inserted four buttons . . . like tapered corkscrews in a bottle in my head.

I got past that and joined the Dodgers in 1954. There were people who looked at me as Pee Wee Reese's successor. It never came to be. I was a "professional" utility player with a metal plate in my head. My lifetime batting average was just .235, but I got into more than a thousand games. Now after fifty years, I am still in baseball. For me, and so many others, it's my life.

A PERSONAL NOTE

Back in 1992 when I wrote *Shoeless Joe and Ragtime Baseball*, I dedicated the book this way: "For my son Freddy, with much love. One day, I know, he will dedicate a book to me."

That day has not yet arrived, but Frederic J. Frommer is getting closer to realizing that prediction. It was such a kick to have the chance to do this book with him.

Harvey Frommer

BOOKS BY HARVEY FROMMER

HARDBACK BOOKS

It Happened in Manhattan [with Myrna Katz Frommer]
Growing Up Baseball [with Frederic J. Frommer]
It Happened on Broadway [with Myrna Katz Frommer]
The New York Yankee Encyclopedia
Growing Up Jewish in America [with Myrna Katz Frommer]
Big Apple Baseball
It Happened in Brooklyn [with Myrna Katz Frommer]
Shoeless Joe and Ragtime Baseball
It Happened in the Catskills [with Myrna Katz Frommer]
Holzman on Hoops [with Red Holzman]
Behind the Lines: The Autobiography of Don Strock
Running Tough: The Autobiography of Tony Dorsett
Growing Up at Bat: 50th Anniversary Book of Little League Baseball
Throwing Heat: The Autobiography of Nolan Ryan
Primitive Baseball
150th Anniversary Album of Baseball
Red on Red: The Autobiography of Red Holzman
Olympic Controversies
Baseball's Greatest Managers
National Baseball Hall of Fame
Games of the XXIIIrd Olympiad
Jackie Robinson
Baseball's Greatest Records, Streaks and Feats
Baseball's Greatest Rivalry
Rickey and Robinson
Basketball My Way: Nancy Lieberman [with Myrna Katz Frommer]
New York City Baseball: 1947–1957
The Great American Soccer Book

Sports Roots
Sports Lingo
The Martial Arts: Judo and Karate
A Sailing Primer [with Ron Weinmann]
A Baseball Century

PAPERBACK BOOKS

Growing Up Jewish in America [with Myrna Katz Frommer]
It Happened in the Catskills [with Myrna Katz Frommer]
It Happened in Brooklyn [with Myrna Katz Frommer]
Shoeless Joe and Ragtime Baseball
New York City Baseball: 1947–1957
Running Tough: The Autobiography of Tony Dorsett
Throwing Heat: The Autobiography of Nolan Ryan
Red on Red: The Autobiography of Red Holzman
New York City Baseball
Baseball's Greatest Rivalry
Basketball My Way: Nancy Lieberman [with Myrna Katz Frommer]
Sports Lingo
Sports Genes [with Myrna Katz Frommer]
· *The Sports Date Book* [with Myrna Katz Frommer]

ABOUT THE AUTHORS

Harvey Frommer is a noted sports author who has been honored by the New York State Legislature and cited in the Congressional Record. His books include the classics *New York City Baseball: 1947–1957* and *Shoeless Joe and Ragtime Baseball*. The author of nearly forty books, Frommer has taught courses in sports and culture at Dartmouth College, Wesleyan University, and New York University.

Frederic J. Frommer, who received his master's degree from Columbia University's Graduate School of Journalism, is a political reporter for the Associated Press in Washington, D.C. He has also written for the *Washington Post*, CNN, and Knight Ridder.